THE ENVIRONMENT OF SCHOOLING

THE ENVIRONMENT
OF SCHOOLING:

Formal Education

as an

Open Social System

ROBERT E. HERRIOTT
Florida State University

BENJAMIN J. HODGKINS
University of Manitoba

PRENTICE-HALL, INC., *Englewood Cliffs, New Jersey*

Library of Congress Cataloging in Publication Data

HERRIOTT, ROBERT E.
  The environment of schooling.
  Includes bibliographical references.
  I. Educational sociology. I. Hodgkins,
Benjamin J., joint author. II. Title.
LC191.H46   370.19   72-6847
ISBN 0-13-283176-7

PRENTICE-HALL INTERNATIONAL, INC., *London*
PRENTICE-HALL OF AUSTRALIA, PTY. LTD., *Sydney*
PRENTICE-HALL OF CANADA, LTD., *Toronto*
PRENTICE-HALL OF INDIA PRIVATE LIMITED, *New Delhi*
PRENTICE-HALL OF JAPAN, INC., *Tokyo*

To
SCOTT, KATHY, NAN, and BEN

Contents

Preface

American social institutions are currently undergoing a barrage of criticism as scathing as any in the history of the United States. The economic system, for example, has been attacked for its obvious inequities and its failure in spite of great societal wealth and productivity to meet the needs of large numbers of American citizens. The system of justice has been taken to task for its inequities and brutality, and the welfare system has reeled under charges of ineptness, insensitivity, and inadequacy. Regardless of the merits of such criticisms, they represent a broadly based disenchantment with the traditional and conventional social processes of American life.

Such social concern has important implications for American education, for dissatisfaction with conventional educational practices has led to criticisms in such basic areas as teacher training, curriculum relevancy, school organization, educational finance, and most fundamentally, educational goals.

Given such turmoil, it may seem audacious to suggest that logic and order underlie these exigencies. And yet, as we shall argue in Chapter One, there is considerable reason to believe that, at least with respect to formal education, the roots of both current and past dissatisfaction stem directly from the interaction of particular social and cultural characteristics of American society with the developmental logic of a modern industrial state. Although significant educational issues may vary in content across time and space, one major factor underlying most educational conflict is the impact of modernization upon the cultural traditions and social institutions of American society. Because the requirements of this process are essentially constant in logical form, if not in specific substance, and because social and cultural phenomena generally are amazingly resistant to rapid change, a basic pattern of conflict and resolution centered upon formal education as a major social institution can be traced. Understanding the basic logic of modernization, particularly as it relates to the society's social and cultural characteristics, will allow fuller understanding of both the contemporary problems of American education and its probable future development.

Past discussion and research on educational outcomes has largely concerned the impact (or more frequently, the lack of "appropriate" impact) of the educational system on the school-age individual. One of the basic criticisms is that the educational system "is not doing what it is supposed to do." Such criticism has focused largely on traditional *cognitive outcomes* and has argued that the educational system has little impact on the school-age individual beyond that attributable to the social characteristics of his family and peers.* Another criticism, perhaps more ominous in implication, presumes that the educational system serves a latent social function detrimental to the well-being of the individual. This latter position has generally focused upon *social outcomes* and has argued that the educational system has a greatly destructive impact upon the school-age individual.**

A clearer understanding of both points of view can best be achieved by putting the issue of educational outcomes in a larger framework, one that emphasizes the impact of the social and cultural (hereafter referred to as sociocultural) context upon educational systems and how this context can constrain the relationship between the educational system and the school-age individual. Using the system rather than the individual as the primary focus reveals the more pervasive, but often less obvious social relationship between formal education and its environment. In this monograph we view the *individual* as being located within an *educational system*, which in turn is located within a *sociocultural environment* and ask, "What is the impact of that environment upon that system?"

Chapters One, Two, and Seven are directed primarily toward educational personnel and interested laymen concerned with the administration or reform of the American educational system. In these chapters we consider

---

*See, for example, James S. Coleman *et al., Equality of Educational Opportunity* (Washington, D. C.: Government Printing Office, 1966); and Central Advisory Council for Education (England), *Children and Their Primary Schools* (London: Her Majesty's Stationery Office, 1967).

**See, for example, Ivan Illich, *Deschooling Society* (New York: Harper & Row, Publishers, 1971); and Everett Reimar, *School is Dead* (Garden City, N. Y.: Doubleday & Company, Inc., 1971).

in general terms the educational system from an "open systems" perspective, review some of what is commonly known about the impact of sociocultural environments on both the individual and the education system, and speculate about the future of American education.

Chapters Three through Six view schools as social organizations and are directed primarily to social scientists interested in extending current knowledge regarding social processes. In these chapters we explicate in considerable detail our perspective on social organizations and wrestle with some of the theoretical and methodological problems in obtaining *systematic* knowledge about the impact of sociocultural environments on educational systems.

Our approach is eclectic. Although we are sociologists, our view of the school as a social organization borrows heavily from "general systems theory," which had its origin after World War II on the frontier between biology and physics. In thinking of the sociocultural contexts of schools we have drawn largely from a cross-cultural perspective developed by anthropologists and economic geographers to compare societies, not social units within a single society. Our methods of data collection and analysis have been primarily those of large-scale survey research, which until recently were applied almost exclusively to individuals. Our primary statistical method is a form of multivariate regression analysis used mostly by economists. Throughout, our major objective has been to synthesize existing theory and method in order to understand better the systemic nature of American public education.

Those readers not accustomed to viewing American education as a *sociocultural* system should guard against a tendency to interpret our sociological ideas and research findings in purely economic terms. Although the reader is urged to be critical of our work, to emphasize simply the economic correlates of sociological phenomena can cause one to overlook an important point: that although money is necessary for educational growth and development, it alone is certainly not sufficient. If the past two decades have taught Americans anything it has been that sociocultural phenomena (such as the persistance of poverty, crime, and alienation in an affluent society) are not explainable solely in economic terms. Although limitations in available data have often forced us to use economic variables as "proxies" for sociocultural ones, our objective in so doing has been to go beyond purely monetary considerations in order to explore the sociocultural dynamics of educational growth and development.

Our efforts in this direction have been aided greatly by others. The bulk of our research and writing was conducted under the auspices of the Center for the Study of Education, a division of the Institute for Social Research at The Florida State University. We are indebted both to our colleagues in the Center and to the Institute's director, Charles M. Grigg, for their assistance in our endeavor. Some of our most useful theoretical insights came during the summer of 1970 when we were affiliated with the American College Testing Program, and could benefit from the many intellectual and material resources made available to us by its president, Fred F. Harcleroad.

The empirical analyses reported in Chapter Five were greatly facilitated by the cooperation of the National Center for Educational Statistics of the U. S. Office of Education, which made available to us the detailed data from its 1967 Elementary-Secondary General Information Survey. The analyses reported in Chapter Six were facilitated by grant number OEG-2-6-062972-2095 from the Bureau of Research of the U. S. Office of Education, which permitted a further examination of data originally collected by our colleague, Charles B. Nam, under contract number OE-5-99-150.

Able bibliographic assistance and editorial criticism has been received from students in the Graduate Training Program in the Sociology of Education at The Florida State University. We are particularly indebted to Richard L. Bale and Ronald P. Estes, Jr. for their tireless efforts in helping us to locate source materials. Helen Means served as our secretary and labored most efficiently and patiently with the many manuscript revisions made during the past three years.

Earlier drafts of our manuscript were read and criticized by Walter Buckley, Daniel E. Griffiths, Archibald O. Haller, G. Alan Hickrod, James McPartland, A. Lewis Rhodes, and David F. Sly. We are especially indebted to Ronald G. Corwin for his most extensive and helpful criticism of the entire final draft. Although we have made a concerted effort to strengthen our manuscript in the light of all suggestions, we have no doubt fallen short and must remain solely responsible for the limitations of our work.

ROBERT E. HERRIOTT
BENJAMIN J. HODGKINS

THE ENVIRONMENT OF SCHOOLING

one

Introduction*

There is little doubt that, for better or for worse, the educational systems of contemporary industrialized societies constitute an integral part of their social life. Many students of social change have noted the extreme pressures for formal education found in all "emerging" nations. Anderson, for example, suggests that the perceived need for formal education stems from its importance for technological progress, cultural unity, and literate administrative personnel.[1] Beyond these immediate needs, he notes the role education plays in the preservation of "intellectual systems," in the development of needed skills and attitudes in a modern society, and in sorting and screening individuals for new social roles.[2]

In America, formal education has evolved from a haphazard, elitist and largely private system in the eighteenth and early nineteenth century to today's highly organized, relatively equalitarian, and largely public system. This transition can be attributed to several changes in America since its founding, not the least of which has been industrialization. Like other social institutions during the period of rapid industrialization, education was shaped by a combination of the cultural heritage of American society and the demands of a largely undeveloped physical environment and new technology.

---

*Throughout this book, numbered footnotes are placed at the end of each chapter. Those identified by letter are situated at the bottom of the page where the text reference occurs.

1

In contemporary America, more youths are going to school longer, and the schooling itself is becoming more complex in organization. Instead of spending his entire educational career in one school, as was often the case in the early part of the eighteenth century, the typical youth in mid-twentieth-century America goes to a series of schools of increasing organizational complexity. Some insight into this development can be gained by considering in detail the growth of the American system of formal education during the past 100 years.

Particularly dramatic has been the increase in the number of young people attending school or college. In 1890 less than 7 percent of the 14–17-year-olds were enrolled in high school. In 1969 the corresponding figure was close to 95 percent (Figure 1–1). A similar dramatic increase can be noted with respect to college and university attendance. For example, in 1870 less than 1 percent of the 18–21-year-olds were enrolled in an institution of higher learning, in 1967 almost 50 percent were enrolled (Figure 1–1).

Not only has the proportion of students enrolled in school been increasing dramatically during the past 100 years, but the time the typical pupil spends in school has also been increasing. According to the best available estimates, in 1870 the average pupil at the elementary or secondary level spent just under 80 days per year in school. His counterpart in 1966 was spending over 160 days in school each year.[3]

There have also been important changes in the organization of formal education. Figure 1–2 presents in idealized form, four general stages of increasing organizational complexity that characterize the development of the American educational system. In the earliest stage, characteristic of much of Colonial America, no system of formal education existed for most people (Figure 1–2A). Systematic instruction took place largely in the family (through fathers and mothers teaching their children) or within the larger society directly (through apprenticeships in skilled and technical occupations).

In the second stage of American educational development, formal schools appeared (Figure 1–2B). Although the first American school was established as early as 1635, this stage is most characteristic of American education during the early part of the nineteenth century at the height of the "common school" movement.

In the third stage of American educational development a differentiation was made between schools and colleges, with some youth still going directly from the family into the larger society, many more going from family to school to the larger society, and a few going from family to school to college and then into the larger society (Figure 1–2C). This stage was particularly characteristic of American society during the latter part of the nineteenth century and the early part of the twentieth century.

The fourth stage of educational development, characteristic of contemporary America, is noted by the highly differentiated array of formal organizations portrayed in Figure 1–2D. All children now attend an "elementary" school (ES) and most go on to a "junior high" school (JHS). A few leave junior high school to enter the larger society directly, but most first enter either a "comprehensive" high school (CHS) (which tends to emphasize college preparation) or a "specialized" high school (SHS) (which tends to emphasize vocational training). After high school the pattern is more diffuse. In 1967 slightly more than half of the high school graduates entered the larger

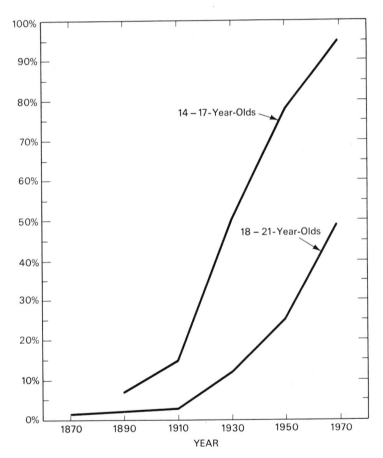

FIGURE 1–1. Percent of American 14–17-year-olds enrolled in secondary education, and of 18–21-year-olds enrolled in higher education: 1870–1970 [Sources: Kenneth A. Simon and W. Vance Grant, Digest of Educational Statistics, 1970 Edition (Washington, D.C.: U. S. Government Print Office, 1970), Table 31; Abbott L. Ferriss, Indicators of Trends in American Education (New York: Russell Sage Foundation, 1969), Figure 2.15].

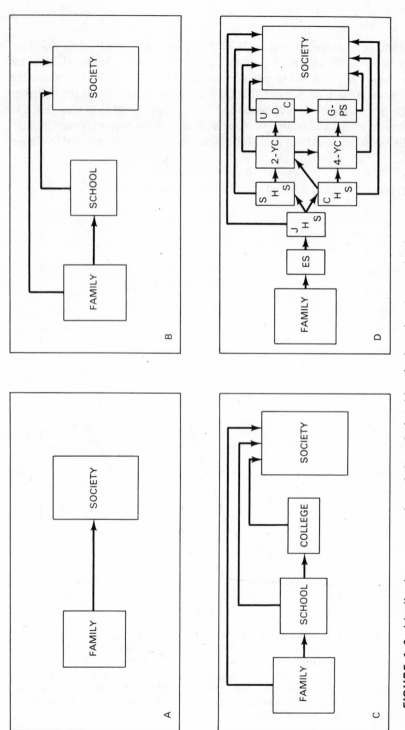

FIGURE 1-2. Idealized representation of the relationship of educational organizations to the family and the society at four stages of educational development. [See text for discussion of symbols.]

society, but (as was noted in Figure 1–1) a rapidly increasing proportion has been attending either a two-year "junior" college (2–YC), or a four-year "senior" college (4-YC). Many students who complete two-year colleges or four-year colleges enter the larger society. But increasingly, students who complete a two-year college go on to "upper divisional" colleges (UDC) or transfer into four-year colleges, and those who have completed four-year colleges go on to "graduate or professional" school (G–PS) before entering the larger society.

This brief account of the growth in size and structural complexity of American education reveals that a system has evolved in the last 100 years wherein a large part of the average American's early life is taken up in "educational concerns." By accentuating the importance of education for *all* youth, and by lengthening the time young people spend in the system, American society has in effect created a major social institution that rivals in many respects the family as a socializing agent. Although such a development is consistent with the industrial and urban requirements of a modern society, as witnessed by the increasingly close relationship between formal education and the occupational status hierarchy,[a] it has created problems, for it makes the individual American increasingly dependent upon institutional arrangements that can be in conflict with his freedom as an individual.[4] At the same time that education has contributed to freeing most Americans from the constraints of ignorance, poverty (in an absolute sense), and the strictures of the small local community, it has forced them to be dependent upon a formal educational system that in some respects is more antithetical to their personal needs than were earlier social arrangements.[b]

---

[a]For a general discussion of the dynamics of this process, see Gerhard Lenski, *Power and Privilege: A Theory of Social Stratification* (New York: McGraw-Hill, 1966), pp. 389–95. Some of the implications of this development for higher education are well developed in a recent work on higher education in Britain. See A. H. Halsey and M. A. Trow, *The British Academics* (Cambridge, Mass.: Harvard University Press, 1971).

[b]Many earlier sociologists were acutely aware of this paradox in the development of modern societies, the locus of which was seen by some as the perceived duality of man's nature. Thus, after discussing the nature of this duality, Durkheim concludes that ". . . since the role of the social being in our single selves will grow ever more important as history moves ahead. . . . All evidence compels us to expect our effort in the struggle between the two beings within us to increase with the growth of civilization." See *Essays on Sociology and Philosophy by Emile Durkheim et al.,* ed. Kurt H. Wolff (New York: Harper Torchbooks, 1964), pp. 339. Simmel expressed this concern somewhat differently. "In an advanced civilization, the community group to which the individual belongs with the whole of his personality has become so large that he is robbed of the advantages and support which membership in a small group could give him. . . . But the formation of purposive associations creates a compensation for this isolation which has resulted from the ever growing extension of the community circle." See Nicholas J. Spykman, *The Social Theory of Georg Simmel* (New York: Atherton Press, 1965), pp. 194–95. And, finally, Toennies, in his classical essay on *Gemienschaft* and *Gesellschaft,* suggests the basic social dynamics surrounding the "emergent" type of constraints associated with modern life when he noted, "Since all relations in the *Gesellschaft* are based upon comparison of

The dynamics of the process that has produced this paradox are far from clear. However, to the extent that modernization has impinged upon the development of schooling, the pattern it has taken was in some unknown measure inevitable.[5] Nevertheless, other patterns of development than that described above might have met the demands of modernization. One need only look at educational systems in Europe to recognize a variety of patterns that serve basically the same ends. Therefore, one must look to the peculiar cultural characteristics of American society itself, as they relate to the development process, in order to gain some insight into the uniqueness of our educational form. In this respect the traditional emphasis upon the individual, reflected in the dominant value orientations of American society, seems particularly important to an understanding not only of the educational system's development, but of the conflicts attendant to that development.

INDIVIDUAL NEEDS VERSUS SOCIETAL NEEDS

All societies have been faced with the dilemma of having to meet the needs of the individual at least minimally and at the same time meet societal requirements.[c] Given the impact of the Industrial Revolution, the current history of Western civilization suggests that the dilemma has been resolved primarily through the mechanism of the formal educational system by redefining individual needs in terms of societal requirements. This has been particularly true of American society, where cultural values have stressed the importance of the individual and his achievement. But beyond this the historical development of American education has systematically reflected a concern alternating between individual and societal needs.

American Values

As in all human societies, some American values are contradictory in

---

possible and offered services, it is evident that the relations with visible material matters have preference, and that more activities and words form the foundation for such relationships only in an unreal way. In contrast to this, *Gemienschaft* as a bond of blood is in the first place a physical relation, therefore, in deeds and words. Here the common relation to the material objects is of a secondary nature and such objects are not exchanged as often as they are used and possessed in common." Ferdinand Toennies, "*Gemienschaft* and *Gesellschaft*," in *Theories of Society*, Vol. I, ed. Talcott Parsons *et al.* (New York: The Free Press, 1961), pp. 191–201.

[c]As Parsons points out, however, it is not a simple matter to define what the "minimum needs" of individuals are. He suggests that from the viewpont of the social system, ". . . it is not the needs of all the participant actors which must be met, nor all the needs of any one, but only a sufficient proportion for a sufficient fraction of the population." See Talcott Parsons, *The Social System* (New York: The Free Press, 1951, paperback edition), p. 28.

their assumptions regarding the relationship of man to society.[d] For example, the emphasis upon personal achievement and success in America accentuates the personal qualities of the individual who ideally through his own efforts can overcome severe obstacles in the realization of his aspirations. Society's role, according to such a view, is to maximize the individual's opportunity and to minimize interference. At the same time, Americans also adhere to what has been described by Myrdal as a "moral overstrain,"[6] a strong commitment to a variety of ethical codes by which they judge not only themselves but others as well. Accordingly, society has the responsibility to insure that individuals live by "ethical" standards. These two views conflict. Is the relationship of the individual to society a voluntaristic one, wherein the society does little more than facilitate him? Or is society responsible for molding the character of the individual along particular ethical lines, and for constraining his action if it deviates from the accepted principles of behavior?

Such inconsistencies in values have served as the basis for numerous conflicts in American society. For example, anti-intellectualism has been rooted in a distrust of established cultural precedents and social institutions. When combined with a general cultural disdain for the "reflective mind," anti-intellectualism has led to a rejection of higher education. At the same time, appreciation of the utilitarian worth of a college education to the individual has provided pressure for the extension of higher education to larger numbers.[7] And in current times a great deal of unrest seems to revolve around the extent to which society has a "right and obligation" to enforce individual compliance with laws, customs, or norms considered by some Americans to be outside the purview of societal responsibility.

Notwithstanding the individual discomfort, disillusion, and despair generated by value conflicts, differing values have played an important part in the sociocultural development of American society generally and with respect to education specifically. One apparent reason for this seems to be that at different historical periods, values stressing either the importance of the individual or of the society have tended to dominate. At such times, critics of our institutions, in agitating for reform, seem to appeal to the less dominant values. Social welfare institutions, for example, have alternately been criticized for their laxity, waste, and ineffectiveness (not meeting social

---

[d]The best general discussion of American values is still to be found in Robin M. Williams, *American Society: A Sociological Interpretation* (New York: Alfred A. Knopf, Inc., 1951), pp. 390–442. An important analytical distinction is made by Joachim Israel in discussing theories of society distinguished by being either "individual-oriented" or "society-oriented." Although his discussion is on a higher level of abstraction than ours, the logical implications Israel associates with the perception of a theorist adapting one orientation or another in his study of society are consistent with our discussion of conflicting values relative to the nature of the relationship between individual Americans and their society as they affected the development of education. See Joachim Israel, *Alienation From Marx to Modern Sociology* (New York: Allyn and Bacon, Inc., 1971), pp. 10–17.

requirements) on the one hand, and their impersonality, red tape, and ineptitude (not meeting the needs of individuals) on the other. The type of criticism that dominates at a given point is usually the opposite of prevailing societal values. In other words, where the society stresses meeting individual needs, critics may succeed in reforming an institution so that it serves the needs of society, and vice versa.

Likewise, the role of the educational system is seen differently by those who stress the importance of the individual and those who stress society. One view of education's role appears to stem from those American values that stress individual achievement, humanitarianism, and equality.[8] Early educational reformers such as G. Stanley Hall, William James, and Edward E. Thorndike placed great stress upon the importance of the educational system in identifying the different talents of individuals and encouraging their development. Hall, as an evolutionary psychologist and educator, believed that heredity was much more important than environment in determining the individual's nature and, therefore, stressed the role of the educational system in meeting the needs of the child as an individual.[9] William James, as a philosopher and psychologist, stressed the need for the school to develop habits of proper behavior in the individual but did not attempt to relate such habits to the requirements of the larger social order.[10] Thorndike, as a psychologist and pupil of James, though not placing as much emphasis as did James upon the individual, also stressed the importance of individual differences in the educational process.[11]

Such men as these saw the process of formal education from a "nominalistic perspective," wherein the aggregate of individuals that is society is believed to benefit primarily from the maximum development of each individual's capacities.[e] Because society is simply the sum of the individuals who comprise it, any "improvement" in the social order is, *ipso facto*, a function of the improvement of individuals. The stress upon individualism, a strong value in American society generally, did not preclude a sense of society, of course. Quite the contrary! The very essence of American society, as seen from this perspective, rested upon the fulfillment of individual potential. Thus, the individual's achievement was the primary justification for formal education. Given such a view, the inadequacies of the educational system

---

[e]The nominalistic view of society generally and education in particular was usually combined with a variety of voluntarism and individualism to provide a unique American perspective of the nature of man and society that presupposed the rational development of society as a logical extension of the personal characteristics of its membership. Such a view was widely shared by many American intellectuals, including American sociologists, during this period. See, for example, Roscoe C. Hinkle, Jr., "Durkheim in American Sociology," in Wolff, *Essays on Sociology and Philosophy by Emile Durkheim,* pp. 267–95; and Robert Bierstedt, "Nominal and Real Definitions in Sociological Theory," in *Symposium on Sociological Theory,* ed. by Llewellyn Gross (New York: Harper and Row, Publishers, 1959), pp. 121–44.

were seen to center primarily upon organizational, familial, economic, and cultural conditions that precluded the realization of individual potential.

The fundamental assumption underlying this view is that, since man is the measure of all things, what benefits one man benefits the collectivity of which he is a part. Accordingly, efforts of educators who followed this line of reasoning to "improve" the educational system emphasized testing individual ability, aptitude, and interest, reform of the curriculum, and the introduction of guidance and counseling practices. Each reform was justified on the grounds that it would benefit not only the individual directly, but the larger society indirectly as well.

The second perspective on the role of the educational system was derived from those American values that Williams has identified as emphasizing morality, external conformity, and nationalism.[12] Such a perspective stresses the socialization and integration of youth into the larger society. As did those with the first perspective, many early American educators with this second view emphasized the "moral" or integrative basis of American education. Horace Mann, for example, a leading influence upon nineteenth-century educators, noted that "all those who are worthily laboring to promote the cause of education are laboring to elevate mankind into the upper and purer regions of civilization, Christianity, and the worship of the true God. . . ."[13] Indeed, one of the greatest attributes of the public school, according to Mann, was its opportunity to influence the "whole life" of the child.[14] So, also, did William Torry Harris see "moral" responsibilities associated with public education.[15] More recently, John Dewey, who perhaps more than any other person in the twentieth century influenced the thinking of American educators, argued for the importance of the school's role in the unification of society in a democratic morality.[16]

To each of these educational reformers, the theme of a "moral" or "character" education, serving the collective interest of the society as they saw it, was of paramount importance. Each of these men, it should be noted, considered himself to be supportive of the interests of the individual. Each associated that interest with a sociocultural ethic dominant in his period of American history. Indeed, for Dewey the "pragmatism" of individual development was forever dependent upon man's social life, not upon the internal dynamics of his personality.[17] Thus, the school was viewed as a major socialization agency, one that should influence and shape the child's perception of social reality. Depending on the ideological and political orientation of these earlier educators, such shaping would be directed to "Christian" principles, to a democratic outlook, or to support of the *status quo*.[18] In all instances, however, there was a recognition of the "social responsibility" of the educational system, which waxed and waned between the school as a purveyor of change and as simply a transmitter of values.[19]

The assumption regarding the nature of men and society underlying such a perception of the institutional process of education is not that fulfillment of the intrinsic needs of man benefits society (the nominalistic approach), but rather that the individual's perception of social reality is determined in large measure by his sociocultural context. The individual is, thus, a social product and his values, beliefs, aspirations, and desires, as well as his perception of his capabilities and limitations, are formed as the result of his social experience. Thus, they are not intrinsic to his nature as a human being.

Given such an assumption regarding the social nature of individuals, it logically followed that agencies of socialization, such as schools, perform an extremely important function in articulating an image of society to each new generation far beyond their manifest claims, which are generally couched in utilitarian terms of simply serving the individual. For such agencies must, from this perspective, play a critical role over a period of years in molding the individual's perception of himself, of the larger social order, and of his place within that order. The development of an educational system that merely serves the interests and capacities of the individual seems meaningless to those who believe that the development of such interests and the recognition of such capacities are a function of society. Educational reforms generated by such a view, accordingly, have tended to stress the need of the system to integrate the child more adequately into the larger society.

Trends in Educational Values

Significant as are the differences between these two perspectives on the role of education, it is important to note that few advocates of either have ever been absolute in their advocacy. All advocates tended to reflect a common American value emphasis upon the practical and the rational. Indeed, in some respects the value placed upon pragmatism has been the unifying theme throughout the history of American education. America is, as Hofstadter has noted, a "practical culture."[20]

Because of such a unifying theme, existing educational practices, as well as criticisms of these practices, were inevitably presented in pragmatic terms, thereby providing an underlying continuity to the development of the system which, with the impact of the industrial revolution, ultimately facilitated what has been referred to as the "rationalization" of American education.[f] Thus, the early establishment of a rudimentary educational system was provided in part by the perceived necessity for a social mechanism to instill in children

---

[f]The most noted sociologist to consider this process was Max Weber. For a thorough discussion of his usage of the idea of "rationality" and "rationalization" in Western civilization, see Julien Freund, *The Sociology of Max Weber* (New York: Vintage Books, 1968), pp. 140–49.

the moral virtues appropriate to a Christian upbringing.[21] Much of the criticism of this type of education during this early period hinged upon its inadequacies in preparing colonial youth to assume productive adult roles. Men of stature in the colonies, such as Benjamin Franklin and William Penn, protested both the lack of humanitarian methods and the impractical nature of the curriculum.[22] Later, with the advance of industrialization during the nineteenth century, concern with the practical value of education became consistent with the perceived needs of industrialists and in a crude fashion was incorporated into the "purpose" of public education. Subsequently, new criticism arose over the inadequacies of this "vocational" system and its consequent failure to meet the needs of individuals in a democratic society.[23]

More recently, the rise of the Progressive Movement in the late nineteenth and the early twentieth century, although associated with the name of John Dewey, saw the reassertion of a humanistic concern for the intellectual, emotional, and social development of the child as a dominant philosophical orientation in American schools.[24] Although it was never totally accepted, its linkages with a variety of educational reforms in the first half of the twentieth century has been well documented.[25] As might be anticipated, during the latter half of this period such critics of the educational system as Lippmann, Bell, Smith, Bestor, and Hutchins pointed to the failure of the schools along several fronts, which can be more or less subsumed under the rubric of a loss in "academic rigor and quality" leading to a failure to prepare children to meet the intellectual and social exigencies of the society.[26]

Although the strength of Progressive Education had waned considerably by the late 1950's, due in part to its success, a re-emergence of its original concern for the social role of the school occurred.[27] Related in no small measure to the Cold War need for an educational system that met the ideological, intellectual, and material challenge of communism, pressures to upgrade the academic content of the curriculum, increase the moralistic thrust of "Americanism," and emphasize the role of education as a screening agency for occupations became quite apparent. Although considerable effort was expended during this period to assist the economically and culturally deprived child, its focus was upon preparing the child to meet the demands of the school rather than on modifying the school to meet the needs of the child. So, also, efforts to locate and stimulate intellectually gifted children seemed motivated more by a concern to use their talents in international competition than to provide them with opportunities to develop as individuals.

Currently, criticism of the socially oriented approach to education once again is intense. Thus, Goodman, after berating the contemporary higher educational system for its meaningless structure, content, and formality, argues for a decentralized and humanized arrangement where learning can occur in small face-to-face groups.[28] Kozol's autobiography of his experiences as a teacher in the Boston public schools is representative of many journalistic, analytical, and research efforts emphasizing how the contemporary American urban educational system is devastating to the personal and intellectual development of poor and black children.[29] Further, Illich, from a radical humanist perspective, perhaps best expresses much of the critical feeling toward contemporary education when he suggests that ". . . schools affect individuals and characterize nations. Individuals merely get a bad deal; nations are irreversibly degraded when they build schools to help their citizens play at international competition."[30]

Rationalization and Institutionalization

Of particular importance to an understanding of the development of the American education system since the introduction of industrialization in the nineteenth century are the terms "rationalization" and "institutionalization." Both phenomena are features of any modern society. Their importance for an understanding of the American educational system in particular, however, is tied directly to the manner in which the type of value-oriented conflict discussed above has been integrated into a rational system where individual needs are institutionalized.[31]

The term "rationalization" refers to the organization of social behavior through a division of labor and coordination of collective efforts toward the attainment of stated ends. The basis for this process has been science and technology generally and the industrialization of Western society specifically, which according to Weber did not presuppose increased knowledge or intellectual acumen *per se*. Rather, industrialization represented a logical social outgrowth of the general belief in man's ability to "master all things by calculation."[32] American industrial development was, therefore, facilitated in no small measure by a tendency to equate such mastery by calculation with "social progress." Similarly, the material benefits to individuals from social progress were generally interpreted as "individual progress." Thus in the past the apparent conflict between individual and social needs tended to be reduced—although never fully resolved—through an emphasis on the apparent mutual benefits of the rationalization of social life.

American society, however, has recently witnessed very dramatic social and cultural changes attendant to its growth into an industrial nation. In large measure society's need for education to develop skills and appropriate values in its populace (although more gradual in American historical perspective than in contemporary "emerging" nations) seems to have led to the rapid development of a "rational" educational system. Thus, the increase in numbers of students attending school and in the amount of time spent in the classroom, noted earlier, can be viewed as a rational development of an educational system in a highly technical social order. So, also, the increasing complexity of the educational process itself, as previously illustrated in Figure 1–2, attests to the rationality of the growing division of labor and specialization within the American educational system.

This process of rationalization has continued over the last century, in spite of conflicts over the "purpose" of education *vis à vis* the individual and society. This does not mean that such conflicts were irrelevant, for the rationalization process could not occur in a sociocultural vacuum. What appears to have occurred is an incorporation of the value configurations associated with the individual into the rationalization process. In effect, the process can be described as the institutionalization of individual needs into the formal system of schooling.[g] Educational reforms, generated by those who have perceived the role of education to be that of meeting the needs of the individual, have increasingly been redefined in a rational fashion consistent with societal requirements. For example, the "counseling" of students, which ostensibly is used to assist them to develop as individuals, seems increasingly to be a selection process to facilitate organizational efficiency.[33] Testing programs, created with the idea of helping the student understand his interests, aptitudes, and liabilities, end up helping the educational system to "track" him.[34] Specialized curricula that propose to make education more relevant for the student are reinterpreted to further organizational growth and development.[h]

This rationalization of the American educational system and institutionalization of individual needs can be viewed as dialectical, as shown in Figure 1–3. Beginning in early American society with the "thesis" that the purpose of education was to serve the needs of the community, the seeds for the "antithesis" to this view rested in the American cultural values associated with individualism, humanitarianism, and egalitarianism. Increased emphasis upon these values with the advent of industrialization ultimately resulted in a synthesis—a late nineteenth-century educational system justified in terms of its association of the needs of the individual with the requirements of an industrial society. Such a synthesis placed inadequate emphasis upon individual and humanistic concerns. Accordingly, the basis for subsequent criticism, culminating in the Progressive Education movement of the twentieth century, was assured. The more recent "reaction" in the 1950's to that development, as well as the late 1960's reaction to con-

---

[g]Seen from the viewpoint of the individual, this has been related to the "alienation" of the individual from the system. Formerly personal relationships within the system have become depersonalized, or in Simmel's words "objectified," since the basis for the relationship rests upon abstract principles—in this case the principles associated with rationalized bureaucratic organization. See Israel, *Alienation,* pp. 121–34.

[h]For example, the transformation of Dewey's philosophy for education reform into a social movement bearing little relationship to Dewey's original intent is well described in Cremin, *Transformation of the School.*

sequences following from adjustments to changes wrought in the 1950's, would appear to be simply the most recent manifestation of a dialectical process that is being accelerated by rapid growth in America's affluence and the pressures of international conflict.

The full ramifications of this developmental process for American education are undoubtedly poorly understood—if for no other reason than the deep involvement of Americans in the process itself. At the same time, however, on the basis of the preceding discussion and considering current themes of educational protest, it is reasonable to suggest that two major concerns, the increasing centralization of power in education and the alleged inability of education to respond to the needs of individual students, will ultimately be reflected in future "educational reforms" that will be rationally incorporated into the present structure, although not necessarily in the form advocated by the critics. In the minds of many critics of education, decentralization and sensitivity to individual needs are two sides of the same coin.

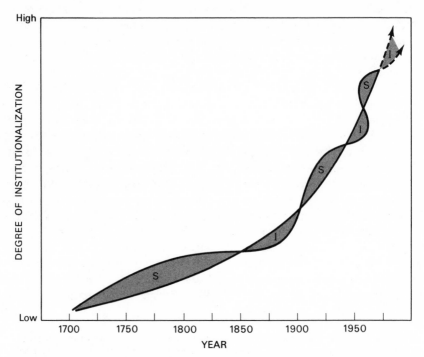

FIGURE 1–3 *Idealized representation of the degree of institutionalization of individual needs within the American educational system: 1700–1975. [Shaded areas above and below the solid line represent the dominant value orientation with respect to the responsibility of the educational system for meeting societal (S) versus individual (I) needs.]*

Thus, many current advocates of decentralization justify their position in terms of the need for a system more sensitive to the individual needs of the student. And many critics of the "dehumanizing" educational experience available to many of today's youth describe the educational system as an impersonal bureaucracy. In fact, however, a decentralized system need not be sensitive to individual needs, nor is it necessary that an individually responsive system be decentralized.[35]

THEORETICAL OVERVIEW

If the preceding observations are accurate, a clearer understanding of both the nature and weaknesses of schooling in contemporary America can be gained by viewing formal education as a sociocultural system open to influences from the larger society. Given such a perspective, the conclusions of many studies that "educational outcomes" are more likely a function of factors outside of the school than of those within it,[36] take on new meaning, for they illustrate the more general fact that as "open" social systems, educational organizations are continually influenced by society. Thus, it is not simply that children within the educational system *fail to learn,* but rather that *what they learn* is determined in large measure by the interaction of school and society.[37]

In addition, as the educational system becomes increasingly rational relative to broad societal needs rather than attuned to the immediate requirements of the various social groups or individuals, subsocietal variation in the perception of the role of the educational system becomes more critical in determining the nature of the learning experience. In contemporary American society in particular, since individual and minority group needs are increasingly rationalized into social ends, the schools' ability to respond to individual or collective needs different from those ends on other than institutionally rational grounds seems limited. Thus, variations in sociocultural constraints *within* the society are likely to assume greater significance than they would if the educational system were isolated from external influence.

Past efforts to explore the dynamics of the relationship between sociocultural forces and the American educational system have been largely descriptive, have treated education as a closed system, or have approached the subject from the standpoint of the individual rather than of the total system.[38] Although such efforts are meritorious, too often they have ignored the dependence of the educational system on sociocultural forces. Because of this oversight, there has been a tendency to interpret the results of such studies in a vacuum, divorced from the mainstream of social concern about acknowledged educational problems.

In the following chapter we will explain more fully what is meant by the concept "modernity" and will view educational contexts as sociocultural environments of different degrees of modernity with at least three major *dimensions* (the cultural, the ecological, and the structural). These environments exist at least at six distinct *layers* (neighborhood, community, state, region, society, and civilization).

In Chapter Three, educational systems will be viewed as open social systems with at least four major *properties* (input, throughput, output, and structure). They will be discussed on six distinct *levels* (school, school district, state, region, nation, and civilization).

Given these definitions and assumptions we will offer this general hypothesis: *The degree of modernity of an educational system varies as a function of the degree of modernity of its sociocultural environment.* Then in Chapters Four, Five, and Six, we will report a series of original analyses of educational systems designed to test this hypothesis at the system levels of nation, region, state, school district, and school. Finally in Chapter Seven we will summarize our findings and reconsider the issues raised in the present chapter in the light of all the evidence we have assembled and explore their implications for the future structure of American education.

REFERENCES

[1]C. Arnold Anderson, "The Modernization of Education," in *Modernization: The Dynamics of Growth,* ed. Myron Weiner (New York: Basic Books, Inc., 1966), pp. 68–80.

[2]*Ibid.,* pp. 70–71. For a skeptical view of the importance of formal education to economic requirements, see Ivar Berg, *Education and Jobs: The Great Training Robbery* (New York: Frederick A. Praeger, Inc., 1970).

[3]Abbott L. Ferriss, *Indicators of Trends in American Education* (New York: Russell Sage Foundation, 1969), Figure 6.2.

[4]Richard Hofstadter, *Anti-Intellectualism in American Life* (New York: Alfred A. Knopf, Inc., 1969).

[5]Whether or not the pattern that American education has taken in the twentieth century was totally inevitable has been extensively considered by Katz, who notes that alternates were actively debated during the nineteenth century. See Michael B. Katz, "From Voluntarism to Bureaucracy in American Education," *Sociology of Education,* 44 (1971), 297–332.

[6]Gunnar Myrdal *et al., An American Dilemma,* Vol. I (New York: Harper & Row, Publishers, 1944), 21.

[7]Hofstadter, *Anti-Intellectualism in American Life,* Part 4.

[8]Williams, *American Society.*

[9]Merle Curti, *The Social Ideas of American Educators* (New York: Charles Scribners Sons, 1935), pp. 404–11.

[10]*Ibid.,* pp. 445–52.

[11]*Ibid.,* pp. 479–80.

[12]Williams, *American Society.*

[13]Neil G. McClusky, *The Public School and Moral Education* (New York: Columbia University Press, 1958), p. 44.

[14]*Ibid.*, p. 52.

[15]*Ibid.*, pp. 159–61.

[16]*Ibid.*, p. 251.

[17]*Ibid.*, p. 256.

[18]Curti, *Social Ideas of American Educators*, pp. 218–45.

[19]*Ibid.*, p. 259.

[20]Hofstadter, *Anti-Intellectualism in American Life.*

[21]Rena L. Vassar, ed., *Social History of American Education*, Vol. I: *Colonial Times to 1860* (Skokie, Ill.: Rand McNally and Company, 1965), 5.

[22]*Ibid.*, pp. 8–14.

[23]Rena L. Vassar, ed., *Social History of American Education*, Vol. II: *1860 to the Present*, 115–25.

[24]Lawrence A. Cremin, *The Transformation of the School: Progressivism in American Education, 1876–1957*, Part II (New York: Vintage Books, 1961).

[25]See, for example, *Ibid.*, chap. 8 and 9, and Curti, *Social Ideas of American Educators.*

[26]Walter Lippmann, "Education Without Culture," *Commonweal*, 33 (1941), 322–25; Bernard I. Bell, *Crises in Education* (New York: Whittlesey, 1949); Mortimer Smith, *And Madly Teach* (Chicago: Henry Regnery Co., 1949); Arthur Bestor, *Educational Wastelands* (Urbana, Ill.: University of Illinois Press, 1953); Robert Hutchins, *The Conflict in Education* (New York: Harper & Row, Inc., 1953).

[27]Cremin, *Transformation of the School*, chap. 8.

[28]Paul Goodman, *The Community of Scholars* (New York: Random House, Inc., 1962), chap. 8.

[29]Jonathan Kozol, *Death at an Early Age: The Destruction of the Hearts and Minds of Negro Children in the Boston Public Schools* (Boston: Houghton Mifflin Company, 1967).

[30]Ivan D. Illich, *Celebration of Awareness: A Call for Institutional Revolution* (Garden City, N. Y.: Doubleday & Company, Inc., 1970), p. 182. See also Ivan D. Illich, *Deschooling Society* (New York: Harper & Row, Publishers, 1970).

[31]For an excellent discussion of the views of Marx, Weber, Simmel, and Durkheim on these subjects, see Israel, *Alienation*, chaps. 1–5.

[32]Freund, *The Sociology of Max Weber* (New York: Vintage Books, 1968).

[33]See, for example, Aaron V. Cicourel and John I. Kitsuse, *The Educational Decision-Makers* (Indianapolis: The Bobbs-Merrill Company, Inc., 1963).

[34]A good summary of the social role of student testing in American education is provided in David A. Goslin, *The Search for Ability: Standardized Testing in Social Perspective* (New York: John Wiley & Sons, Inc., 1966).

[35]See, for example, Michael B. Katz, "The Present Movement in Educational Reform," *Harvard Educational Review*, 41 (1971), 342–59.

[36]See, for example, James W. Guthrie, "A Survey of School Effectiveness Studies," in *Do Teachers Make A Difference?* (Washington, D. C.: U. S. Office of Education, 1970), pp. 25–54.

[37]A similar argument has been advanced in Charles E. Silberman, *Crisis in the Classroom: The Remaking of America* (New York: Doubleday and Company, 1971) pp. 70–80.

[38]For an overview of previous research, see Charles E. Bidwell, "The School as a Formal Organization," in *Handbook of Organizations*, ed. James G. March (Skokie, Ill.: Rand McNally and Company, 1965), pp. 972–1022.

two

The Environment of American Educational Systems

In this chapter, we shall first discuss modernity and modernization generally, then consider in detail three prominent layers of the environment of American educational systems: *region, community,* and *neighborhood*. After defining these terms, we show the relationship of region, community, and neighborhood to the concept of modernity and review what is currently known about how variation in educational phenomena are associated with these aspects of the sociocultural environment. In Chapter Three, we turn to a more abstract conceptualization of the relationship of educational systems to their sociocultural environments, a conceptualization that we will test empirically in Chapters Four, Five, and Six.

MODERNITY AND MODERNIZATION

Modernity and modernization can be analyzed from at least as many perspectives as there are social sciences.[1] While sociologists have tended to stress the structural and functional characteristics of modernity (specialization and differentiation), economists have stressed productive control and economic growth (industrial rewards). Geographers and demographers have usually focused on urbanization and population growth, political scientists have concerned themselves with the emergence and attendant problems of new forms of poltical control, anthropologists have sought to identify general cultural changes associated with the process, and social psychologists have focused upon value and attitudinal changes displayed by individuals in societies evolving toward a more modern state.[2] Each of these concerns is legitimate and reflects to some extent the extremely complex nature of the modernization process. To reduce this complexity, we can postulate one of the primary bases upon which contemporary societies seem to modernize. This basis appears to involve both the introduction of a new technology and the social acceptance of the consequences of that technology in most, if not all, areas of the society.[3] Accordingly, the *modernity of a society* in contemporary times may be defined as *the extent to which it is characterized by a general acceptance and use of the most advanced available technical knowledge. Modernization,* then, refers to *the process by which this acceptance and use occur.*

The introduction of a new technology is often very rapid and can be identified historically as stemming from either innovation or cross-cultural diffusion. The general acceptance of the consequences of that technology, however, is often quite gradual. Lerner has captured the cultural essence of the nontechnological aspects of modernization when he speaks of the challenge to all societies that seek modernization regarding ". . . the infusion of a rationalistic and positivistic spirit."[4] In effect, given increasing technological knowledge, there must be an increasing willingness on the part of a significant and influential segment of a society's membership to restructure social life in order to maximize the potential benefits to be derived from that technology.[5]

Such a restructuring, of course, is never complete, nor does it affect with equal force all segments of the social order. Institutions within a society vary in their susceptibility to the effective and efficient use of the new technology, thereby reducing to a degree the direct impact of that technology upon them, as well as the immediacy of its influence, Thus, the results of early attempts to use technology effectively were first and most dramatically evident in the productive (or economic) sectors of eighteenth- and nineteenth-century Europe. Subsequently, political and familial institutions began to reflect the impact of economic decisions in those societies. Ultimately, religious and social hierarchical arrangements came increasingly and differentially to reflect significant changes in other areas of the social systems. Although it is questionable whether this was the actual order of influence, the historic manifest consequences of "the rationalistic and positivistic spirit" seems to have been expressed in the sequence described. Whether the twentieth century will sustain the continued development of this spirit into all segments of the social order of Western civilization is uncertain, although sociologists such as Ellul and Aron argue for the spirit's inevitability.[6]

Implicit in the above remarks is the assumption that modernization does not occur uniformly within a given society. Because pre-modern societies vary internally in similarity to the modern ideal, as well as in resiliency to pressures for change, the idea that variation occurs cross-culturally is readily accepted. Internal variation in modernization is less commonly considered, although its tenability has been advanced by several authorities.[7] One reason would seem to be the tendency to view a "society" as socioculturally homogeneous, with little internal variation. Such a view is necessary, of course, for most cross-cultural comparisons. However, it bears little resemblance to social reality in other than the smallest of traditional societies.

Many facets of a society influenced by modernization could be elaborated upon. However, in the following discussion we shall restrict ourselves to discussing briefly three major dimensions influenced by modern technology: the ecological, the cultural, and the structural. This is not to suggest that factors other than technology, such as nationalism, religion, or ideology,[8] may not have influenced these dimensions in the course of modernization, but without technology and the acceptance of its ecological, cultural, and structural consequences, modernization as we view it today simply could not exist. Technology and its acceptance, then, are seen as necessary (but probably not sufficient) conditions for modernization, and therefore can be considered as a primary basis for its occurrence. As will become apparent in the following analysis, each dimension can have great relevance for the nature of formal education in contemporary American society.

Ecological Dimension

Human ecology has traditionally been defined by sociologists as the study of man's relationship to his natural environment.[9] In particular, this area of scholarship has focused upon the temporal and spatial arrangements of the human community in its adaptation to the constraints of its environment. Such concern has tended to focus upon the population characteristics of the community as they affect and are affected by the symbiotic nature of the community-environment relationship. Most notably, Durkheim at the end of the nineteenth century observed the importance of population size and density in determining the patterns and bases for relationships within a society.[10] A classical attempt to differentiate and categorize communities using population size, density, and heterogeneity was that of Wirth,[11] wherein *small* communities were characterized as low in density, homogeneous, and having relationships mainly of a primary nature based upon sentiment. Conversely, *large* communities tended to be high in density, heterogeneous, and having most social relationships of a secondary, utilitarian nature. More recent students of community, while acknowledging the importance of Wirth's contribution, question the primacy of size, density, and heterogeneity in determining the nature of the community.[12] Nonetheless, the tenor of ecological research on the human community has stressed the importance of these three population characteristics in determining the nature of the communities' social order.[13]

The relevance of human ecology for modernization is in the fact of mankind's phenomenal increase in numbers. At the end of the neolithic period, the world population has been estimated at between 5 and 10 million.[14] By the time of Christ it had risen to between 200 and 300 million, and by 1650 had reached 500 million. Currently, it is over 3 billion. The rate of increase, in other words, has risen from roughly 2 percent every 1000 years to 2 percent *per year*. In the neolithic period, population increase was accomplished primarily through the development of sedentary life styles and the establishment of small agricultural communities. The growth from these early Neolithic villages to large cities has been fully discussed elsewhere.[15] It is important to note, however, that since at least 1800 this "urbanization" has proceeded at a faster rate than has population growth. According to Hauser, while world population increased 2.5 times between 1800 and 1950, the proportion of the population living in cities of 100,000 and over increased 23 times.[16]

More currently, some ecologists have sought to make explicit the nature of this development by focusing upon the so-called "ecosystem."[17] An ecosystem is characterized as a "natural unit" (a type of system) that exchanges materials, energy, and information with other living and nonliving units in its environment. Further, living systems are complex material structures maintained by such exchange.[18] From an ecological point of view, the significance of man's historical development has been his ability to increase his importance in the ecosystem of the planet through the use of technology to serve his material ends. Through more efficient techniques of food production his numbers increased dramatically. So, also, technology freed large numbers from elementary tasks associated with survival, and through the elaboration of organizational arrangements society was able to further advance its control over the environmental component of the ecosystem.[19]

From the view of the human ecologist, modernization is but the most recent step in man's unending struggle to enhance his position relative to the physical environment. To the human ecologist, the distinguishing impetus of this process is not the introduction of technology as such, but rather the increasing use of inanimate sources of energy to serve man's material ends. A primary change in the social order associated with modernization is the increasing concentration and heterogeneity of the population in metropolitan centers. Although historic civilizations have supported great cities (Rome, Alexandria, Constantinople), and large cities exist in contemporary traditional societies (Bangkok, Saigon, Baghdad), only in the more modern societies have large *proportions* of a society's population been concentrated in urban centers.[20]

This change from a highly dispersed population in traditional societies to a highly concentrated population in modern societies is of particular interest from an ecological perspective, for several developments are derived from it. By the enlargement and concentration of the population in metropolitan centers, societies are able to divert labor from agriculture to other productive pursuits from which yet further technological progress can be achieved. So, also, the collective efforts of large numbers of workers have required the development of managerial and coordination skills.[21]

The beginning of modern society is associated with industrialization of the late eighteenth and early nineteenth century—although as Duncan points out, many technical innovations necessary for industrialization occurred much earlier.[22] The current industrial phase of social development has, however, witnessed the general intensification of the characteristics identified above, with one notable difference. Technology, which originally had been *used* by man in his interchanges with the environment, has become the basis for decisions both in regard to those interchanges and in the organizational arrangements society deems desirable.[23] In effect, a "quantum leap" in man's role in the ecosystem was achieved through the use of inanimate forms of energy to the point where techniques for energy control have been interposed between man and his physical environment. In somewhat different terms, a more functionally general level of complexity has emerged in man's relationship to his environment wherein that relationship is mediated by the state of the technology available. Thus, such modern environmental problems as air and water pollution, urban blight, transportation tieups, breakdowns in waste disposal, and the like become defined as the "costs" of technological sophistication. Further, solutions depend upon available technical resources. The core of modern industrial life is found within areas of concentrated population where the material and organizational benefits of technology can be most effectively exploited and its ecological ramifications (both desirable and undesirable) are most evident. Accordingly, solutions to these "primary" problems rest upon their compatibility with the technical logic of existing services.

Cultural Dimension

One limitation associated with the ecological approach to modernization, as convincing as it is in other respects, is its failure to systematically develop the role of values, beliefs, and norms in the changes associated with the modernization of a society.[24] Therefore we must also look at modernization from the cultural point of view.

If we define *culture* as *that meaning collectively shared by a society, learned as part of the normal socialization experience of its members, and transmitted from generation to generation,*[25] then it is probably fair to contend that the most significant, although intangible, aspect of change associated with modernization is the pattern of meaning relating man to both his natural and his social environments. Whether such change is antecedent to, subsequent to, or coterminous with the ecological component of modernization is open to debate,[26] but there is little doubt that such a cultural change is vital to the total transformation.

In a general sense, the essence of the cultural change associated with modernization can best be understood by recognizing that all men must come to terms with the conditions of their existence and that ways to do this are limited. The manner in which societies collectively define these conditions provide the organizing principles around which culture is developed. Following Kluckhohn and Strodtbeck, these responses can be defined as "value orientations," that is, "generalized and organized principle(s) concerning basic human problems which pervasively and profoundly influence(s) man's behavior."[27]

Four major problems important to an understanding of cultural change are the society's man-to-nature orientation, its time orientation, its orientation toward activity, and its relational orientation.[a] Essentially, the man-to-nature orientation stems from the basic problem of how man relates to nature or his physical environment. Three fundamental alternatives are mastery over environment, subjugation to it, or harmony with it. As to time, a society may be oriented primarily toward the past, the present, or the future. In respect to action, the emphasis may be upon "doing," "being," or "being in becoming." And, finally, the dominant relations of men may be upon the extended family, the group, or the individual.[28]

In modern societies, the value orientation regarding the environment is predominantly one of mastery over nature, if the ecological changes noted earlier may be explained as an attempt to more effectively control man's place in the ecosystem. Verification of this conclusion may be adduced from studies by anthropologists and sociologists regarding the man-nature orientation in more contemporary traditional societies,[b] which display fatalistic

---

[a]Kluckhohn and Strodtbeck, *ibid.*, originally identified *five* problems. We have chosen to exclude "the nature of man" problem from this analysis, however, because of our dominant concern with the environmental and social characteristics of the system and, further, we have some reservations as to whether the nature of man problem as developed by Kluckhohn and Stroddteck is logically consistent with the other four problems.

[b]For a summary of much of the cross-cultural research supportive of this generalization, as well as other differences between modern and traditional attitudes, beliefs, and values, see Alex Inkeles, "The Modernization of Man," in Weiner, "Introduction," in *Modernization*; and David H. Smith and Alex Inkeles, "The OM Scale: A Comparative Social Psychological Measure of Individual Modernity," *Sociometry*, 29 (1966), 353–77.

acceptance of nature's order. Studies of the values, attitudes, and beliefs of modernizing societies themselves suggest that faith in an active mastery of the environment is a dominant orientation of these societies.[29]

The dominant time orientation in more modern societies is toward the future. This would seem to follow naturally from the necessity to invent techniques for handling technical problems, or to accept the diffusion of an innovation from another culture. Traditional societies tend to sanctify not only past events, but traditional norms and customs as well, thereby reducing the likelihood of either developing or accepting modern techniques to replace sacrosanct traditional techniques.[30] An orientation toward the present also does not stress the importance of new solutions to technical problems. Rather, the emphasis in traditional societies seems to be upon either acceptance of current alternatives or the inevitability that particular consequences follow from possible impending events.[31]

Modern societies stress doing, rather than being or being in becoming. Where emotional gratification is important, a being orientation is common; and a being in becoming orientation finds expression in those social orders with highly stylized and idealistic definitions of the individual. On the other hand, emphasis on doing is congruent with active mastery over the environment and future time orientation. Evidence in support of such reasoning is most apparent in American society, where achievement has tended to be equated with "the American way of life."[32]

Relational orientations in modern society, at least within Western civilization,[c] would seem to be consistent with an emphasis upon the individual, as opposed to the family or the larger social group, in keeping with the constraints of a technological proficiency associated with mastery over nature and a concern with achievement. Further, the interdependent nature of specialized social relationships based upon "differences in kind"[33] rather than upon a "likeness of kind," as Durkheim noted in the nineteenth century, would further accentuate the importance of the individual in dominant patterns of social relations. Evidence of this emphasis, in both its positive and negative forms, is suggested by the concern in modern societies for the individual's "equal rights," regardless of his ascribed social or

---

[c]Just how appropriate such a relational emphasis upon the individual in modern societies is outside of Western civilization is a debatable point. Certainly Abegglen's study of Japanese industrial development, as well as Berger's analysis of Egyptian bureaucracy, suggests that the emergence of the relational emphasis upon the individual may be less a product of industrialization than of the interaction of industrialization and dominant values associated with Western civilization generally and Western Christianity specifically. See James G. Abegglen, *The Japanese Factory* (New York: The Free Press, 1968); and Morroe Berger, *Bureaucracy and Society in Modern Egypt* (Princeton, N.J.: Princeton University Press, 1957).

physical characteristics, and by the concern for "alienation" as a result of modern conditions.[d]

At a less abstract level, values consistent with the orientations noted above may be anticipated in the more modern "ideal" society. Specifically, defining values as the "primary connecting element between . . . social and cultural systems" which in effect determine the action taken by members of that society,[34] we would expect patterns of behavior indicative of value orientations previously associated with modernity. Such patterns would reflect, among other things: a) an openness to new experiences, b) an emphasis upon individual qualities, as opposed to group attributes, c) a positive orientation toward the solution of both individual and collective problems, d) a concern for time and the planning of activities, e) a propensity for interest and participation in activities affecting individuals' political and economic status in the group.[35] Undoubtedly, other patterns could also reflect modern values. These, however, would appear to be some of the major patterns for which there is some empirical support,[36] and the obverse of these patterns would be anticipated in the "ideal" traditional society.

In reality, of course, no modern society could be expected to exhibit uniformly attitudes and beliefs appropriate to such values, any more than the ecological dynamics noted in the previous section could be expected to reflect completely the spatial and temporal arrangements within every sector of a modern society. However, the general pattern of evolutionary change does appear to be evident in both cases. The empirical question then, is not one of demonstrating the totality of modernization in terms of other ecological arrangements or operative values, but rather the extent to which a society or sociocultural units within a society have advanced in that direction.

Structural Dimension

The ecological expansion of modern societies with the introduction of a new technology expresses itself in concentration of population and reordering of organizational arrangements. Further, values arise consistent with the effective and efficient use of the new technology for man's adaptation to his

---

[d]The various militant efforts for equal rights most commonly associated today with racial and ethnic minorities, or various women's groups, has found its expression historically in numerous social movements over the last two centuries. For an interesting discussion of this historic thrust, see R. R. Palmer, *The Age of Democratic Revolution* (Princeton, N. J.: Princeton University Press, 1959). On the other hand, writings on the alienation of the individual in modern society, generated in part by a similar emphasis upon the individual, can be found in such works as Kenneth Keniston, *The Uncommitted* (New York: Harcourt Brace Jovanovich, 1965), Robert Presthus, *The Organizational Society* (New York: Random House, Inc., 1962), and more recently Charles A. Reich, *The Greening of America* (New York: Random House, Inc., 1970).

environment. The interrelated nature of the ecological and cultural dimensions of modernization is, perhaps, most evident in the structural dimension of the modernization process.

A *social structure* may be defined as *the relatively enduring stable pattern of social interaction which integrates the various and sundry elements of a social system.*[37] New organizational arrangements, legitimated by appropriate norms and values, presuppose the evolvement of new stable patterns of interaction supportive of these changes. Almost a century ago Durkheim noted the transition in patterns of behavior as a function of increased population size and density.[38] The cultural aspect of this structural change is reflected in new emphasis upon impersonality and utility in social relationships wherein the interdependence of members of the collectivity is the basis for group solidarity. Other cultural changes include the emphasis upon "secular" aspects of social life such as material progress and rewards.

The basic feature of structural change associated with modernization is differentiation, or increasing complexity of structure. At the societal level, such growth is not random but appears to follow a general principle that Parsons has referred to as "adaptive upgrading."[39] This means that structural differentiation enhances the system's ability to control its environment; the assumption being that specialized groups can be more effective in fulfilling societal requirements than groups with many functions. Thus, in a traditional society a family serves not only as the residential group but as the primary economic unit. In the structurally complex modern society, on the other hand, the family's economic function has been assumed by specialized economic groups (for example, stores and factories).

Norms supportive of such specialization of function can be described in terms of Parsons' "pattern variables" of universalism, affective neutrality, diffuseness, and achievement.[40] However, the normative characteristics of differentiation can also be understood generally in terms of a view of social reality in which the desirability of means are determined in large measure by their efficiency and effectiveness relative to specific ends.[41] Although the source of differentiation has been ascribed by some to the nature of modern technology,[42] in point of fact it appears to be a consequence of that technology, along with ecological changes wrought by its adoption and the emergence of dominant values and norms determining what is "functionally rational." Stated more technically, the emergent institutional structure of modern societies (constituting the guidelines of stable patterns of interaction) is derived from a meaning of life whose parameters are defined by the cultural dimension of the modernization process.

The "adaptive upgrading" of a society undergoing modernization, according to Parsons, is most evident in the economic institutions of that society wherein are found those patterns of behavior most clearly associated with environmental constraints.[43] Thus, for example, work patterns become more narrow in scope and purpose. So also, new work roles associated with coordination and control emerge to facilitate the complex interaction of goods and services. Accordingly, entirely new services, with their attendent occupational roles, emerge in response to new social needs for goods and services produced by the new technology. Less apparent but equally important structural changes occur in noneconomic institutions as well. Thus, the political structure gets a new, more systematic hierarchy of control at the same time that the limits of its influence in man's life are more clearly delineated. Religious structure also tends to lose its significance in social behavior not directly associated with "otherworldly" concerns, and the role of the family is more narrowly limited to welfare and the socialization of children.

We can summarize our discussion of the ecological, cultural, and structural components of modernization by noting that the ecological characteristic of population concentration has as one of its prerequisites a technology sufficiently advanced to support both increased numbers and a greater proportion of people engaged in activities not directly associated with the production of food. Cultural characteristics of modernization presuppose the potential, if not the actual, existence of technical means to master the environment and bring about material progress. Since humans, individually and collectively, interpret reality in ways learned both from experience and from socialization, it is reasonable to expect that the ultimate success of new technological innovations in overcoming previously accepted constraints would facilitate a new definition of reality consistent with the changes noted previously. Structural changes, too, reflect the organizational requirements of technological change. The cultural mechanism underlying the reordering of the social structure is the emphasis placed upon a rationality directed toward the more efficient and effective attainment of specific material ends.

It should be emphasized, of course, that the pattern of modernization is not necessarily the same in all societies. It may evolve over a long time, as in Western Europe, or it may be thrust upon traditional societies "in toto," as in many contemporary Asian and African countries. Changes may occur in modified form, or the process itself may never effectively become part of the sociocultural context for a variety of historic, economic, or ideological reasons. There is nothing inevitable, in other words, about the changes described. What does seem to be inevitable, however, is that once a society places a high priority upon those goals most effectively attained by modernization and has access to the technology necessary for their attainment, its ecological, cultural, and structural characteristics generally evolve in the fashion described above.

Analytic Layers of Sociocultural Environments

In addition to the three *dimensions* of sociocultural environments, described above, one can speak of a series of "analytic" *layers*. For example, a school may be located in a community virtually unaffected by modernization, which in turn may be part of a state that has been moderately influenced by modernization. And that state could be part of a nation that overall has been strongly influenced by modernization. Though such a combination of environmental layers is unlikely, it is not impossible,[e] and is suggestive of a second environmental characteristic upon which modernization can have a differential effect.

Thus, the environments of educational systems may be distinguished by the extent to which they have been influenced by modernization. The manner in which environmental layers can best be distinguished depends upon the problem considered. Since this monograph is primarily concerned with variations in environmental modernity within a given society, we have chosen to view the layers spatially. Specifically, for purposes of analysis, the scope of functional relevance of our environmental layers for the system under consideration is clearly associated with the size of the physical space to which it refers.

With the above distinction in mind, it is crucial to note that each analytic layer of the environment can be considered in terms of its ecological, cultural, and structural dimension, and each dimension in every layer of the environment can vary in the extent to which it has been influenced by modernization.

Figure 2–1 shows that American society has at least six environmental layers that are relevant to the educational system as an open sociocultural

LAYERS	DIMENSIONS		
	Cultural	Ecological	Structural
Western Civilization	1	2	3
American Society	4	5	6
Region	7	8	9
State	10	11	12
Community	13	14	15
Neighborhood	16	17	18

FIGURE 2–1. *Layers and dimensions of the environments of American schools as open sociocultural systems.*

system. The largest consists of the ecological, cultural, and structural dimensions of Western civilization. Next largest is American society. However, since we are concerned here primarily with *internal* variation in American

---

[e]A case in point is the recent development of Huntsville, Alabama as a scientifically oriented, cosmopolitan community in one of the least modern states and regions of the United States.

society, these most general layers will not be discussed further except to note that by definition Western civilization in general and American society in particular are *at the present time* the most modern known environments. The remainder of this chapter is devoted to a consideration of the environmental layers of "region," "community," and "neighborhood."

AMERICAN REGIONS

The term "region" has been used in many ways by different individuals and agencies.[44] In contemporary America, "north," "south," "east," and "west" are used with varying degrees of precision to distinguish geographical areas of the United States. In addition, geographical areas have often been roughly identified by their proximity to rivers (for example, Tennessee Valley region) or mountains (for example, Appalachian region), and by factors associated with their settlement (for example, New England region). Originally there were two American regions, a North and a South. As settlement began to expand westward beyond the Appalachian mountains, the North was differentiated into an East and a West and then the West into Northwest, Midwest, Southwest, and Far West.[45]

By far the most systematic attempt to develop the "best possible" regional delineation of the United States is that of Odum and Moore, published in 1938. They sought answers to a series of important questions:

> What . . . are adequate regions, acceptable as frames of reference for research and portraiture, as basic divisions for administrations and planning, and as fundamental, yet flexible, units in the totality and union of the states . . .? What is the nature and size of those regions best suited to the largest number of purposes and how may they be determined? What are the limitations of regions too small and too numerous or too large and too few? What are the limitations of the incidental regions chosen for convenience or for political ends?[46]

After surveying the use of the term "region" in literature, journalism, and historical works, as well as in social research and governmental administration, and after extensive evaluation of several hundred statistical indices, Odum and Moore identified six major regions of the United States: Northeast, Southeast, Middle States, Northwest, Southwest, and Far West. Their six regions maintain the integrity of state boundaries and "approximate the largest degree of homogeneity measured by the largest number of purposes."[47] However, they point out that an even closer approximation of sociocultural homogeneity could be represented if it were not necessary (for data collection purposes) to adhere to state lines as regional boundaries.

A more recent, rather thorough analysis of American regions was conducted by Ira Sharkansky in a comparative examination of political systems. Like Odum and Moore, Sharkansky examined the relationship between various statistical indices in an attempt to uncover basic similarities and differences among geographic regions. Unlike Odum and Moore, however, Sharkansky was interested in developing multiple demarcations of regions, rather than identifying a single "ideal" set of regions.[48] Sharkansky's subsequent analysis of regional variations in political behavior strongly supports his contention that the American states can be classified into different regions in various ways, and that the nature of such classifications varies with the researcher's interests.

The work of Odum and Moore, as well as that of Sharkansky, exemplifies many considerations important for our examination of regional effects on educational phenomena. However, in any study of regional effects on the school as an open social system it is necessary to delineate a series of sociocultural areas sufficiently different from each other to reflect expected differences in the characteristics of the educational system. Although we would ascribe the uniqueness of each region to sociocultural factors, it would be a major oversight to ignore the additional effect of important historical and geographical factors. Thus, in identifying a set of regions one needs to take into account all three elements.

For purposes of the present discussion and subsequent analysis, then, we define a *region* as *a limited cluster of coterminous geopolitical states in American society sharing a similar sociocultural environment, which differs to a significant degree from other clusters by virtue of historical circumstance, geographic conditions, and cultural traits.* We will pay particular attention to those cultural traits associated with modernization. It must be noted, of course, that any regional designation is arbitrary. As Wirth has pointed out, regional variations do not in reality end at political boundaries, nor are they shared equally by all groups in the region.[49] Still, the term has both heuristic and analytical utility in distinguishing among the significant sociocultural forces that influence the modernization process and thus the educational system.

The definition of region given above led us to the identification of five basic American regions, shown in Figure 2–2. Although Chapter Four will include a more detailed description of the methods used in identifying the regions, a brief statement of procedures seems appropriate at this point. Our approach consisted of the following three general steps; 1) carefully examining previous attempts at delineating American regions; 2) considering the contradictions and alternatives offered by previous classificatory schemes; and 3) examining and comparing the available statistical information that reflects the level of development for each state and region. After having followed these three steps, the states were grouped into regions identified as the "Northeast," "Southeast," "Great Lakes," "Plains," and "West," as portrayed in Figure 2–2.

FIGURE 2–2.   Five "ideal" sociocultural regions of the United States.

Unfortunately, social science research data documenting regional variations in ideology and values are not as readily available as are data on the ecological and structural manifestations of modernization. However, what little data exist tend to support our thesis that beliefs and values vary in a systematic way between less and more modern regions. In studies of voting, authoritarianism, values, attitudes, and opinions, significant regional differences have been reported.[1] It would appear to be generally true that the less modern regions of the United States (as defined in Figure 2–2) are more conservative and traditional in their ideology and values than are the more modern regions.

---

[1]Some relevant studies on regional differences directly or indirectly supportive of regional variation in ideology and values include: Irving Crespi, "The Structural Basis for Right-Wing Conservatism: The Goldwater Case," *Public Opinion Quarterly*, 29 (1965–1966), 523–43; Norval D. Glenn and J. L. Simmons, "Are Regional Cultural Differences Diminishing?" *Public Opinion Quarterly*, 31 (1967), 176–93; David Gottlieb, "Regional Differences as a Variable in Sociological Research," *Social Problems*, 10 (1963), 251–56; Rose K. Goldsen *et al.*, *What College Students Think* (Princeton, N. J.: D. Van Nostrand Co., Inc., 1960); Duncan MacRae, Jr., *Dimensions of Congressional Voting* (Berkeley, Calif.: University of California Press, 1958), pp. 256–80; Allen J. Williams, Jr., "Regional Differences in Authoritarianism," *Social Forces*, 45 (1966), 273–77; Sharkansky, *Regionalism in American Politics*; Raymond D. Gastil, "Homicide and a Regional Culture of Violence," *American Sociological Review*, 36 (1971), 412–26; and Raymond C. Rymph and Jeffrey Kotladden, "The Persistence of Regionalism in Racial Attitudes of Methodist Clergy," *Social Forces*, 49 (1970), 41–50.

Sociocultural Variation Among Regions

Although "hard" data regarding differences in ideology and values are limited, a wealth of literary evidence attests to their existence. Based upon historical documentation, ecological considerations, and personal observation by such keen observers of the American scene as de Tocqueville, Brogan, Beals, and Turner, the vignettes we shall present below offer a synthesis of the historical and contemporary factors associated with regional variation in ideology and values.[50] Because the Northeast and the Southeast are both the oldest regions in American society and at the extremes of the modernization index to be presented in Chapter Four, we shall discuss them first and in greater detail than the three other regions (the Great Lakes, the Plains, and the West), for which we will identify only their sociocultural uniqueness. We turn first to the most modern of our five regions, the Northeast.

NORTHEAST. The legendary story of America before the great nineteenth-century westward migration belongs primarily to the establishment and growth of the Northeast. Although the Southeast was colonized at the same time, most Americans see in the symbols of Plymouth Rock, Bunker Hill, Lexington and Concord, Valley Forge, the Puritans, the Boston Tea Party, and Independence Hall a representation of America's ideals and beliefs. The escape from religious tyranny, the fight to establish a viable Western civilization on the shores of a hostile continent, the resourcefulness of the early settlers in overcoming a wilderness and its natives, and ultimately the fight against foreign rule leading to the establishment of a republic, are historical materials derived from the Northeast. From such experience, the ideological elements and values generally identified with the larger contemporary American society emerged.

There seems little doubt that religious conviction played a significant part in the early settlement patterns of the Northeast.[51] Protestant in large measure, and in rebellion against the established Church of England, many New England colonies were essentially attempts to set up autonomous theocracies. Curiously, the pattern of religious persecution from which these groups fled was repeated by them in America. In contrast to New England, the so-called "Middle Colonies"[52] (including New York, New Jersey, Pennsylvania, Delaware, and Maryland) did not stress religious conformity to the same extent, although the pattern of flight from the religious dogmas of the Church of England was basic to these colonies as well as to those in New England. Differences to an extent are explained by the more heterogeneous ethnic settlement of the middle colonies.[53] In both instances, however, morality based upon religious beliefs had from the beginning been a significant characteristic. In an age when formal religion was an integral part of man's daily life, behavior was consistently judged according to absolute religious principles of right and wrong, good and bad.

Although it is true that the early Northeast was characterized in large measure by an absolutist religious philosophy regarding the nature of man (particularly in New England), it is equally true that the content of this philosophy was instrumental in establishing the importance of individualism, work activity, and material reward to the American credo. Weber and others have described how Protestant convictions accentuated the importance of the individual's working to achieve salvation. Since this end was not something that could be attained by inheritance, little credence was given to wealth *per se,* but a great deal was given to the man who "proved" his worth by his own efforts. Material wealth, as a consequence, was desirable not only for itself but for its social and religious connotations. Achievement as a manifestation of one's efforts was also valued in its own right.

It has frequently been said that beliefs in pragmatic rationality, progress, and equality are also attributable to the role of Protestant theology in American society. Although there is little doubt that these beliefs are not antithetical to Protestantism, one may question the appropriateness of their being so designated in the case of the Northeast's historical development. Much cross-cultural evidence is available to the contrary.[g] However, more germane to this development historically have been the environmental constraints and experiences to which settlers in the northeastern region were exposed. Faced with the exigencies of frontier life, lacking support from the mother country, and imbued with the credo of work and material rewards, early northeastern settlers had to be pragmatic in order to survive.[54] Such pragmatism required a discarding of beliefs regarding ascribed differences among men in favor of a belief in man's intrinsic equality, the variability of which was distinguished on the basis of performance in meeting the needs of the larger group. In large measure it was the success of this approach over time in an environment highly favorable to its articulation that was the basis for the development in the Northeast of a belief in progress and achievement, especially of a secular and material nature.

Finally, in considering the belief and value placed upon external conformity in the Northeast historically, it is necessary to recognize that, at least for this region, Riesman's thesis that Americans have become outer-directed rather than inner-directed is suspect. As de Tocqueville, Brogan, and others have observed, Americans have always been extremely sensitive to the wishes of others.[55] Indeed, if one but considers the intolerance of

---

[g]For interesting discussions of the role of beliefs and values associated with social development in various societies, see S. N. Eisenstadt, *Modernization: Protest and Change* (Englewood Cliffs, N. J.: Prentice-Hall, Inc., 1966); Wilbert E. Moore, *The Impact of Industry* (Englewood Cliffs, N. J.: Prentice-Hall, Inc., 1965); and Joel M. Halpern, *The Changing Village Community* (Englewood Cliffs, N. J.: Prentice-Hall, Inc., 1967).

dissent found in early New England, the subsequent pattern of community migration from New England, and the expulsion of the conservative Tories from New England and the Middle Atlantic states following the Revolutionary War, it is apparent that conformity has long been characteristic of this region. The expression of individualism, though highly cherished as an ideal, has been tolerated only within the limits of the communities' values and norms. Historically, it has not been pervasive in all social behavior.[h]

We have stressed the historical basis for the ideology and values often cited as characteristic of the Northeast. While these values would explain in part its emergence as the most modern region of America, other regions share to some extent the same beliefs and values. Thus, an analysis of why this region should have developed more rapidly than the other four must include its history and geography. We shall comment briefly upon each of these.

In part, the Northeast's high level of modernization may be attributed to its early development. Having quickly established an industrial base and a surplus of labor to utilize in its growth, being less encumbered than the Southeast by a traditional agrarian heritage, and emerging early as the commercial and financial center of the new nation, the Northeast early reached a relatively high level of modernization. Having initially outstripped its only regional competitor early in the nineteenth century (if not before), it could benefit from the subsequent exploitation and development of the other regions. The much-vaunted "know-how" of the Yankee can be attributed in no small measure to the secure commercial, industrial, and financial base from which he operated. Supplying skills and products needed for the development of a nation produced an accumulation of capital that was reinvested in the Northeast, leading to its further development. As the center of the national culture, it attracted talents from other regions, which further contributed to its relative stature.[56]

This early development of the Northeast may be attributed in part also to geography. Its land, never considered particularly good for agriculture, was rapidly exploited. Thus, a surplus of population for westward and urban migration quickly developed. Additionally, by virtue of serving as the nation's major port of entry (New York, Philadelphia, and Boston), this region received many immigrants with values and skills compatible with urban life and industrial requirements. There was, therefore, a ready supply of manpower in excess of agricultural needs quite early in the region's history. The fact that beliefs and values dominant in the region enhanced its susceptibility

---

[h]In his comparative and historical analysis of American society, Lipset observes that "uniformity and conformity" have been attributed to Americans as a national characteristic since pre-Civil War days. See Seymour Martin Lipset, *The First New Nation: The United States in Historical and Comparative Perspective* (New York: Basic Books, Inc., 1963), p. 106; see also Arensberg, "American Communities."

to modernization is, in some respects, fortuitous in that geographic circumstance provided the most favorable conditions for its development.[57]

In discussing the ideology and value orientation of the Northeast, we must remember that these beliefs and values are shared by other regions as well. The uniqueness of this region rests in the emphasis it places on certain values, as well as the manner in which a particular belief or value is construed within the region. With these qualifications in mind, the Northeast may be said to emphasize material reward and progress to a greater extent than other regions (with the possible exception of the West). The historical emphasis in this region has been upon technological and economic development. The achievement of these material ends has required a commitment to, a belief in, and a value of progress highly consistent with the cumulative effects of technical and economic growth.

Other major beliefs and values have assumed a lesser importance and have, to some extent, been modified over time from those of the larger society. The belief and value placed upon traditional morality has become increasingly redefined in terms of social morality — more relativistic than absolute, more secular than sacred.[i] Consistent with the interpretation of Kluckhohn and others, the demands placed upon the individual in a highly modern region for conformity in organizational life appears to have led to a growth of belief in, and valuation of, individual development (as opposed to individualism).[58] This modification, in turn, is associated with a relative deemphasis of work activity and increased emphasis of activities associated with individual growth and gratification. One of the apparent paradoxes of modern society seems to be that as organizational constraints increase, individual constraints are reduced, thereby relaxing the requirement of conformity in many areas of life outside of one's occupation. Whether this is attributable to the ecology of urban life, or a concomitant of the universalistic social relationships necessary in a highly specialized society, is unclear. However, the influence of this relative autonomy upon the life style of residents in the Northeast has to some measure differentiated them from residents in other regions of the country, with the possible exception of the West.

SOUTHEAST. The Southeast is the least modern of the five regions of the United States identified in Figure 2–2. Although it is one of the older regions, its history is, in many respects, a story of resistance to the modernization so apparent in the Northeast. It is by contrasting the Southeast to the

---

[i]Secularization in American society in general is systematically analyzed by Herberg. See Will Herberg, *Protestant, Catholic, Jew*, rev. ed. (Garden City, N. Y.: Doubleday & Company, Inc., 1960), particularly chap. 6.

Northeast that the most pronounced regional differences in the United States in beliefs and values can be articulated.

To understand the sociocultural uniqueness of the Southeast, it is necessary to consider its historical development. Unlike the Northeast, settlement of the Southeast by and large was not a settlement of religious dissenters. It was, rather, a colonial settlement pattern based largely upon commercial exploitation or personal gain. Many settlers were originally brought over to clear and develop large royal grants of land for the British aristocracy. Others came to seek their fortunes. Accordingly, no real opposition to traditional authority existed in the initial settlement of the region.[j]

The fact that such a close connection with the mother country ultimately was broken by the Revolutionary War in no way detracts from the conservative political and economic origins of the region's early settlement. Ample evidence suggests in fact that in both Northeast and Southeast, from one-third to better than half the colonists were loyal to the crown. Zimmerman and DuWors suggest that beyond this, commercial interests of the Southeast had more to lose by the Revolution and thus were more reluctant to participate than those of the Northeast.[59] Further, although Virginia contributed disproportionately to Revolutionary leadership, it was a leadership seeking colonial autonomy to perpetuate the existing agrarian system rather than to develop a different political and economic order.[60]

This pattern of traditional political and economic forces holding dominance in the Southeast was matched in large measure in southeastern religious institutions. Before the Revolutionary War, the Anglican Church was the established religious authority in the southeastern colonies.[61] With the end of the war and the subsequent westward expansion, fundamentalism (ideologically conservative in nature) succeeded Anglicanism as the dominant religious ethos of the region. The success of fundamentalist denominations in the Southeast introduced a religious morality and individualism heretofore lacking. Unlike the morality and individualism of the Northeast, however, their theological base was not Calvinist in origin and thus did not lead, as in New England, to an emphasis upon worldly achievement and collective responsibility. Rather, the morality was based upon submission to God's will in making the best of a generally poor lot. Such a morality, based upon scripture and emotional commitment, was highly personal and associated with salvation through individual reform. This reform inevitably was cast in terms of absolute good or its absence. Morality of this type narrowed rather than broadened toleration for nonconformity in the southern community. Fur-

---

[j]Georgia was a partial exception to this generalization. But even in that case, the trustees anticipated the colony would ultimately grow into an economically profitable enterprise. See Roger Burlingame, *The American Conscience* (New York: Alfred A. Knopf, Inc., 1957), chap. 7; and Boorstin, *The Americans*, parts III and IV.

ther, as Nichols suggests, the individualism justified by such a morality quickly degenerated to an extreme form of social Darwinism supportive of the existing class structure.[62]

As in the Northeast, the early frontier experience in the Southeast tempered the value and belief in traditional authority, conservative morality, and "rugged individualism" with a particular appreciation for the pragmatically rational solution to the demands of frontier life. The notion of equality, also, emerged from the rigors and isolation of early backwoods existence. The early strength of these changes was, in fact, the basis for the egalitarianism in American society associated with the Jacksonian movement of the early nineteenth century. Such a movement reflected the incipient growth of what was to be the populist movement later in the century. Ultimately, however, the conservative strength of the region's tradition was successful in containing the growth of populism in the Southeast by interpreting its impact as a threat to the "civilized authority" of the existing institutions.[63] That this same device was far less successful in other frontier regions at that time speaks both of the strength of traditional forces in the Southeast and of their weakness in other frontier regions.

The social and economic factors leading to the Civil War and Reconstruction have been thoroughly explored elsewhere. Their relevance for our discussion of sociocultural regions rests upon the values and beliefs influenced by those events. "Progress," to the extent that it was identified with social change, abolition, and reconstruction efforts imposed by the North, became the antithesis of the southern tradition in the southeasterner's eyes. What little industry was developed in the South following the Civil War was rapidly coopted into sharing the sociocultural traditions held by the aristocracy of the region.[64] Progress, never a strongly held belief in the area, became increasingly seen as material exploitation of the masses (generally black) by the few (generally white). Thus, progress as defined in the Northeast was impeded by the maintenance of a mythology of the supremacy of traditional economic, social, and political institutions associated with the southern life style.

In maintaining what essentially was an agrarian belief and value system in the face of industrial change elsewhere in American society, the Southeast had to de-emphasize the pragmatic rationality originally nurtured in the frontier areas of the region, while increasingly emphasizing the desirable qualities of southern morality, particularly as expressed in the antebellum South. The pattern of individual violence and physical solutions to community problems already associated with the region in de Tocqueville's time[65] continued to be supported as part of the cultural heritage of southern society.[66] So, also, the early belief in and value placed upon egalitarianism became subverted by racist fears generated by the southern power structure.[67]

Yet another aspect of southeastern historical development of importance to an understanding of its belief and value system is its immigration and

emigration. Compared to the Northeast, the Southeast received disproportionately few immigrants in the nineteenth century. One consequence of this
was the ability of the Southeast to maintain a fairly endogamous belief and
value system in the face of little competition. Compounding this isolation
was the high soil fertility of the region, which reduced manpower needs in
agriculture, leading to the large emigration of primarily unskilled workers
to other regions. These two patterns (low immigration and high emigration
of labor surplus) have, until very recently, permitted the traditional southeastern ideology and values to go relatively unchallenged.[68]

The contemporary southeastern region is, then, a region wherein the
dominant beliefs and values center upon a traditional morality generally
resistant to the requirements of modern industrial life. Although desirous of
the material well-being associated with industrial technology, southeasterners
frequently see the introduction of technical innovations as a threat to traditional life styles. To an extent not shared by its neighboring region to the
north, the Southeast has tended to romanticize its past at the expense of
progress and the pragmatic rationality associated with changes in social
organization needed to bring about modernization. Having little history of
dissent, turning in upon itself following defeat, clinging to an agricultural
past, and faced with the dilemma of a large unwanted racial minority, the
Southeast has only recently begun to break out of its ideological constraints.
In general its ideology is conservative and traditional, and its values are primarily those associated with a preindustrial society.[69]

GREAT LAKES. This region, frequently referred to as the "most typically American" region in America, is in many respects a merging of the ideologies of the Northeast and Southeast. As in the Northeast, progress, hard
work, and material success are emphasized. On the other hand, the morality
and insularity of this region are similar in many respects to those of the South.
Populated by both regions, as well as by large numbers of immigrants during
the early and middle nineteenth century, favored by both agricultural and
industrial potential, the Great Lakes region has been marked by an emphasis
upon egalitarianism, which has found expression in both material achievement and tendencies toward isolationism. The political conservatism of this
region tends not to be the conservatism of tradition, but that of material
success.[70]

Although this region has several large metropolitan areas, it lacks the
more urbane characteristics of the Northeast. Its ideology, in many respects,
is best typified in the various community studies that point to beliefs and
values highly moralistic and committed to the "American way," which tends
to be interpreted in terms of equality, individual effort, and material reward.[71]
Not particularly tolerant of social and philosophical deviation, it nonetheless

has been marked in its history by a great deal of economic and political diversity.[k]

Thus, the ideology and values of the Great Lakes region center upon material success, equality, and morality. The region's position relative to other regions on the modernization index points to its commitment to progress, tempered by a somewhat irrational enthnocentrism and its dependence upon the Northeast as the financial and cultural center of the society.

PLAINS. This region of the United States is not generally treated separately in regional studies. The northern section is usually included with the Great Lakes region (as part of the Midwest), and the southern section is generally associated with the Southeast (as part of the South). Yet, both in degree of modernization and in ecological and economic characteristics, this region is quite homogeneous. The economy of these states is predominantly agricultural; their climate uniformly harsh; and their history (with the exception of that of Texas) relatively brief.[72]

Climate and resources have played a highly significant role in the development of the regional subculture of the Plains. Arid or semiarid climatic conditions have restricted agricultural development to primarily grain crops in the northern area and cotton, grain, sheep, and cattle in the southern area. Such products have been highly amenable to technological improvements in farming, but not particularly conducive to the growth of large urban centers. Accordingly, the Plains region has been strongly agrarian. Such a cultural disposition has been reflected in the pragmatic conservatism of this region's politics and social life. Subscribing to the essentially nineteenth-century ideology of individualism and hard work, the Plains culture has been quick to adapt technological innovation to agricultural and mineral exploitation but reluctant to extend that adaptive tendency to other areas of social life. This somewhat narrow view of "progress" has, to some extent, led to a depopulation of much of the Plains area as technological improvements have forced the marginal farmer off the land, but offered him little in the way of occupational alternatives within the region. Only in Texas, which has benefited from great mineral advantages, has this pattern deviated to any extent.[1]

The plains area as "the last frontier" is a region characterized by the pragmatism of rural life, highly optimistic in a narrow material and tech-

---

[k]Wisconsin was one of the few states in American history to successfully develop a Progressive party outside the boundaries of the major political parties. Also, a great measure of support for early populist movements was garnered in this region.

[l]Texas, as Odum and Moore have observed, is a dominant force in the southern segment of the Plains region. However, because of its size, history, and wealth, it is in many ways least typical of the Plains region.

nological sense, priding itself on an external conformity in its belief in individualism as "the American way." It is, in short, a reflection of a way of life consistent with the "frontier spirit" of nineteenth-century America. The belief in equality, strongly reflected in the Great Lakes region, exists here also, but it is more an economic equality than the broader social and political equality of the Great Lakes (laissez faire equality versus social equality).[73]

WEST. For many Americans, the West is close to the Promised Land; a land of opportunity, scenery, sunshine, and wealth. It is a region strongly committed to a belief in, and valuation of, progress. Favored by bountiful natural resources, a relatively sparse population, and scenic grandeur, it has witnessed tremendous development during the current century.[74] Individualism is strong in this region, but it is an individualism tempered by the need for cooperative efforts in overcoming the economic and technical problems presented by the vastness of the region.[m] Its configuration of ideology and values is similar to that associated with the Northeast. Differences in large measure seem attributable to the history of the Northeast and the ecological features of the two regions. Having developed an early lead in the industrial and commercial growth of the society, the Northeast has a greater commitment to the morality of work and achievement than does the West. So, also, the vast expanse and great natural wealth of the West have encouraged economic individualism, long since weakened in the Northeast by the limitations of a less bountiful environment. External conformity too varies between the regions, consistent with the maintenance of western individualism. Although the rapid growth of large-scale industry has led to the same needs for external conformity in the West as in the Northeast, it is a conformity more restricted to occupational life than in the Northeast, thus allowing for a comparatively greater expression of individuality.[n]

Educational Variation Among Regions

Although it is possible to relate all three dimensions of the regional environment to variations in the educational system, when one links the

---

[m]Odum and Moore, *American Regionalism*, pp. 550–71. Indirect corroboration for this observation on the strength of individualism in this region is evidenced by the relatively high level of support Goldwater was able to gain in the 1964 presidential election in the West. See Crespi, "The Goldwater Case." Its temperance, however, is suggested by congressional voting records, where western representatives are more responsive to federal legislation consistent with controlled development. See MacRae, *Congressional Voting*.

[n]Gillin, "National and Regional Cultural Values in the United States," p. 113; Zimmerman and DuWors, *Graphic Regional Sociology*, pp. 122–29. The somewhat amorphous position of the Far West in values and beliefs may be attributable in part to the large number of newcomers from other regions. The contemporary fluctuations in political and social behavior in the Far West suggests that many of these groups are not totally assimilated into a coherent regional orientation.

extremes in ideology and values associated with the degree of cultural modernization in different regions of American society to the institutional role of education, it can be expected that educational organizations will vary appreciably from one region to another. In the three most modern regions (the Northeast, West, and Great Lakes), the emphasis upon individuality, progress, social morality, and material reward are higher than in the less modern regions (the Plains and Southeast). On the other hand, the less modern regions tend to be relatively higher in conservatism, individualism, and traditional morality. Conformity and pragmatism were observed to be fairly evenly distributed over all regions with the exception of the Southeast. In anticipating the effects of the regional culture on the educational system, we shall concentrate on these dominant beliefs and values.

"Progress," of critical importance to an understanding of regional variation in American education, has a definite meaning in American society, especially in the more modern regions. The essential aspects of progress are illustrated by Williams when he states that the term encompasses the belief that ". . . human nature is subject to continuous improvement and that society as a whole is inevitably moving toward a better order of life."[75] Thus, in this sense, the belief in and high evaluation of progress make acceptable changes in the educational system that are justified in terms of both individual achievement and the group's status.

The criteria for proposed change, of course, must be consistent with what is socially defined as "improvement." There seems little doubt that improvement in the systemic rational sense generally means increased material well-being achieved through greater efficiency.[76] As critics of American society have correctly pointed out, materialism is its primary motif and is consistent with the dominant cultural orientation noted earlier of "the mastery over nature." More simply in contemporary America, increased economic returns seem to be the principal basis for considering a change as "progress." Thus, a higher standard of living, more extensive medical care, more efficient communication, and faster transportation constitute progress to the extent that they contribute to the well-being of the members of society. A newer car, a bigger home, a job promotion, or a longer vacation are generally viewed as evidence of individual progress.

Progress defined in terms of these material rewards is also expressed in the more modern regions through a social ethic, as Niebuhr and Herberg have suggested, oriented toward helping others who are materially less well off than oneself.[77] Such morality does not violate the individualistic thesis of the Protestant Ethic. Rather, it tends to confirm in a secular manner the effect of what has been referred to as the "social gospel," that is, being one's brother's keeper. In contrast, the traditional morality identified with the less modern environments is much more absolutist, the focus of behavior being not progress and change but a transcendental state divorced from existing or future material conditions.

Ideally, an educational system within one of the more modern American regions can be characterized as a sociocultural system whose properties are evaluated in terms of progress, material reward, and social morality. Thus the region would be supportive of progress in that the educational changes felt to result in better student achievement would be defined in terms of the skills and orientations necessary to contribute to the larger society as well. Such a sociocultural milieu would be particularly amenable to both the school's specialization of function and its structural differentiation associated with the increasing complexity of the educational system, since these are consistent with the notion of "progressive" improvement and efficiency in the services provided for the environment by the educational system. Further, "feedback" would consist of tangible measures of progress associated with education's institutional role, such as the proportion of pupils who graduate and go on to further education. The educational system's sensitivity to such matters would encourage a high emphasis upon the system's adaptability to societal demands relatively independent of the local social context.

In contrast, the emphasis on individualism, conservatism, and traditional morality characteristic of the less modern American regions is associated with a view of education wherein respect for order and authority, tempered by a belief in the individual's "right" to succeed or fail by virtue of his own efforts. Thus, the sociocultural milieu is deemed by its membership as a "natural" state of affairs wherein status differences and the accompanying differential treatment patterns are consistent with the individual's proven worth to the community. Therefore, perceived changes (with the possible exception of some technological changes) in the educational system frequently are interpreted as inappropriate since they generally threaten the "natural" balance of the sociocultural milieu. Within such a context, education manifests a greater concern with legitimating its role in the traditional environment than with the development of more progressive "reforms." Increasing complexity of the educational system is construed as a bureaucratic threat to the individual rather than an aid to his progress, and is frowned upon. Subscription to the modern institutional role as the purpose of the educational system is less clearly evident because of the greater emphasis upon the maintenance of existing standards of performance associated with local traditions rather than in terms of the needs of the larger society.

Empirical evidence on regional variations in education is limited but consistent. In respect to input to education, regional variation in enrollment rates,[78] teacher-pupil ratio,[79] and per-pupil expenditure[80] has been shown.[o]

---

[o]Regional variations in such educational inputs as school facilities, services, curricula, and the characteristics of teachers can also be observed in James S. Coleman et al., *Equality of Educational Opportunity*, Vol. I (Washington, D.C.; Government Printing Office, 1966). However, since the focus of Coleman and his associates was on educational differences among racial and ethnic groups *within* regions, educational variations among regions can only be estimated indirectly from these data.

In output, regional variation in educational attainment,[81] college enrollment,[82] and professional and scientific productivity,[83] have also been demonstrated. With a few exceptions (noticeably in the Plains area) these studies point to the positive association between the degree of modernity of a region and of the inputs and outputs of its educational system. This pattern is particularly apparent when the Northeast, the most modern region, is compared to the Southeast, the least modern region. Other less direct evidence suggests the cultural dynamics associated with the slower development of education in the Southeast. Thus, Cartter, in an analysis of southern higher education, argues that the South tends to overvalue " . . . the social aspects of higher education . . . and has undervalued the intellectual and economic benefits."[84] Indirect documentation for this contention is available from Ryans' study of teacher characteristics. Southern teachers scored the lowest on verbal understanding and held the most traditional educational perspectives.[85] Elsewhere, Nichols argues that the South has historically been antagonistic toward public education generally, and intellectual freedom and inquiry specifically.[86]

AMERICAN COMMUNITIES

Like regions, communities vary as to the modernity of their sociocultural life. Of particular importance is their degree of urbanization. Increasingly, urban life is the community life form most indicative of a modern society.

In our subsequent discussion we will use the term "urbanization" to refer to the process by which some members of a society come increasingly to reflect ecological characteristics associated with metropolitan life *in modern societies.* Although to be consistent with historical usage we will discuss "rural-urban" differences, a metropolitan community is more than simply urban, for it represents a special configuration of life styles not found in pre-industrial cities. Further, it is fairly evident that "rural" in contemporary American life does not refer to the classical peasant community of preindustrial societies. Our discussion, therefore, refers to a broader sociocultural phenomenon: how social settings of varying degrees of ecological concentration reflect different degrees of modernity.

The meanings of "rural" and "urban" in American society are far from clear, particularly with the rapid pace of modernization. Bealer, Willits, and Kuvlesky have identified three meanings of rural that underlie past research efforts—the ecological (rurality determined by population size, density, and urban proximity), the occupational (the proportion of a population engaged in agriculture), and the sociocultural (particular social and cultural characteristics).[87] Although the three components need not reflect the same phenomena in a given society,[88] they are generally associated. Accordingly, the realities of research often necessitate their combination in some form.

Rurality and urbanness are traditionally associated with the concept of "community." This concept also has several meanings,[89] but it is most commonly defined in terms of territory, social ties, and group identity.[90] Further, as Sjoberg has noted, "In order to analyze rural-urban [differences] effectively, one must recognize that rural and urban communities are subsystems within larger wholes such as nation-state systems. Neither the local urban community nor its rural counterpart are macroscopic representations of the broader society."[91] Sjoberg notes further that rural and urban are primarily analytic constructs employed in the study of aspects of social systems. He warns that "we must not confuse an analytical distinction with empirical reality, for obviously a gradation exists from the relatively small, isolated village, through the larger village, to the market town, the largest city, and finally to the dominant community (or communities)."[92]

A rural community, ideal-typically, is characterized as a community of small population and low population density, sufficiently removed from the closest urban area to be considered organizationally autonomous, whose male population is predominantly engaged in agricultural pursuits or in occupations directly supportive of agriculture, with a total population who identify themselves as members of that community, and with solidarity (or unity) based upon a high consensus of the membership as to appropriate ideology and values. In contrast, an urban community is, ideal-typically, characterized as a community of large population and high population density, organizationally autonomous from other urban communities, whose male population is predominantly engaged in commercial or industrial pursuits, with a total population who identify themselves as members of that community, and with solidarity (or unity) based primarily upon the division of labor.

The underlying ecological and structural differences between rural and urban communities are apparent in the above characterizations. A word is necessary about the cultural differences, however. In the case of the rural community, as Toennies, Weber, and others have shown, it is the shared sentiment, based upon similar ideology and values, that leads to the traditionalism of the rural community, that is, support of existing norms based upon their being handed down from a past considered sacred.[93] Such emphasis upon traditionalism is supportive of the particularistic, diffuse, and ascriptive nature of rural community relationships, wherein family and friendship frequently determine behavior and influence patterns in community action. In contrast, the cohesion of the urban community is manifest in the division of labor and rests upon what we have previously referred to as functional rationality, and what Becker has referred to as "pursuant rationality,"[94] that is, a recognition of the need for cohesion and cooperation in order to attain individual ends. Such cohesion is maintained by universalistic, specific, and achievement norms associated with social relationships required in complex commercial and industrial life, and is functional in a modern society.

Sociocultural Variation Among Communities

The preceding characterizations must, of course, be seen within the larger context of American society. It seems apparent that although, in the final analysis, differences among communities rest upon ecological and structural variation associated with the technological level of American society, the basis for differences in rural and urban communities rests primarily upon the different roles played by ideology and values *per se*. Among regions, distinctions in ideology and values are distinctions in emphasis, but the differences in ideology and values between rural and urban communities are in the role they play in the maintenance of community cohesion. Socioculturally, in contemporary American society, the main basis for the traditionalistic[95] posture associated with the rural community is seen to be the "sacred" role ascribed to values and beliefs held by members of the community as important for community life. These same values and beliefs are generally held by members of the urban community, but in much more of a "secular" fashion, and, therefore, tend to be less associated with the basic integrity of the community itself.[96]

It should be noted, however, that most students of the rural-ruban continuum agree that in American society rural-urban differences of the type just noted have been lessening.[97] Larson and Rogers, for example, in a broad review of relevant literature, report that rural communities are becoming linked to the larger society through the increasing number of farmers who work in nonfarm occupations to supplement their incomes, a trend to "agribusiness" and contract farming, the integration of rural communities into centralized organizations, and increased rural-urban interaction.[98] These social linkages are important, of course, in reducing sociocultural differences. Yet, there is ample evidence to suggest that significant differences still exist—differences that could influence the structure and function of the educational system.[99] Community studies, such as the work of Vidich and Bensman, suggest that the small rural community, to some extent, subverts the rationality of urban-based organizations in order to maintain the particularistic and ascriptive solidarity of rural life.[100] Furthermore, as Schnore observes, rural and urban communities still vary along a wide spectrum of demographic, social, economic, and residential characteristics.[101] We turn, therefore, to a brief summary of selected research on such variations in areas of interpersonal relations, the family, socialization, attitudes, and values.

INTERPERSONAL RELATIONS. Historically, students of the subject have seen rural and urban life styles as varying in several ways. Generally, interpersonal behavior in rural settings has been found to emphasize primary relationships consistent with the particularistic, diffuse, and ascriptive qualities of rural life mentioned earlier. In contrast, interpersonal relations in urban settings are found to emphasize secondary relationships in keeping with universalistic, specific, and achievement orientations in modern life.[p] However, research on the subject is not always consistent in supporting this distinction regarding American society.[102] Some evidence points to a reduction of rural group solidarity, particularly in the urban fringe areas, and other evidence suggests that the particularistic and diffuse aspects of urban relationships have been greatly overlooked. In essentially rural areas, informal contacts appear to be increasing, and in some cases small primary groups are assuming less importance, to be replaced by the village as the "social and institutional center of rural life."[103] Similarly, recent research has suggested that particularistic relationships are more important in urban areas than has been assumed in the past.[104]

FAMILY RELATIONS AND SOCIALIZATION PATTERNS.   The family as an integral unit of any community has also been found to vary between rural and urban settings. As Burchinal has noted, "A considerable body of data points to the . . . conclusion that there are significant differences in the socialization experiences of rural and urban youth."[105] Such differences in socialization experiences suggest, of course, that familial patterns are different as well. Thus, it is not surprising to find rural-urban differences in the household division of labor, with farm women fulfilling a higher proportion of household tasks as well as helping the husband in his occupational role.[106] Further, although research findings are not entirely consistent, Burchinal has suggested that farm living produces less marital and personal satisfaction than nonfarm living.[107] In spite of such differences, however, the frequency of divorce is much higher in urban areas.[108]

Other differences directly associated with rural and urban socialization experiences include less child satisfaction with parental-child relationships in rural homes,[109] a lower level of personality adjustment in rural children,[110] less parental encouragement of advanced education for rural children,[111] less involvement in the occupational planning of adolescent boys by rural parents,[112] and less opportunity for children to develop financial responsibility.[113] Athough in many ways there is indication of increasing similarity in the attitudes and behavior of rural and urban families, differences are still quite noticeable.

---

[p]The classic statement of interpersonal relations in the two types of communities can be found in Louis Wirth, "Urbanism As A Way of Life," *American Journal of Sociology*, 44 (1938), 1–24. A great deal of criticism has been directed toward this statement. For an extensive review of this criticism and a recent defense of Wirth's position, see Stanley S. Guterman, "In Defense of Wirth's Urbanism As A Way of Life," *American Journal of Sociology*, 74 (1969), 492–99. See also Claude S. Fischer, "A Research Note on Urbanism and Tolerancy," *American Journal of Sociology*, 76 (1971), 847–56; and Murray A. Strauss,

IDEOLOGY AND VALUES.   Differences in patterns of social behavior such as those noted above may be clarified in some measure by research pointing to differences in ideology and values dominant in rural or urban settings. Beers, for example, found in an analysis of several public opinion pools conducted between 1946 and 1950 that farmers (relative to other groups in American society) were generally more opposed to government welfare and control measures, to labor unions and pro-union issues, to social legislation, and to Negro occupational equality, but more in favor of universal military training and the "control of communism" in American society.[114] Farmers also indicate less support for college training and more satisfaction with their lot in life. However, they do not appear to differ generally from the rest of the population on international issues and occupational preferences. Beers also suggests that such differences as he found indicate a greater degree of conservatism, traditionalism, and puritan morality among farmers than among nonfarmers. Some measure of additional support for these tentative findings is offered by the results of a study of religious beliefs and practices of farm and nonfarm families that indicates that farm-reared college students are raised in a more religiously conservative environment.[115]

There have also been some comparative studies of rural and urban youth. Willits and Bealer report rural high school students to be more socially conservative than town or village high school students, although they suggest the difference may not be prominent enough for "rurality" to serve as an indicator of levels of conservatism.[116] Straus and Sudia indicated that farm boys had a lower "entreprenurial orientation" and less business knowledge than urban boys.[117] Further support for this finding is available from Haller and Wolff, who report that "urban boys tend to score higher on personality measures related to performance in urban work situations."[118] Thus, although rural-urban differences in American society are probably being reduced, such distinctions continue to constitute a meaningful basis for differentiating contemporary sociocultural environments.

Educational Variation Among Communities

The preceding discussion and evidence suggest the importance of differences in the sociocultural environments of metropolitan and nonmetropolitan life. Beyond values associated with the region, a nonmetropolitan community tends to support a view of the educational system's purpose consistent with its concern for the solidarity of the community. Thus, the educational system is defined to a large extent as an agent for community cohesion and continuity. Therefore, it is not surprising that the use of schools

---

"Social Class and Farm-City Differences in Interaction with Kin in Relation to Societal Modernization," *Rural Sociology*, 34 (1969), 476–95.

for noneducational activities associated with community life is a commonly accepted practice in nonmetropolitan areas. On the other hand, metropolitan life depends upon the meeting of material and social needs of a highly complex industrial and commercial order. For the metropolitan community, then, social systems like the educational system tend to be perceived less as agents for community cohesion than as means to both individual and community progress.

Given the above differences in the community perception of education, it is reasonable to anticipate differences in structural emphasis within school districts serving the differing communities. In the nonmetropolitan districts, concern with the maintenance of community requirements would receive much more attention than would efforts to improve the efficiency and effectiveness of the systems. Accordingly, administrative control and conformity to existing educational practices would express themselves in high sensitivity to feedback from the local environment. Institutional requirements, as reflected in accreditation and certification practices, on the other hand, would tend to be seen as less constraining, since their importance to the community would be viewed as peripheral to the purpose of education.

In contrast, we would anticipate that the structure of metropolitan educational systems would place a relatively greater emphasis upon the rationalization of the system. Education, being associated with both individual and social progress, would be focused upon processes directly concerned with education's institutional role. Thus, concern with curriculum, teacher qualification, testing practices, and student performance, on the one hand, would be matched by adaptation to the changing needs of society on the other hand.

Directly related to the above differences in schools found in metropolitan and nonmetropolitan areas would be the greater tendency for metropolitan schools to differentiate by specialization. Through specialized subject matter, specialized services such as counseling or coaching, and grouping of students close in age, metropolitan schools can more efficiently adapt to both their institutional role and the complex requirements of metropolitan life. Thus, specialized high schools to meet particular vocational, social, or academic requirements are not uncommon.

Some idea as to the effect of these differing community environments upon educational systems can be inferred from research findings regarding differences between rural and urban schooling. Rural schools have been found to be smaller than urban schools, in number of pupils and number of teachers per school, as well as number of students per schoolroom.[119] Not only are rural schools smaller on the average than urban schools, but they offer less service to the community in kindergartens, summer school programs, and adult education programs.[120] Similarly, urban schools have been shown to have more specialized staffs (for example, art teacher, reading teacher, librarian) than rural schools have.[121] Rural teachers are generally older[122] and more mobile between school districts than are urban teachers; urban students are more mobile between schools than are rural students.[123] In addition, rural teachers are more likely to teach several grades and subjects simultaneously, and are likely to spend more hours in teaching.[124] Finally, the proportion of rural teachers with less than a college degree or without full certification is much greater than that of urban teachers, and rural principals are not as well trained as are urban principals.[125]

Since the fewest kindergartens are in the rural areas, it is understandable that the proportion of 5-year-olds in elementary or kindergarten classes ranges from 57 percent in the urban central city to 24 percent among farm families.[126] In addition, school retardation is highest among the rural non-farm population and lowest in the urban fringe.[127] This unfavorable position of rural youth is maintained both in dropouts and in proportion of high school graduates who enter college. More rural children are generally found to drop out of school and in rural areas fewer high school graduates go on to college than in urban areas.[128] Such differences are also reflected in the proportion of young adults who graduate from high school. In 1960, 64 percent of urban young adults, but only 55 percent of rural young adults, were high school graduates.[129]

Part of these difference, of course, can be attributed to economic factors. Rural school teachers, for example, are paid appreciably less than are urban teachers.[130] On the other hand, there would appear to be general agreement from many studies that rural farm youth lack educational and occupational aspirations as high as those held by urban youth.[131] While differences are not as clearcut for rural nonfarm youth, considerable evidence suggests they fall in an intermediate position on aspirations between rural farm and urban youth.[132] This difference in aspirations at the high school level may explain in part the fact the rural farm youth are less likely to have definite college plans than are rural nonfarm or urban youth,[133] or to perform as well academically at the college level.[q] It has been suggested, for example, that educational achievement is depressed for rural youth by the larger family size characteristic of rural areas.[134] Another factor influencing

---

[q]Merville C. Shaw and Donald J. Brown, "Scholastic Underachievement of Bright College Students," *Personnel and Guidance Journal*, 36 (1957), 195–99; Norman F. Washburne, "Socioeconomic Status, Urbanism, and Academic Performance in College," *Journal of Educational Research*, 53 (1959), 130–37. Lavin and Sanders *et al.* point to the uncertainty of these results since rural students tend to enroll in different schools or choose different majors, thereby making strict comparisons difficult. See David Lavin, *The Prediction of Academic Performance: A Theoretical Analysis and Review of Research* (New York: John Wiley & Sons, Inc., 1965), p. 132; William B. Sanders, R. Travis Osborn, and Joel E. Green, "Intelligence and Academic Performance of College Students of Urban, Rural, and Mixed Backgrounds," *Journal of Educational Research*, 49 (1955), 185–93.

differences in academic performance is suggested by the finding that rural college students are more vocationally oriented than urban students,[135] and more traditional in their educational values.[136]

AMERICAN NEIGHBORHOODS

In the preceding sections we addressed ourselves to the transitional nature of modernization, discussed regional and community variations within American society, and considered the general effects of such variation upon educational phenomena. In this section we consider the neighborhood served by the school.

Sociocultural Variation Among Neighborhoods

Although ideally we would like to examine the sociocultural characteristics of neighborhoods as environments of schools generally, by considering religious, ethnic, and racial differences, we have chosen to focus solely on social class differences in order to emphasize one of the more dominant concerns of American sociology with respect to the structure of the neighborhood and the school. Social class, as a major form of social differentiation, is of particular importance in a modern industrialized society. Although some degree of social differentiation based upon class considerations has very likely existed in all historical societies, its importance in determining the *Zeitgeist* of a society's sociocultural milieu is associated primarily with the industrialization process of modern societies.[137] Several factors contribute to its emergent importance in this capacity, but its relevance in determining dominant social role orientations would appear to be critical.

DEFINITIONS OF SOCIAL CLASS. Unfortunately, the meaning of "social class" is far from clear. According to Barber, social stratification is the product of the interaction of social differentiation and social evaluation resulting in an arrangement of differential rankings.[138] Social class is a term used to represent one form of social differentiation found to be an important explanatory factor in modern society.[139]

The classical Marxian view of social class emphasized the production process as the primary basis for social differentiation and evaluation. Specifically, according to Marx, in capitalist societies the major social distinction is between those who own capital and control the means of production (capitalists, *grande bourgeoisie*) and the workers who are without property or control over the production process upon which they are dependent.ʳ Social differentiation based upon one's relationship to the means of production was in turn associated with a social evaluation based upon economic criteria leading to high prestige and rank for the capitalist and low prestige and rank for the worker. By virtue of common experience, the members within each group share a common income, standard of living, mode of life, ideology, culture, psychology, and political view.[140] Social class, though based upon economic factors, is to the Marxian a "multi-bonded" phenomena (using Sorokin's term),[141] wherein homogeneous attributes of the collectivity lend themselves to a consensus of solidarity within the production group that separates that group from the other economic groups within the society.

Weber agreed in many respects with the Marxian view of the intrinsic nature of social class. He sought, however, to clarify and bring into balance the strong economic bias of the Marxian interpretation.[142] To achieve these ends he introduced a tripartite distinction to the stratification system seen by Marx. His stratification factors were *class, status,* and *party.* Class, in Weberian terms, refers to stratification based upon one's economic position in society. Status stratification is based upon social ranking by "life style" and patterns of social interaction. Party stratification is based upon the distribution of social power within the society. To Marx, status and power were merely reflections of economic classes, but Weber sought to establish their difference. Weber acknowledged their correlation with economic position, but he argued that status and power were not solely dependent upon social class considerations, but rather varied with circumstances.[143]

Contemporary American students of social stratification, greatly influenced by the general empiricist trend in American sociology, have sought to operationalize the definition of social class provided by Weber. In doing so they have to some extent moved away from his tripartite distinction. Mayer, for example, defines social classes as " . . . aggregates of persons with similar amounts of wealth and property and similar sources of income . . . expressed in different ways of life: patterns of consumption, types of education, speech, manners, dress, tastes, and other cultural attributes."[144] This nominalistic definition is shared by others. To Kahl, "If a large group of families are approximately equal to each other and clearly differentiated from other families we call them a social class."[145] For him, the "equality" and "differentiation" in this definition refer to prestige, occupation, possessions, interaction, class consciousness, and value orientations.[146] Gordon, on the other hand, in a well-developed argument, sees social classes as "major status divisions which stratify a community . . . "[147] and argues that major

---

ʳThere are many discussions of the Marxian view of stratification, but that by G. D. H. Cole is particularly lucid. See G. D. H. Cole, *Studies in Class Structure* (London: Routledge and Kegan Paul, Ltd., 1955), pp. 86–100.

factors of stratification (economic, political, and occupational) are closely associated with the social status system.[148] At the same time, Williams refers to social class as " . . . an aggregate of individuals who occupy a broadly similar position in the scale of prestige."[149] Williams identified such prestige ranking primarily in terms of the extrinsic valuations placed upon power, wealth, group membership, and authority by the society.[150] Thus, his view seems reasonably close to that of Gordon. Finally, Barber sees a social class as consisting of " . . . a set of families that share equal or near equal prestige according to the criteria of evaluation in the system of stratification. . . . " He further notes that " . . . the inclusiveness . . . of a social class can be set in not one but several ways."[151]

It is apparent from these brief examples that although attempts have been made to define social class in fairly explicit terms, agreement as to its meaning is lacking. The suggestion of ambiguity becomes even more apparent when it is recognized that at least four criteria are used in measuring social class for purposes of analysis: life style, others' evaluation, self-evaluation, and occupation.[152] It would seem, therefore, that in spite of its predictive utility, the term "social class" lacks a clear referent. This is not necessarily an indictment of theory and research in this area of sociological inquiry, for as Reissman has noted, there are many "facets and nuances" to social class.[153] To expect any theory or operational measure of social class to spell out clearly its total complexities, in terms of its antecedents and consequences for social life, is to grant to sociology a wisdom and body of knowledge not yet attained. However, it is possible to consider the body of knowledge on social class by clearly delineating what is meant by the term in a particular setting, justifying its usage in the most logical and parsimonious manner possible, and applying it in research efforts in a way consistent with that usage. For, in the final analysis, the validity and utility of most sociological concepts rests upon the judgment of the informed critic rather than upon an absolute consensus.

SOCIAL CLASS AND MODERNIZATION.   In general the primary basis for social class in modern society is production. Although race, ethnicity, ideology, law, and other forms of stratification are important as well.[s] Moreover, the production process can be viewed as primarily descriptive of the technological order rather than of the economic order—although the two are obviously related. However, in modern society, men are differentiated primarily on the basis of occupational roles. The social evaluation of those roles, accordingly, is based upon the perceived worth of knowledge, skills, and orientations

---

[s]For a discussion of these and other forms of stratification, see Barber, *Social Stratification*, chap. 3.

required to fulfill occupational role requirements.[t] Thus, status inconsistencies between occupational roles and income (for example, in the case of clergymen, professors, or morticians) can be interpreted as arising from evaluative discrepancies associated with different systems of social differentiation.

This view of social class is consistent, we would suggest, with much of the theory and research concerned with stratification in both traditional and modern societies. All societies require a division of labor. What distinguishes the division of labor in traditional societies from that found in modern societies, however, is that the division of labor in traditional society is not based primarily upon the technological order. It is related, of course, but in a vestigial way associated with the society's past. Thus, the basis for the division of labor in traditional societies is primarily kinship and wealth.[u] By way of contrast, division of labor in a high modern society apparently rests on a *particular combinations of skills and orientations,* associated with jobs, which are consistent with the requirements of the technical system.[v]

The transition from a division of labor based upon kinship and wealth to a stratification system based upon the technical requirements of the society (wherein occupational requirements emerge as a dominant principle of stratification) is, of course, not instantaneous, nor is it ever complete in a particular society. Resistance to change and oligarchial tendencies, among other things, can prevent a completely "functional rationalization"[w] of occupations. Still, in a comparative sense occupation has become an increasingly important factor in determining the structural arrangements of a society as it moves toward modernity.

---

[t]This is not to suggest that such evaluation presupposes a societal worth or value attached to a given occupation to the extent that it is functionally important to some sort of abstract need of society. Rather, the social psychological evaluation of an occupation regardless of its absolute worth to the larger society is increasingly determined by criteria of the technological order, such as knowledge and skills, rather than nontechnological factors. For a discussion of the functional view of stratification and problems related to it, see "The Continuing Debate on Equality," in *Class, Status and Power: Social Stratification in Comparative Perspective,* 2d ed., ed. Reinhard Bendix and Seymour Martin Lipset (New York: The Free Press, 1966), pp. 47–72.

[u]There is no doubt that kinship and wealth remain important in modern societies, as well as in traditional societies, but in modern societies the importance of the technological order appears to be rapidly replacing these conventional criteria as society becomes more "rationalized" in terms of the needs of modern life.

[v]Again, we stress that such a view should not be equated with a classical functional view of stratification—that the worth of a given position to society somehow determines the status of its role occupant.

[w]We are using the term "functional rationality" in a slightly different way than did Karl Mannheim, who defined it as "a series of actions organized in such a way that it leads to a previously defined goal." Here we refer to the hierarchical ranking of occupations consistent with their contribution to the needs of the technological order. See Karl Mannheim, *Man and Society in an Age of Reconstruction* (New York: Harcourt Brace Jovanovich, 1940), p. 53.

Max Weber, as noted earlier, identified the term "social class" with the economic aspects of social life.[154] It seems, however, that to the extent that technology has become crucial in modern life, economic factors do not wholly determine social status or prestige as they once did. Although income derived from occupation determines in large measure the normative patterns of interaction reflective of one's life style in modern society, the social evaluation placed upon the occupation is increasingly critical. For this reason we shall use the term social class to refer to stratification based upon occupational position.[155]

FUNDAMENTAL DIFFERENCES AMONG AMERICAN SOCIAL CLASSES.   People with higher-ranked occupations form what is generally referred to as the "middle class" and can be roughly contrasted to those with lower-ranked occupations (generally referred to as the "lower class") on a variety of social characteristics of particular relevance to the study of American education. The following characteristics are only a few of the differences between the middle and lower classes in American society.[x]

Evidence is neither complete nor fully consistent, but it seems that parental roles in the middle-class family are more equalitarian and diffuse than are those in the lower-class family, where parental roles are more authoritarian and highly structured. Attitudes toward children are more permissive in middle-class families, with high emphasis placed upon achievement and upon intellectual and personal development. In the lower-class family the emphasis is upon control and respect for parental authority. The middle-class family is more socially stable than the lower-class family.[156]

Middle-class adults also tend to place a high value on social activity, which is reflected in their greater rate of membership in formal organizations. In addition, among the higher groups in the middle class, business and social interaction are frequently mixed. Conversely, lower-class adults tend to be socially inactive, restricting much of their informal activity to relatives.[157]

Middle-class persons tend to be associated with "modern" Protestant or Catholic churches. They tend to support the social gospel and favor such Protestant denominations as the Methodist, Presbyterian, or Episcopalian. Lower-class persons, in contrast, are either unaffiliated or tend to belong to Protestant sects or fundamentalist Protestant denominations such as the Baptist church. A large number of Catholics are also found in the lower class.[158]

The range of life styles in the middle class is, of course, great. Certain underlying features tend to be consistent, however. Most middle-class

---

[x]We are excluding the upper class from this discussion because it constitutes a very small segment of American society (1 percent to 3 percent, depending upon one's criteria). Further, its members do not usually avail themselves of the public school system.

families own or will own a home. They possess one or two cars and indulge in a moderate amount of television watching and occasional light reading. The highlight of their year is usually a two- or three-week vacation involving travel away from home. Frequently, the wife works to better the family's standard of living or to help send the children to college. In contrast, the lower-class family usually lives in an apartment or rents a small home. They may own a car, generally purchased secondhand. They do little reading, but a great deal of television watching. They are restricted financially and plagued by intermittent work schedules. They rarely take vacations, dinners out, or Sunday outings. Their style of living has been characterized as one of "boredom and quiet desperation."[159]

The values of the middle class are more distinctively "modern" than those of the lower class. Middle-class persons tend to emphasize work, achievement, rationality, and individuality. While more pronounced in the upper reaches of the middle class, these values are subscribed to by lower-level middle-class people as well, although their expression frequently is blunted by economic and social circumstance. Lower-class people, in contrast, tend to verbalize these values, but adopt what is essentially a more circumspect and fatalistic approach to their validity. Work becomes a way of making a living; achievement is for the lucky. This is a rationale that lends itself to immediate returns. Individual autonomy is to be found only in specific activities with family or friends. The lower class, in other words, is often observed to be indifferent to, if not alienated from, the dominant values of modern society.[160]

Middle-class individuals may be roughly characterized as optimistic and positive in their attitudes toward life, whereas lower-class persons tend to be characterized as pessimistic and negative. Thus, it seems to follow that middle-class members tend to stress opportunity and lower-class members security, not only in work but in personal relations. Lower-class males in particular seem to adopt defensive or aggressive attitudes toward society generally. In addition, middle-class members have been found to be less authoritarian and less biased in their attitudes toward minority groups than have lower-class persons, although the evidence is not overwhelming.[161]

The above characterizations of the middle and lower classes are, of course, broad generalizations. Classes are not discrete categories, nor are generalizations always valid. However, there is heuristic as well as analytic value in presenting such generalizations, for they allow us to identify some of the neighborhood constraints upon schooling.

Educational Variation Among Neighborhoods

Although there is a growing body of literature on the impact of the social class of American neighborhoods upon educational phenomena, much greater attention has been paid to the impact of the social-class origin of pupils' families. For this reason, and because normally the neighborhood of a school contains the families that send their children to that school, we have chosen to consider the available evidence on the relationship of educational phenomena to *family* social class as well as that with respect to *neighborhood* social class.

Societal needs within modern America center upon the use of formal education to prepare students for adult roles through transmitting knowledge and skills and by instilling appropriate values.[y] Although such needs tend to be congruent with the experiences of the child raised by a middle-class family, the literature on class differences suggests that this is not the case for the child raised by a lower-class family. Middle-class life experience in American society is generally associated with the type of behavior necessary to execute the complex requirements of large-scale organizations. Middle-class families stress the importance of achievement (intellectually as well as socially), and at the same time try to channel its expression within the boundaries of socially approved organizational life. Thus, membership in highly institutionalized churches and participation in social, athletic, and community organizations furnishes the young middle-class child with experiences not unlike those he is required to undergo in school. Given such experiences, values supporting work achievement, rationality, and individuality are reinforced positively and form the basis for an orientation toward social life. Role behavior is defined by general standards rather than specific relationships, with priority given to achievement as opposed to particular social attributes, and tends to be restricted to a given situation free from emotional considerations.[z]

By way of contrast, the experiences of the lower-class child, even though he may share these "middle-class values," contain neither encouragement for them nor the opportunity to express them. Experiences lead to roles being defined in terms of loyalty to family or friends, and interaction with others is categorized and applied uniformly in different situations, dependent upon the emotional loading of any specific situation. Thus, lower-class children, by virtue of relatively unstable family relationships and limited adult-organized social participation outside of school, seek and find rewards in personal relationships among others like themselves by building loyalties that cut across situational boundaries. Since achievement in socially approved areas of life is limited, the lower-class child rationally seeks achievement in non–work-related activities that do not involve participation in

---

[y]See Chapter Three for the development of the argument upon which this assertion is based.

[z]This discussion is derived primarily from Parsons' application of the pattern variables to the social system. See *Toward A General Theory of Action*, ed. Talcott Parsons and Edward A. Shils (New York: Harper Torchbooks, 1962), pp. 80–84.

middle-class organizational life. Under such circumstances his opportunity to practice behavior that would be appropriate in school is limited.[aa]

Given these different experiences, the basic difference between a predominantly lower-class and a predominantly middle-class neighborhood may be viewed as a difference in role orientations learned by lower-class and by middle-class children. Such differences are significant for the school in several respects. Middle-class role expectations are not unlike those that the school seeks to inculcate, and, accordingly, middle-class pupils are much more amenable to organizational influence. Further, because middle-class pupils closely associate achievement with occupational status (which, in turn, is highly dependent upon education in American society), the discrepancy between institutional demands and local environmental constraints is slight. This congruence increases sensitivity to feedback from institutional sources. Lower-class attitudes toward education generally tend to be particularistic and diffuse. Accordingly, parents frequently see the school as they view other public agencies—with a large measure of distrust or indifference. Lower-class pupils, feeling the same way, are quickly defined as "problems" by the school. Such school-environment relationships quickly force a defensive posture upon the school, leading to a great emphasis upon internal control and school-environment relations. Thus, schools in lower-class neighborhoods allocate a great deal of energy to controlling student behavior and to attempting to isolate themselves from potential or real conflicts with their lower-class environment.[162]

EDUCATION AND FAMILY SOCIAL CLASS.   A great deal of research on the relationship of family social class to student behavior, motivation, and attitudes lends support to the interpretation above. It is known, for example, that although there is little difference in initial school enrollment rates among the social classes,[163] the dropout rate of lower-class children is greater than that of middle-class children.[164] For lower-class students, dropping out of school may mean great difficulty in getting a job.[165] Directly related to dropping out is age-grade retardation; the lower the social class of the child, the greater the probability of his repeating a grade.[166]

The relationship of social class to academic achievement in high school is well known also, although its relative importance is uncertain.[167] However, the association of social class with academic performance does not end with high school. Going to college is class-related as well. Folger and Nam report that ". . . among those who actually attend college in the year that they graduated from high school, the proportion coming from white-collar families was about twice that from other families. . . ."[168] Although early

---

[aa]For a more extended discussion of lower-class life, see Frank Reissman, *The Culturally Deprived Child* (New York: Harper and Row, Publishers, 1962).

research by Wolfle suggested that the influence of socioeconomic factors vanished once the student was in college,[169] subsequent research by Eckland[170] and by Sewell and Shah,[171] using longitudinal designs, suggest that social class is important in the probability of college graduation as well.

Given the consistent association of social class and school-related behavior in American society, research has quite naturally sought explanations. Early research attempted to show that social class differences were little more than differences in intelligence. However, numerous studies have since shown that intelligence, as measured by standardized tests, though attenuating the social class-school behavior relationship slightly, does not eliminate it.[172] Recent research has focused more on motivational differences among the social classes and tends to show that students from higher classes are more highly motivated to achieve in school than are students from lower classes.[173]

Motivation, in turn, has been related to the attitudes, values, and beliefs regarding life generally and education specifically. This research has led some investigators to conclude that differences in the behavior of students from different social classes are due, by and large, to differences in achievement aspiration resulting from values and beliefs regarding education learned in the home. The conclusion appears to be that since lower-class families have different values and beliefs than middle-class families, their children do less well in school.[174] It is basically this line of reasoning that led Coleman and his associates to the conclusion that the school itself has little effect upon children beyond that attributable to variation in the nature of their home environments.[175] However, the issues (both theoretical and methodological) involved in attributing pupil behavior to the influences of home or school are very complex.[176]

EDUCATION AND NEIGHBORHOOD SOCIAL CLASS. A more central question than that of the effect of family social class on educational performance is whether the social class characteristics of a school's *neighborhood* affect the school's performance of its institutional role, and further, whether such an effect exists in addition to the effects of the family social class of the student body itself. There have been two major approaches to this question. One approach, basically social psychological and behavioristic, has been to determine the social class composition of a school's student body and to posit the development of a "normative climate" that influences student attitudes, aspirations, and achievement independent of the effects of the pupils' own social class background. The second approach, more sociological and structural-functional, has been to study the effects of the social class context upon particular aspects of the school as a social organization—effects that in turn may influence pupil behavior independently of the pupils' social origins.

Research on the effects of the social class composition of the student body upon student attitudes, aspirations, and achievement is somewhat inconsistent in its findings. Early research led to the conclusion that the social class composition of the student body produces "normative climates" that vary in the degree to which they support appropriate attitudes and achievement.[177] Specifically, this research suggests that schools having a high proportion of middle-class students develop climates positively associated with high aspiration and achievement, whereas schools with a high proportion of lower-class students develop climates negatively associated with high aspirations and achievement. More recently, however, Sewell and Armer, using an elaborate research design in which sex, I.Q., and the social class of the students' family were controlled, found that the social class composition of the student body contributed little to the college-going plans of students above and beyond that attributable to the characteristics of the individual and his family.[178] Such a finding, though hardly conclusive, suggests the complexities associated with a behavioristic approach to the problem.

The second major approach, studying the effects of the social context upon aspects of the school as a social organization, is also limited but has resulted in more conclusive findings. Research has consistently shown middle-class predominance in teacher origins.[179] Thus, it is not surprising to find that teachers tend to prefer locations in which the student body is predominantly middle class.[180] More importantly, perhaps, principal and teacher morale, performance, and qualifications have been shown to be lower in lower-class schools than in middle-class schools.[181] Other differences have been reported between schools serving middle- and lower-class areas in textbooks,[182] facilities,[183] pupil-teacher interaction,[184] counseling,[185] and other pupil services.[186]

The bases for these differences are undoubtedly numerous. However, as Corwin and others have pointed out, the predominance of middle-class personnel in teaching, administrative, and school board positions has led to the conclusion that the school is a "middle-class agency."[187] Thus, one might explain the lack of success of lower-class children in school by saying that their families have failed to instill appropriate attitudes, values, or role-orientations for adaptation to middle-class schools. On the other hand, such an explanation begs a more fundamental set of questions centering upon *why* the school should emphasize middle-class achievement. Certainly, the often-stated explanation that America is a middle-class society tells us less about the reasons for middle-class emphasis in the schools than it does about the ideological predilection of the informant. Insight into this issue would seem to lie in a larger view of the importance of the social class context for schools as open sociocultural systems *vis à vis* their institutional role, which in contemporary America includes the development of a role orientation highly congruent with that fostered in the middle class. The inability of lower-class families to adequately socialize their children according to the institutional requirements of the educational system places them at an initial disadvantage that appears to be compounded by the defensive posture of the school in a lower-class neighborhood.

SUMMARY

In this chapter, after explaining "modernity," we have briefly considered three layers of the sociocultural environment of contemporary American education, noting how variations in dimensions of modernity at each layer could be reflected in differences in the nature of the educational system. Empirical research supportive of this interpretation was also discussed. Ideally, a more thorough explication of this relationship at all layers of the environment with respect to each of the three major dimensions should be carried out.

In the following chapter the theoretical underpinnings for our open-systems perspective on American education, which were introduced in Chapter One, will be developed more fully. In Chapters Four, Five, and Six, empirical tests of the association of some of the social characteristics discussed in this chapter with specific properties of the educational system will be reported. The implications of that analysis for much of the material in this chapter, as well as that in Chapter Three, will be considered in Chapter Seven.

REFERENCES

[1] Myron Weiner, "Introduction," in *Modernization: The Dynamics of Growth,* ed. Myron Weiner (New York: Basic Books, Inc., 1966), pp. 1–14.

[2] *Ibid.,* p. 3.

[3] See, for example, Marion J. Levy, Jr., *Modernization and the Structure of Societies,* Vol. I (Princeton, N. J.: Princeton University Press, 1966) or Daniel Lerner, *The Passing of Traditional Society: Modernizing the Middle East* (New York: The Free Press, 1958).

[4] Lerner, *The Passing of Traditional Society,* p. 45.

[5] Talcott Parsons, "An Outline of the Social System," in *Theories of Society,* Vol. I., ed. Talcott Parsons *et al.* (New York: The Free Press, 1961).

[6] Jacques Ellul, *The Technological Society* (New York: Vintage Books, 1967); Raymond Aron, *The Industrial Society* (New York: Frederick A. Praeger, Inc., 1967).

[7] Levy, *Modernization and the Structure of Societies;* Lerner, *The Passing of Traditional Society;* Bert F. Hoselitz, "Main Concepts in the Analysis of the Social Implications of Technical Change," in *Industrialization and Society,* ed. Bert F. Hoselitz and Wilbert E. Moore (New York: UNESCO, 1963), pp. 11–31.

[8] For an interesting discussion of the limitations associated with this theoretical approach to the problem, see Marvin E. Olsen, *The Process of Social Organization* (New York: Holt, Rinehart and Winston, Inc., 1968), esp. chap. 16.

[9] George A. Theodorson, *A Modern Dictionary of Sociology* (New York: Thomas Y. Crowell Company, 1969), p. 124.

[10] Emile Durkheim, *The Division of Labor in Society,* trans. George Simpson (New York: The Free Press, Paperback edition, 1964).

[11] Louis Wirth, *Community Life and Social Policy: Selected Papers,* ed. Elizabeth Wirth Marvick and Albert J. Reiss, Jr. (Chicago: University of Chicago Press, 1956).

[12]O. Dudley Duncan, "Community Size and the Rural Urban Continuum," in *Cities and Society*, ed. Paul K. Hatt and Albert J. Reiss, Jr. (New York: The Free Press, 1957), pp. 35–45; and Gideon Sjoberg, "The Rural-Urban Dimension in Preindustrial, Transitional, and Industrial Societies" in *Handbook of Modern Sociology*, ed. R. E. Faris (Skokie, Ill.: Rand McNally and Company, 1964), p. 131.

[13]W. Richard Scott, *Social Processes and Social Structures: An Introduction to Sociology* (New York: Holt, Rinehart and Winston, Inc., 1970), pp. 432–33.

[14]Philip M. Hauser, "Urbanization: An Overview," in *The Study of Urbanization*, ed. Philip M. Hauser and Leo F. Schnore (New York: John Wiley & Sons, Inc., 1965), pp. 1–47.

[15]Sjoberg, "The Rural-Urban Dimension"; Hauser, "Urbanization."

[16]Hauser, "Urbanization."

[17]O. Dudley Duncan, "Social Organization and the Ecosystem," in Faris, *Handbook of Modern Sociology*, pp. 37–82.

[18]*Ibid.*, pp. 37–40.

[19]*Ibid.*, p. 40.

[20]*Ibid.*

[21]*Ibid.*, p. 58.

[22]*Ibid.*, p. 62.

[23]*Ibid.*, p. 63; Ellul, *The Technological Society*; Aron, *The Industrial Society*.

[24]Olsen, *The Process of Social Organization*; Scott, *Social Processes and Social Structure*.

[25]Talcott Parsons, *The Social System* (New York: Free Press, 1951), pp. 15–17.

[26]Hauser, "Urbanization."

[27]Florence Kluckhohn and Fred Strodtbeck, *Variations in Value Orientations* (New York: Harper and Row, Publishers, 1961), p. 341.

[28]*Ibid.*, p. 341.

[29]Alex Inkeles, "Industrial Man: The Relation of Status to Experience, Perception and Value," *American Journal of Sociology*, 66 (1960), 1–31.

[30]Hoselitz, "Social Implications of Technological Change."

[31]Kluckhohn and Strodbeck, *Variations in Value Orientations*.

[32]*Ibid.*, p. 17.

[33]Durkheim, *Division of Laber in Society*.

[34]Talcott Parsons, *Societies: Evolutionary and Comparative Perspectives* (Englewood Cliffs, N. J.: Prentice-Hall, Inc., 1966), p. 18; Talcott Parsons, *Structure and Process in Modern Societies* (New York: The Free Press, 1967), p. 172.

[35]Alex Inkeles, "Making Man Modern: On the Causes and Consequences of Individual Change in Six Developing Countries," *American Journal of Sociology*, 79 (1969), 208–25.

[36]*Ibid.*; Lerner, *The Passing of Traditional Society*.

[37]Parsons, *The Social System*, p. 36.

[38]Durkheim, *Division of Labor in Society*.

[39]Parsons, *Societies*, p. 22.

[40]Parsons, *The Social System*.

[41]Max Weber, *The Theory of Social and Economic Organization*, trans. A. M. Henderson and Talcott Parsons (New York: Oxford University Press, 1947).

[42]Ellul, *The Technological Society*.

[43]Parsons, *Societies*.

[44]Writing in 1938, Odum and Moore report 28 varying definitions for regions. See Howard Odum and Harry E. Moore, *American Regionalism* (New York: Holt, Rinehart and Winston, Inc., 1938), pp. 2–34.

[45]*Ibid.*, pp. 438–39.

[46]*Ibid.*, p. 433.

[47]*Ibid.*, p. 436.

[48]Ira Sharkansky, *Regionalism in American Politics* (Indianapolis: The Bobbs-Merrill Company, Inc., 1969).

[49]Louis Wirth, "The Limitations of Regionalism," in *Regionalism in America*, ed. Merrill Jensen (Madison, Wis.: University of Wisconsin Press, 1951), pp. 381–93.

[50]Alexis de Tocqueville, *Democracy in America*, ed. J. P. Mayer and Max Lerner (New York: Harper and Row, Publishers, 1966); D. W. Brogan, *America in the Modern World* (New Brunswick, N. J.: Rutgers University Press, 1960); Carleton Beals, *Our Yankee Heritage: New England's Contribution to American Civilization* (New York: David McKay Co., 1955); and Frederick Jackson Turner, *The Frontier in American History* (New York: Holt and Co., 1921).

[51]H. Richard Niebuhr, *The Social Sources of Denominationalism* (Cleveland: Meridian Books, Inc., 1957).

[52]Conrad M. Arensberg, "American Communities," *American Anthropologist*, 57 (1955), 1143–62.

[53]*Ibid.*, p. 1153.

[54]Frederick Jackson Turner, *The Frontier in American History*; Daniel J. Boorstin, *The Americans: The Colonial Experience* (New York: Random House, Inc., 1958), parts I and II.

[55]de Tocqueville, *Journey to America*; Brogan, *America in the Modern World*.

[56]Carle C. Zimmerman and Richard E. DuWors, *Graphic Regional Sociology* (Cambridge, Mass.: The Phillips Book Store, 1952), pp. 54–55.

[57]*Ibid.*, pp. 55–57.

[58]Clyde Kluckhohn, "Have There Been Discernible Shifts in American Values during the Past Generation?" in *The American Style*, ed. Elting E. Morrison (New York: Harper and Row, Publishers, 1958), pp. 145–219.

[59]Burlingame, *The American Conscience*, pp. 140–42; Zimmerman and DuWors, *Graphic Regional Sociology*, p. 28.

[60]Boorstin, *The Americans*, pp. 109–11.

[61]*Ibid.*

[62]William N. Nichols, *Southern Tradition and Regional Progress* (Chapel Hill. N. C.: University of North Carolina Press, 1960), pp. 64–65, and p. 104.

[63]*Ibid.*, pp. 82–86.

[64]*Ibid.*, pp. 43–79.

[65]de Tocqueville, *Journey to America*, pp. 106–10.

[66]Nichols, *Southern Tradition and Regional Progress*, pp. 134–40.

[67]*Ibid.*, pp. 73–92.

[68]*Ibid.*, pp. 18–21.

[69]*Ibid.*, chap. 2.

[70]Odum and Moore, *American Regionalism*, pp. 462–81; John Gillin, "National and Regional Cultural Values in the United States," *Social Forces*, 34 (1955), 107–13.

[71]*Ibid.*

[72]Odum and Moore, *American Regionalism*, pp. 576–617; Perloff *et al.*, *Regions, Resources, and Economic Growth* (Baltimore: The Johns Hopkins Press, 1960).

[73]Gillin, "National and Regional Cultural Values in the United States," pp. 112–13.

[74]Perloff *et al.*, *Regions, Resources, and Economic Growth*.

[75]Robin Williams, *American Society*, 2d ed. (New York: Alfred A. Knopf, Inc., 1960), p. 432.

[76]*Ibid.*, pp. 433–36.

[77]Niebuhr, *The Social Sources of Denominationalism*; and Herberg, *Protestant, Catholic, Jew*.

[78]John K. Folger and Charles B. Nam, *Education of the American Population* (Washington, D.C.: Government Printing Office, 1967), p. 21.

[79]*Ibid.*, p. 92.

[80]U.S. Bureau of the Census, *Statistical Abstract of the United States*: 1963 (Washington, D.C.: Government Printing Office, 1963), tables 19 and 144.

[81]Folger and Nam. *Education of the American Population*, pp. 152–55.

[82]Charles C. Cole, *Encouraging Scientific Talent* (New York: College Entrance Examination Board, 1956), p. 64.

[83]*Ibid.*, pp. 14–18.

[84]Alan M. Cartter, "Qualitative Aspects of Southern University Education," *Southern Economic Journal*, 32 (1965), No. 1, Part II, 39–69, esp. p. 40.

[85]David Ryans, *Characteristics of Teachers* (Washington, D.C.: American Council on Education, 1960), p. 397.

[86]Nichols, *Southern Tradition and Regional Progress*, pp. 106–53.

[87]Robert C. Bealer, Fern K. Willits, and William P. Kuvlesky, "The Meaning of 'Rurality' in American Society: Some Implications of Alternative Definitions," *Rural Sociology*, 30 (1965), 255–66.

[88]Thomas R. Ford and Willis A. Sutton, Jr., "The Impact of Change on Rural Communities and Fringe Areas: Review of a Decade's Research," in *Our Changing Rural Society: Perspectives and Trends*, ed. James H. Copp (Ames, Ia.: Iowa State University, 1964), p. 199.

[89]Otis Dudley Duncan and Albert J. Reiss, Jr., *Social Characteristics of Urban and Rural Communities, 1950* (New York: John Wiley & Sons, Inc., 1956), chap. 2.

[90]Pitirim A. Sorokin and Carl Zimmerman, *Principles of Rural-Urban Sociology* (New York: Henry Holt and Co., 1929).

[91]Gideon Sjoberg, "The Rural-Urban Dimension," p. 131.

[92]*Ibid.*

[93]Bert F. Hoselitz, "Social Implications of Technical Change," p. 15.

[94]Howard Becker, *Man in Reciprocity: Introductory Lectures on Culture, Society and Personality* (New York: Frederick A. Praeger, Inc., 1956).

[95]Hoselitz, "Social Implications of Technical Change."

[96]Howard Becker, *Through Values to Social Interpretation* (Durham, N. C.: Duke University Press, 1950).

[97]Sjoberg, "The Rural-Urban Dimension," pp. 149–50; Glen V. Fuguitt, "The City and Country Side," *Rural Sociology*, 28 (1963), 246–61.

[98]Olaf F. Larson and Everett M. Rogers, "Rural Society in Transition: The American Setting," in Copp, *Our Changing Rural Society*, pp. 47–52.

[99]Leo F. Schnore, "The Rural-Urban Variable: An Urbanite's Perspective," *Rural Sociology*, 31 (1966), 131–55.

[100]Arthur J. Vidich and Joseph Bensman, *Small Town in Mass Society* (Princeton, N. J.: Princeton University Press, 1958), esp. chaps. 8, 10, and 11; Ford and Sutton, "Impact of Change on Rural Communities and Fringe Areas," pp. 206–207.

[101]Schnore, "The Rural-Urban Variable."

[102]Ford and Sutton, "Impact of Change on Rural Communities and Fringe Areas."

[103]*Ibid.*, p. 208.

[104]See, for example, Gordon L. Buttena, "Rural-Urban Differences in the Familial Interaction of the Aged," *Rural Sociology*, 34 (1969), 5–15; Marvin B. Sussman and Lee Burchinal, "Kin Family Network: Unheralded Structure in Current Conceptualizations of Family Functioning," *Marriage and Family Living*, 24 (1962), 231–40; Aidak Tomch, "Participation in a Metropolitan Community," *Sociological Quarterly*, 8 (1967), 85–102; John P. Sutcliffe and B. D. Crabbe, "Incidence and Degrees of Friendship in Urban and Rural Areas," *Social Forces*, 42 (1963), 60–67.

[105]Lee G. Burchinal, "The Rural Family of the Future," in Copp, *Our Changing Rural Society*, p. 180.

[106]Robert O. Blood, "The Division of Labor in City and Farm Families," *Marriage and Family Living*, 20 (1958), 170–74.

[107]Burchinal, "The Rural Family of the Future," p. 175. See also James D. Tarver, "Gradients of Urban Influence on Educational Attainment, Employment, and Fertility Patterns of Women," *Rural Sociology*, 38 (1969), 356–67.

[108]Burchinal, "The Rural Family of the Future," p. 178.

[109]Ivan F. Nye, "Adolescent-Parent Adjustment: Rurality as a Variable," *Rural Sociology*, 15 (1950), 334–39; Burchinal, "The Rural Family of the Future," p. 180.

[110]Hart M. Nelsen and Stuart E. Storey, "Personality Adjustment of Rural and Urban Youth: The Formation of a Rural Disadvantaged Subculture," *Rural Sociology*, 34 (1969), 43–55.

[111]Burchinal, "The Rural Family of the Future," p. 182.

[112]*Ibid.*

[113]Murray A. Straus, "Work Roles and Financial Responsibility," *Rural Sociology*, 27 (1962) 257–74.

[114]Howard W. Beers, "Rural-Urban Differences: Some Evidence from Public Opinion Polls," *Rural Sociology*, 18 (1953), 1–11.

[115]Lee Burchinal, "Farm–Non-Farm Differences in Religious Beliefs and Practices," *Rural Sociology*, 26 (1961), 416.

[116]Fern K. Willits and Robert C. Bealer, "The Utility of Residence for Differentiating Social Conservation in Rural Youth," *Rural Sociology*, 28 (1963), 70–80.

[117]Murray A. Straus and Cecelia E. Sudia, "Entreprenurial Orientation of Farm, Working Class, and Middle Class Boys," *Rural Sociology*, 30 (1965), 291–98.

[118]A. O. Haller and Carole Ellis Wolff, "A Note on 'Personality Orientations of Farm, Village, and Urban Boys,' " *Rural Sociology*, 30 (1965), 338–40.

[119]M. C. S. Noble, Jr., and Howard A. Dawson, *Handbook on Rural Education: Factual Data on Rural Education, Its Social and Economic Backgrounds* (Washington, D.C.: Department of Rural Education of the National Education Association, 1961), p. 76; George W. Mayeske *et al.*, *A Study of Our Nation's Schools* (Washington, D.C.: U. S. Office of Education, 1969), p. 101.

[120]Noble and Dawson, *Handbook on Rural Education.*

[121]Mayeske *et al., A Study of Our Nation's Schools*, p. 100.

[122]*Ibid.*, p. 100; see also Folger and Nam, *Education of the American Population*, p. 94.

[123]Mayeske *et al., A Study of Our Nation's Schools*, p. 100; Noble and Dawson, *Handbook on Rural Education*, pp. 30–31.

[124]Mayeske *et al., A Study of Our Nation's Schools*, p. 100.

[125]*Ibid.*, pp. 27–29.

[126]Folger and Nam, *Education of the American Population*, p. 34.

[127]*Ibid.*, p. 52.

[128]*Ibid.*, p. 58.

[129]*Ibid.*, pp. 155–57.

[130]Noble and Dawson, *Handbook on Rural Education*, p. 32.

[131]Lee G. Burchinal, "The Rural Family of the Future"; William H. Sewell, "Community of Residence and College Plans," *American Sociological Review*, 29 (1964), 24–38.

[132]Lee G. Burchinal and Hilda Siff, "Rural Poverty," *Journal of Marriage and the Family*, 26 (1964), 399–405; Dael Wolfle, "Educational Opportunity, Measured Intelligence, and Social Background," in *Education, Economy, and Society*, ed. A. H. Halsey, Jean Floud, and C. Arnold Anderson (New York: The Free Press, 1961), pp. 216–40; Natalie Rogoff, "Local Social Structure and Educational Selection," in Halsey, Floud, and Anderson, *Ibid.*, pp. 241–51; Folger and Nam, *Education of the American Population*, p. 58.

[133]Folger and Nam, *Education of the American Population*, p. 58.

[134]David L. Featherman, "Residential Background and Socioeconomic Achievements in Metropolital Stratification Systems," *Rural Sociology*, 36 (1971), 107–24.

[135]Benjamin J. Hodgkins, *Student Subcultures—An Analysis of Their Origins and Affects on Student Attitude and Value Change* (unpublished Ph. D. dissertation, Michigan

State University, 1964), pp. 119–21.

[136]Irving J. Lehmann and Paul L. Dressel, *Critical Thinking, Attitudes, Values in Higher Education* (East Lansing, Mich.: Michigan State University Press, 1962).

[137]Pitirim A. Sorokin, *Society, Culture and Personality: Their Structure and Dynamics* (New York: Harper and Bros., 1947), pp. 271–72.

[138]Bernard Barber, *Social Stratification* (New York: Harcourt, Brace Jovanovich, 1957), p. 2.

[139]Milton M. Gordon, *Social Class in American Sociology* (Durham, N. C.: Duke University Press, 1958), p. 13; Leonard Reissman, *Class in American Society* (New York: The Free Press, 1959), p. 43.

[140]Sorokin, *Society, Culture and Personality*, p. 267.

[141]*Ibid.*, p. 261.

[142]*From Max Weber: Essays in Sociology*, trans. and ed. H. H. Gerth and C. Wright Mills (New York: Oxford University Press, 1946), pp. 46–47.

[143]*Ibid.*, pp. 180–94.

[144]Kurt B. Mayer, *Class and Society*, rev. ed. (New York: Random House, Inc., 1955), p. 8.

[145]Joseph A. Kahl, *The American Class Structure* (New York: Holt, Rinehart and Winston, Inc., 1959), p. 12.

[146]*Ibid.*, pp. 8–10.

[147]Gordon, *Social Class in American Sociology*, p. 250.

[148]*Ibid.*, p. 251.

[149]Williams, *American Society*, p. 98.

[150]*Ibid.*, p. 97.

[151]Barber, *Social Stratification*, p. 73.

[152]Reissman, *Class in American Society*, p. 116.

[153]*Ibid.*, p. 37.

[154]Gerth and Mills, *From Max Weber*, p. 181.

[155]Peter M. Blau and Otis Dudley Duncan, *The American Occupational Structure* (New York: John Wiley & Sons, Inc., 1967), pp. 6–7.

[156]John A. Clausen and Judith R. Williams, "Sociological Correlates of Child Behavior," in *Child Psychology: The Sixty-second Yearbook of the National Society for the Study of Education*, ed. Harold W. Stevenson (Chicago, Ill.: University of Chicago Press, 1963), pp. 62–107.

[157]Kahl, *The American Class Structure*, pp. 141–50; Harold M. Hodges, Jr., *Social Stratification: Class in America* (Cambridge, Mass.: Schenkman Publishing Company, 1964), pp. 113–14.

[158]Hodges, *Social Stratification*, pp. 154–56.

[159]Kahl, *The American Class Structure*, pp. 100–10.

[160]*Ibid.*, pp. 193–217; Hodges, *Social Stratification*, pp. 198–201.

[161]Hodges, *Social Stratification*, pp. 195–220.

[162]See, for example, Lynn Nicholas *et al.*, *Effects of Socioeconomic Setting and Organizational Climate on Problems Brought to Elementary School Offices*, U.S. Office of Education Project 2394 (OE-4-10-084).

[163]Folger and Nam, *Education of the American Population*, p. 46.

[164]*Ibid.*, p. 41.

[165]*Ibid.*, p. 50.

[166]*Ibid.*, p. 56.

[167]Wilbur B. Brookover and David Gottlieb, "Social Class and Education," in *Readings in the Social Psychology of Education*, ed. W. W. Charters, Jr., and N. L. Gage (Boston: Allyn and Bacon, Inc., 1963), pp. 3–11; Peter H. Rossi, "Social Factors in Academic Achievement: A Brief Review," in Halsey, Floud, and Anderson, *Education, Economy, and Society*, pp. 269–72.

[168]Folger and Nam, *Education of the American Population*, p. 60.

[169]Dael Wolfle, *America's Resources of Specialized Talent* (New York: Harper and Row, Publishers, 1954), p. 163.

[170]Bruce K. Eckland, "Social Class and College Graduation: Some Misconceptions Corrected," *American Journal of Sociology*, 70 (1964), 36–50.

[171]William H. Sewell and Vimal P. Shah, "Socioeconomic Status, Intelligence, and the Attainment of Higher Education," *Sociology of Education*, 40 (1967), 1–23.

[172]W. W. Charters, Jr., "Social Class and Intelligence Tests," in Charters and Gage, *Readings in the Social Psychology of Education*, pp. 12–21.

[173]Ronald G. Corwin, *A Sociology of Education: Emerging Patterns of Class, Status, and Power in the Public Schools* (New York: Appleton-Century-Crofts, 1965), p. 205.

[174]See, for example, Bernard Rosen, "The Achievement Syndrome," *American Sociological Review*, 21 (1956), 203–11; Robert J. Havighurst and Bernice Neugarten, *Society and Education*, 3d ed. (Boston: Allyn and Bacon, Inc., 1967), pp. 20–32.

[175]Coleman *et al.*, *Equality of Educational Opportunity*, Vol. I.

[176]See, for example, Samuel S. Bowles and Henry M. Levin, "The Determinants of Scholastic Achievement: An Appraisal of Some Recent Evidence," *Journal of Human Resources*, 3 (1968), 3–29; Robert C. Nichols, "Schools and the Disadvantaged," *Science*, 154 (December 9, 1966), 1312–14; Glen G. Cain and Harold W. Watts, "Problems in Making Policy Inferences from the Coleman Report," *American Sociological Review*, 35 (1970), 228–42.

[177]Alan B. Wilson, "Residential Segregation of Social Classes and Aspirations of High School Boys," *American Sociological Review*, 24 (1959), 836–45; Natalie Rogoff, "Local Social Structure and Educational Selection," in Halsey, Floud, and Anderson, *Education, Economy, and Society*, pp. 241–51; John A. Michael, "High School Climates and Plans for Entering College," *Public Opinion Quarterly*, 24 (1961), 585–95; James A. Coleman, *The Adolescent Society* (New York: The Free Press, 1962); Irving Krauss, "Sources of Educational Aspirations Among Working-Class Youth," *American Sociological Review*, 29 (1964), 867–79; Ralph H. Turner, *The Social Context of Ambition* (San Francisco: Chandler Publishing Co., 1964); Coleman *et al.*, *Equality of Educational Opportunity*, Vol. I.

[178]William H. Sewell and J. Michael Armer, "Neighborhood Context and College Plans," *American Sociological Review*, 31 (1966), 159–68.

[179]Robert J. Havighurst and Bernice L. Neugarten, *Society and Education*, pp. 410–12.

[180]Howard S. Becker, "The Career of the Chicago Public School Teacher," *American Journal of Sociology*, 57 (1952), 470–77; Robert E. Herriott and Nancy Hoyt St. John, *Social Class and the Urban School: The Impact of Pupil Background on Teachers and Principals* (New York: John Wiley & Sons, Inc., 1966), pp. 85–88.

[181]Herriott and St. John, *Social Class and the Urban School*, p. 109; Patricia Cayo Sexton, *The American School: A Sociological Analysis* (Englewood Cliffs, N.J.: Prentice-Hall, Inc., 1966), p. 54.

[182]Edgar Litt, "Civic Education, Community Norms, and Political Indoctrination," *American Sociological Review*, 28 (1963), 69–75; Corwin, *A Sociology of Education*, p. 164.

[183]Sexton, *The American School*, p. 54.

[184]Howard Becker, "Social Class Variations in the Teacher-Pupil Relationship," *Journal of Educational Sociology*, 25 (1952), 451–65; Helen H. Davidson and Gerhard Lang, "Children's Perception of Their Teachers' Feelings Toward Them Related to Self-Perception, School Achievement and Behavior," *Journal of Experimental Education*, 29 (1960), 107–18.

[185]Sexton, *The American School*, p. 54; Aaron V. Cicourel and John I. Kitsuse, *The Educational Decision Makers* (Indianapolis: The Bobbs-Merrill Company, Inc., 1963).

[186]Sexton, *The American School*.

[187]Corwin, *A Sociology of Education*, pp. 162–66.

three

American Public Education as an Open Sociocultural System

Formal education, as we know it today, is generally considered an integral part of modern American society. However, it is difficult for individuals within a society to identify the form and purpose of education. As suggested by our discussion in Chapter Two, such form and purpose can vary appreciably from one school—and one period of history—to another. Yet, as noted in Chapter One, it is possible to identify an underlying developmental theme throughout the historical growth of education in America. To perform an analysis of the type we shall report in subsequent chapters requires the development of a conceptual model within which both variation and unity can be not only logically related, but also used for empirical study. It is the purpose of this chapter to present such a model, first verbally, then symbolically.

The existential basis for this model is critical to its understanding. Accordingly, our discussion begins with several assumptions that underlie our model regarding the nature of social reality. For the reader accustomed to viewing social phenomena solely in terms of individuals interacting in some specified situation, the perspective to be set forth in this chapter will undoubtedly be disturbing. Nevertheless, without at least a minimal awareness of a sociological perception of social phenomena, an understanding of our model and its implications would be problematic. The model itself, it should be noted, is not intended in any sense to be a "theory." Nor, in all candor, can we claim it to be isomorphically derived from some set of universal principles and applicable to all social phenomena, although structural properties introduced subsequently are considered to be isomorphically similar in "open systems" generally.[1] Rather, our model is an analytic and heuristic device that can provide a better understanding of a highly complex subject. After presenting a series of assumptions and definitions, this chapter explains how we perceive education as an open sociocultural system to be influenced by modernization. Subsequently, intrasocietal variation in modernity and its effects upon education is considered, and our model is presented in formal symbolic terms.

SOME ASSUMPTIONS REGARDING SOCIAL REALITY

An assumption underlying much of the analytic discussion to follow relates to the distinction noted in Chapter One between the interests of the group and those of the individual. Such interests may at points coincide, but they are not necessarily identical. Emergent levels of social reality, arising out of the prolonged interaction of individuals in any social system, can generate collective interests independent of the intent of individual members at a given point in time and space.[2] This, of course, does not prevent individual initiative (either singularly or collectively) as it is interpreted by the individual or others, nor the possibility of an individual's influencing the shape or direction of the *social reality* associated with his group. It does assume, however, that the individual, as a part of a group, will perceive, act, emote, and know largely within the dominant framework of the social reality as it is defined by the collectivities of which he is a member. Therefore, in considering the analysis that follows, it is important to note that we are directing our attention not to the behavior or perception of *individuals*—except insofar as such action or perception is seen to reflect the larger definition or social reality—but rather to characteristics of the *society* and its subsidiary sociocultural elements.

Although foreign to most contemporary American thinking regarding the nature of reality (particularly that associated with research on education), the idea of an emergent social reality can provide a powerful analytic tool for studying the effects over time of large-scale social forces upon social systems, as well as permitting a partial resolution to the problem of relating the individual to the social order discussed in Chapter One.[a] Although such

---

[a]The question of how an individual relates to society has been problematic for social philosophers back at least to Aristotle and continues to be debated by social scientists. "Social realists," such as Emile Durkheim, have argued that society and social facts exist independent of the individuals who are their carriers. On the other hand, most American sociologists have explicitly or implicitly taken the position of social behaviorism, that "structure of all social groups is the consequence of the aggregate of its separate component individuals and that social phenomena ultimately derive from the motivations of those

social reality is an analytic abstraction, as in fact are all such attempts to explain "reality," it is both theoretically sound and heuristically useful in the study of environmental forces that affect education. We do not, however, assume the impact of these forces to be inevitable. Nevertheless, given an understanding of the current state of a society and the nature of its social and historical development, the consequences of such forces often are predictable.

A major assumption directly related to the view of the nature of social reality as emergent is that there are inherent developmental tendencies in all societies that will, if given the appropriate circumstances, move them in fairly well-defined directions. Such transitions are not evolutionary in the sense that they are inevitable,[3] nor are they even vaguely related to the mechanistic concoctions of the "Social Darwinist" school of thought, which sought to connect the evolutionary theory of Darwin to a social ideology supportive of the status quo.[b] The developmental tendencies to which we refer are, rather, the uniform directional propensities that societies demonstrate as a result of their adaptation to particular exigencies (such as major climatic, ecological, or technological changes) that require major adjustments in their social order. For example, in prehistoric times the introduction of agriculture required the development of sedentary life styles and the reordering of many social relationships. So, also, industrialization in both historic and contemporary societies leads to a concentration of population in urban areas and a more complex division of labor.[4] Again, we are not assuming that such tendencies inevitably occur, or that every society responds identically to the same exigency. However, we do assume that given a specified initial state, the adaptation to a particular exigency is always in the same *general* direction.

To adopt such an evolutionary stance implies to many an assumption of some end state toward which society is moving. However, as we are viewing it, this process of socio-historical change has not been simply one of moving "upward" toward an ideal state, but rather one of increasing adaptation to and control of the physical environment.[5] Such a view does

---

knowing, feeling, and willing individuals." [Roscoe C. Hinkle, Jr. and Gisela J. Hinkle, *The Development of Modern Sociology: Its Nature and Growth in the United States* (Garden City, N. Y.: Doubleday and Co., Inc., 1954), p. 7.] Both positions have their strengths and weaknesses and we view them as essentially complementary in explaining social phenomena. In this instance, for analytic purposes we have chosen to take essentially a "neo-realist" position regarding the relationship of the individual to society.

[b]Social Darwinism, or the belief that natural selection through conflict and competition occurs both within and between societies in order for the "best" to dominate or at least survive, has been popular in some circles since the original work of Darwin. A good summary of much of the nineteenth- and early twentieth-century writing on this subject is to be found in Don Martindale, *The Nature and Type of Sociological Theory* (Boston: Houghton Mifflin Company, 1960).

not presuppose any end state. Quite the contrary! Given man's imperfections, the developmental process is, for all practical purposes, perpetual and not completely predictable.

The significance of the idea of "level" in the subsequent discussion should also be understood. As Edel notes, level has many meanings in the natural and social sciences but is most closely associated with a historical evolutionary perspective. Generally, it refers to "the emergence of qualities in the process of historical development."[6] Such qualities are associated with different empirical forms and can be considered a transformation of the phenomena, for purposes of analysis. It is for this reason that chemical attributes of an organism generally are not analyzed in the same way as are the organism's physiological attributes. The physiological attributes in this case are a "higher level" of the phenomena considered, with traits and properties unique to that level and not directly attributable to the phenomenon's "lower level" chemical attributes. A variant of this usage, suggested by Edel and employed in this work, is that such levels may be considered levels of "group generalization";[c] that is, analytically the attributes of a phenomena to be studied are determined by the basic unit of analysis selected. Thus, for example, interest in the chemical "form" of an organism leads to a concern with its chemical attributes. Such a perspective tells one little, directly, of its physiological processes. So, also, an analytic decision to evaluate the physiological attributes of the organism presupposes a perception of its physiological form. Both concerns are directed toward the same object and are equally valid. However, a view of the chemical form of an organism does not presuppose its physiological attributes, and a physiological analysis does assume the organism's chemical properties. They are simply at different levels of "group generalization."

It is also possible to distinguish between levels of systems in terms of the system's functional generalizability. Thus, there are subsystems within systems, which are in turn subsystems of yet larger "suprasystems." Accordingly, one may speak of a carburetor system within an internal combustion system within an automobile system within a transportation system within a social system. Such a discussion may focus upon the internal dynamics of a system at any given level or upon the relationships between systems at the same or different levels, depending upon the problem being considered.

Just as different *levels* of social systems can be conceptualized, the environment of a social system, as noted in Chapter Two, may be seen in

___

[c]Edel, "The Concept of Levels in Social Theory," p. 175. Examples of such usage in sociological theory can be found in work of both Parsons and Sorokin. See Talcott Parsons, "An Outline of the Social System," in *Theories of Society,* Vol. I, ed. Talcott Parsons *et al.* (New York: The Free Press, 1961), 30–79; and Pitirim Sorokin, *Social and Cultural Dynamics: A Study of Change in Major Systems of Art, Truth, Ethics, Law and Social Relationships,* revised and abridged ed. (Boston: Porter Sargent, 1957).

layers (for example, region, community, and neighborhood), which also are relative and transitional in nature. That is, a social environment is defined relative to a given social system, not by its apparent physical reality. "Transitional" indicates that the social environment is never static, but changes over time as its parameters are reinterpreted by the social system. The term "layers" refers to differences in function in a social environment analagous to system levels of group generalization within the total social context.[7] Accordingly, one may speak of the environment of a formal organization as constituting elements extraneous to the system that are important to the organization in meeting its requirements. Such elements may include available material resources, sociocultural characteristics of the local community, the potential market for the organization's product, government restrictions, and the like. In turn, at a more general level, the formal organization may be seen as part of a corporation or industry with an environmental context incorporating not only concerns of the organization itself but extending to concerns of the corporation or industry. Analytically an environment can be defined in terms of its relevance to the purpose of the system under consideration, and thus the definition of the scope of that environment is a function of the level of system generalization being considered.

AN OPEN-SYSTEMS PERSPECTIVE

Basic Concepts

We begin our formal discussion with a consideration of some of the basic concepts of systems theory. Our discussion draws primarily upon the works of Parsons, Katz and Kahn, Buckley, and von Bertalanffy.[8] However, our reliance on them is selective and aimed at developing a limited explanatory framework for the study of the American public educational system. Accordingly, our approach is less an attempt to present a "theory" than to present the conceptual basis for a "heuristic model."

As we noted in the previous section, the two most fundamental concepts in a general systems framework are those of "system" and "environment." In scientific literature, "system" is typically used in a highly general manner. To von Bertalanffy, a system is simply ". . . complexes of elements standing in interaction."[9] Hall and Fagen present a more complete definition. To them a system is ". . . a set of objects together with relationships between the objects and between their attributes."[10] Objects, according to Hall and Fagen, are components of the system, whereas attributes are properties of those objects.[11] In general, it is the relationship between objects and their attributes that forms a system. Hall and Fagen emphasize "relationships" in their definition, rather than physical objects, although objects and their attributes are seen as part of the system. The most important relationships between objects and their attributes are a function of the problem being considered by the investigator of the system.[12]

In general terms we agree with the above definitions. There is, however, a certain "static" and deterministic quality to them, for they are essentially descriptive and make no reference to the dynamic nature of the system or to changes that may occur in it for either immanent or extrasystem reasons. Hall and Fagen resolve these problems to their own satisfaction by avoiding the question of causality, and speak instead of change as a function of modification in attributes of the system, which in turn results in changes in the object's relationships.[13] This somewhat "scholastic" view of change would appear to stem from an assumption that the reality of any system is an aggregate phenomenon derived from the properties of its constituent objects.[14] A more comprehensive view would be that a system is qualitatively different from its objects. Given such a view, it is no longer necessary to "explain" the nature of the system or its change in terms of the characteristics of its components.[15] Thus the system is qualitatively different from (although functionally dependent upon) its component properties, behaving intrinsically consistent with what Bunge has referred to as the "principle of determinacy," wherein everything is determined by something else in accordance with specific law.[16] From such an ontological position a *system* can be conceptualized as *a set of lawfully related complex relationships evidencing a high degree of stability.*[d]

Every system, of course, exists within an environment. Hall and Fagen define an environment as ". . . a set of objects a change of whose attributes affect the system and also those objects whose attributes are changed by the behavior of the system.[17] The emphasis in this definition is upon those objects influencing or being influenced by the system. Von Foerster goes a step further, however, in viewing the environment as ". . . an accumulation of successful solutions (for the system) to the problem of selecting such conditions in the physical world which are at least survivable."[18] This latter view of the environment implies, according to von Foerster, that a specific system has a specific environment and vice versa. Further, such a definition recognizes the predominantly functional nature of the system-environment nexus, wherein the interaction of the two is somewhat symmetrical in that changes in either one are associated with changes in the other. Given our previous definition of a system, *environment* is defined as *those objects and patterns of relationships that exist outside a system but significantly influence*

---

[d]The expression "lawfully related" should be understood in the philosophical sense of a conditional and regular association between two or more objects, events, and so forth. See Bunge, *Ibid.*

it or are influenced by it. Implicit in this definition is the assumption that although transitional in nature, at a specific point in time a system is particular to its environment and must come to terms with it. Also implicit is the view that the boundary between a system and its environment is neither static nor clearcut.[e]

The conceptual linkage between a system and its environment is incorporated in the term "energy." *Energy is that which is exchanged between a system and its environment.* In physics, energy is traditionally defined in operational terms (for example, as the capacity for doing work, or as that which diminishes when work is done).[19] Energy can assume many forms (kinetic, heat, electro-magnetic, and so forth) with a variety of properties.[20] When applying the term to the interrelation of a system and its environment, consistent with our earlier discussion, it would seem appropriate to emphasize the source of energy relevant to the type of relationship under consideration (physical, biological, psychological, social, and so on). Thus, a physical system, such as a diesel engine, derives its energy (the capacity for work) from oil, whereas a biological system, such as an animal, uses energy from food.

This energy exchange between a system and its environment has several characteristics important to an understanding of any given system. One is the degree to which the system is open or closed in regard to the exchange of energy. *Closed systems,* once established, exchange no energy with their environments.[21] Classical thermodynamics has dealt with such systems, as have laboratory experiments in physical chemistry where one combines various chemicals in isolation from any environment in order to bring about particular effects.[22] In contrast, an *open system* continually exchanges energy with its environment. Biological organisms, such as animals or men, are the traditional examples of open systems. As we have said, the American public school is also an open system.

In considering an open system, a problem arises as to the manner and type of exchanges the system has with its environment. With which elements of the environment does exchange occur? Von Foerster's definition of environment suggests selectivity in the exchange process. Those significant elements of the environment, as von Foerster suggests, are those upon which the system depends for survival.

As a rule it seems reasonable to suggest that for open systems generally,

---

[e]Berrien extends the physical analogy of the boundary concept beyond that suggested by our definition. To him, a boundary is defined as "that region through which inputs and outputs must pass, during which exchanges with the system's environment undergo some modification or transformation." [F. Kenneth Berrien, *General and Social Systems* (New Brunswick, N. J.: Rutgers University Press, 1968), p. 23]. Although such a definition may have utility when the individual is the system under consideration, its usefulness in discussing systems at the collective level, where personal relationships are basic, is less clear.

the initial actual environment is determined almost exclusively by survival consideration. To the extent that such considerations remain paramount, other elements that might be included in the system's environment are ignored. However, survival is not the sole criterion in the determination of a system's actual environment. But only when the constraints of survival are reduced by changes in the total environment, or in the system, do other elements take on significance. Thus, the environment of the newborn animal is sharply delimited by his immediate biological needs. Subsequently, however, maturation leads to an expansion of the animal's awareness of and response to other elements that were there all along. In effect, to use William James' expression, the "blooming buzzing confusion" becomes meaningfully structured. Or, to give an example of another type, harsh physical conditions may reduce an organism's environment to the point where it contains only consumable or potentially destructive objects. A modification of the physical environment could reduce the energy required to survive, thereby permitting other elements, neither consumable nor threatening, to become environmentally relevant. Such an expansion of environment occurs with the domestication of certain animal species. Generally, then, on the biological level, such things as climate, food, and natural enemies, constitute the environment of the organism. They, in effect, are significant constraints upon the organism's behavior. More generally, such constraints constitute the environment of any open system and determine the type of exchange that ensues.

The term "purpose," which is directly related to the nature of system-environment exchange, must also be considered in discussing open systems. For individual biological organisms, purpose is frequently viewed as simply another way of saying "survival." The specific organism exchanges energy with its environment for the purpose of survival. Beyond the individual biological system, however, the concept of purpose becomes much more difficult to explain and is frequently used in a teleological manner. For example, one can discuss the "survival" of a biological species, or nature's maintenance of a given "ecosystem." Therefore, it is important to note that our usage of purpose does not presuppose an anthropomorphic "awareness" on the part of the organism. As we shall use the term in the following discussion, *purpose* refers only to *an inferred directional state of the system consistent with its structural properties and dominant environmental constraint* (for example, the primary focus of system activities at a given point in time).[f] There are, of course, similarities between the above definition of purpose and Merton's

---

[f]Bertalanffy refers to this aspect of open systems as a "dynamic teleology" wherein the directiveness of the system is based upon its structure and is governed by feedback mechanisms. [Ludwig von Bertalanffy, *General Systems Theory* (New York: George Braziller, 1968), p. 78.]

concept of "function," which is defined as ". . . those observed consequences which make for the adaptation or adjustment of a given system.
. . ."[23] In contrast, our definition of purpose does not presuppose the
subjective dispositions of individuals in the system and, therefore, the problem of manifest and latent functions (for example, intended and unintended
consequences) is irrelevant to the definition. Further, this definition of purpose
is neither time-bound nor predicated upon the idea of an end state governing the system's behavior. Rather, purpose is inferred by the observer, given
his knowledge of the system's structural properties and dominant environmental constraint, as the apparent *direction* in which the system is moving.

Characteristics of Sociocultural Systems

To this point we have restricted our discussion to a brief explication
of general systems theory through the introduction of some of the basic
concepts. Our perspective, which is holistic and organic, was derived in
large measure from principles developed in the biological and physical
sciences. Its relevance to sociocultural systems rests upon the assumption
that open systems exhibit similar structural properties regardless of their
content, and therefore, are isomorphically similar.[24] Given such structural
isomorphism, it is reasonable to expect principles appropriate to properties
of biological or physical systems to affect sociocultural systems as well. Our
basic description of the system characteristics of sociocultural systems, accordingly, will seek to demonstrate in homological fashion that "lawful principles" apply similarly to all sociocultural systems regardless of substance.[25]

Parsons defines a social system as ". . . a mode of organization of
action elements relative to the persistence or ordered processes of change
of the interactive patterns of a plurality of individual actors."[26] Although
Parsons views the act as the elementary unit of the system, he argues that
the participation of the actor in patterned relationships is more useful as
a basic unit of analysis. This participation has two principal aspects—the
position of the actor relative to others in the system (that is, his status) and
what the actor does (that is, his role).[27] A similar approach is taken by
Katz and Kahn, who define an organization as a system that ". . . consists
of the patterned activities of a number of individuals."[28]

These definitions have utility for considering individual participation
in the system. They become problematic, however, when one wants to
consider the intrinsic qualities of the system distinguishable from the acts
of its members. For although it is true that social systems are contrived,[29]
in the sense that without the individual there is no social system, it is also
true that a system possesses specific attributes, structure, function, and purpose independent of its membership.

As noted earlier, the purpose of an open system must enter into its specification. For sociocultural systems below the societal level, purpose can be viewed as the primary environmental constraint, imposed by the larger society, which determines the directional state of the system. This constraint may be identified as the sociocultural system's institutional role. Thus, for example, if we acknowledge the societal role of the economic institution to be primarily that of the effective and efficient distribution of goods and services, the "purpose" of the business organization would be defined accordingly. This, of course, says nothing about individual motives for profit or an ultimate end state for the business organization. Adding this characteristic of purpose to our previously stated definition focusing upon relationships, an *open sociocultural system* may be defined as *a set of lawfully related complex social relationships evidencing a high degree of stability in order to affect societally determined ends.*

Some understanding of this perspective can be gained by turning to the work of Max Weber, who conceptualized social action in terms of the subjective motivation of men to act and with respect to the type of social organization and authority[30] Essentially, according to Weber, in an ideal sense, motivation comes from either tradition, rationality, or emotion. We will discuss only the former two. Traditional action stems primarily from habit. Rational action is derived either from a commitment to an ideal or value (*wertrational*), or from calculated self-interest in selecting appropriate means to attain specific ends (*zweckrational*). Traditional authority and organization thus rest upon the "sanctity" of past custom, belief, and status. Rational authority and organization, on the other hand, are legitimated in terms of ". . . a system of rules that is applied judicially and administratively in accordance with ascertainable principles. . . ."[31] An example of a traditional social system is the family, and the classic example of a rational social system is what Weber has referred to as a legal-rational system, modern bureaucracy.

It is rational participation, social organization, and authority that are the focus of interest at this point in our discussion. By appealing to rationality based upon enacted rules and regulations as the basis for participation, the individual participant must assume that such participation will contribute to his desired ends.[32] This kind of rationality may be referred to as *subjective* rationality and can be used to explain why individuals participate in a sociocultural system. But, there is a form of *objective* rationality associated with this type of organization as well. By virtue of its contrived nature, the social system must constantly legitimate its actions, not by referring to past customs and mores but by establishing that it meets the requirements of its institutional role in efficiency and effectiveness.[g]

---

[g] It should be noted that our usage of the terms "objective" rationality and "subjective" rationality departs somewhat from previous usage. For instance, Simon dis-

This distinction between subjective and objective rationality is important in that the latter type of rationality is a characteristic of the social system rather than of its membership. At the societal level, several sociologists have touched upon a major determinant of such rationality for collective life in modern societies in their discussion of the influence of technology upon social development.[33] Myrdal's analysis of the economic basis for the development of the welfare state, and Galbraith's thesis regarding the "inevitable" spread of the international corporate structure, are also suggestive of this form of rationality, which appears to be particularly strong in modern industrial life.[34] At the same time, however, because a system is contrived and emerges out of the subjectively perceived reality of individuals who make up the collectivity, its *apparent* legitimacy rests upon subjective rationality cast in terms of the ideology and values dominant in its immediate environment. That congruency between the "subjective" and "objective" forms of rationality associated with this type of social organization is neither inevitable nor universal is evident in many complaints about "the system," or the innocuous "they" forcing individuals within a society into patterns of action inconsistent with their subjectively perceived rational behavior.

Properties of Open Sociocultural Systems

Having related sociocultural systems to a systems framework generally, we can now discuss the manner in which particular properties of open systems may be interpreted when applied to sociocultural systems. The properties to be elaborated upon are input, throughput, output, negative entropy, feedback, homeostasis, and structural differentiation.

INPUT.   At the most abstract level an open system receives energy from its environment. This imported energy is referred to as input. In sociocultural systems, input energy is generally perceived as information, materials, and personnel. At the societal level, input is usually couched in terms of the society's relationship to other societies that form part of the larger societal environment, or in terms of a society's relationship to its physical environment. More frequently, however, sociocultural systems are discussed at the level of the institution or organization. Subsystems of the larger society can be viewed as sociocultural systems existing in a largely sociocultural environment.

---

tinguishes between "objective" and "subjective" rationality on the basis that objective rationality "is the correct behavior for maximizing given values in a given situation" whereas behavior is subjectively rational" if it maximizes attainment relative to the actual knowledge of the subject." See Herbert A. Simon, *Administrative Behavior,* 2d ed. (New York: The Free Press, 1957), p. 63.

Although inputs of material and personnel are patently homologous to energy inputs in nonsocial systems, insofar as they are tangibly "resources," information as input is more complex and less self-evident. One can best understand its significance by recognizing that sociocultural systems are both created and constrained by the meaning associated with them ("symbolism," in von Bertalanffy's terms).[35] Meaning then is integral to the continuity of such systems, and its transmission constitutes information. Seen in this perspective, informational input is qualitatively different from material or personnel input. This input is not energy, but rather acts as a catalyst insofar as it has the power to stimulate, direct, or constrain the social relationships that constitute the system. Whether or not the input's potential is realized for a given system is dependent upon the openness of the system to the social environment and the energy available to it for response. As "contrived systems,"[36] sociocultural systems are never totally open, but rather selective—contingent upon the primary institutional meaning associated with the particular system-environmental relationship. Thus, for example, the meaning associated with a hospital as a system normally insures its relative openness to inputs from medical associations or community economic groups and its "closedness" to inputs from other (for example, political) aspects of its sociocultural environment.

Like physical systems, as Buckley observes, society may be viewed as a "complex, adaptive system."[37] Like any open system, the society seeks to sustain itself through the use of materials, information, and personnel. Subsocietal sociocultural systems are more complex analytically, however. Major social institutions, as subsystems of the larger society, are by definition functionally related to its requirements. Organizations, in turn, operate within these institutional frameworks, which provide their purpose. Thus, as noted, businesses operate within the economy, which is concerned with the distribution of goods and services, political parties operate within the political institution, which is concerned with the distribution of legitimate power. Such organizations, on the one hand, use resources to sustain and perpetuate themselves.[38] On the other hand, organizations effect changes in some aspect of the environment consistent with their institutional role. For example, a business may take raw materials and transform them before distributing them, or a political party may seek to transform the electorate so that it will redistribute legitimate power. Conventionally, that which is acted upon by a system is also considered to be input. Logically, however, the system energies associated with efforts to bring about changes in one or more elements of the environment do not require those elements to be part of the system but only that they be exposed to the appropriate application of system energies. For this reason, we shall restrict our use of the term input to only that energy (materials or personnel) or meaning (information) that is imported by a sociocultural system in order to sustain and perpetuate itself over time.

THROUGHPUT AND OUTPUT. Given the distinction noted above, material, personnel, or information acted upon by the system in performing its institutional role need not be thought of as input. Rather, materials used in the manufacturing of a product, patients entering a hospital, or customers in a service organization, or the information used in a public relations firm, are all example of *throughput*. Necessary for the system, given its social direction, throughput is the focus of system energies, consistent with its structural characteristics and the constraints of the environment of which it is a part.[h]

In the most general sense, *output* is simply the energy expended by a sociocultural system in performing its institutional role. However, it is useful to distinguish between two major forms of output: *organizational output,* which is the energy expended by the system in the form of consumed input, and *production output,* which is throughput at some terminal stage. One can see this distinction in sociocultural systems by considering the hospital as a social organization. Patients (throughput), having entered the hospital, are treated by the physicians and staff (input). Subsequently, upon their discharge from the hospital, the former patients (production output) reenter the environment. The skills used during their stay to bring about their recovery, as well as those materials consumed in treatment (such as drugs or bandages), are organizational output.

NEGATIVE ENTROPY. A closed system, according to the second principle of thermodynamics, experiences ultimate entropy (the final dissipation of energy within the system). An open system, through exchange with its environment, permits new energy to enter the system. This characteristic of an open system is critical, for it permits the system to reverse the entropic process characteristic of closed systems by developing a surplus of energy to be stored or used in a variety of purposive ways, thus sustaining itself beyond the use of energies present in the system at any given time.[39]

At the level of sociocultural systems, according to Katz and Kahn, there is a general tendency for the system to attempt to "maximize its ratio of imported energy to expended energy."[40] Commercial organizations do so by efforts to minimize costs of production, by attempts to maximize returns on investments, and the like. As the result of such negative entropic tendencies, social systems have the potential to sustain themselves beyond

---

[h]Although the term "throughput" is not as widely discussed in the systems literature as "input" and "output," our usage is consistent with that of Katz and Kahn, *Ibid.,* p. 20.

the life span of their membership, as well as to adjust to changes in the environment through modifications of their organizational properties. Some systems do not so adjust, and thus cease to exist.

FEEDBACK.   At the most abstract level, all purposeful systems receive environmental energy. However, although most of such input is associated directly with the maintenance or productive concerns of the system, and hence is destined for system consumption, some fraction of it is a result of previous system dynamics associated with the system's primary directional state. Inputs of this type are generally referred to as *feedback*. The classic examples of feedback, servomechanisms, are designed to react to environmental contingencies in a compensatory manner to redirect deviant system efforts toward some end state. Though both are informational, a distinction should be made between negative and positive feedback. *Negative feedback* is information about previous system activities considered to be deviations of the system from its directional state. *Positive feedback,* on the other hand, is information about previous system activities tending to accentuate the deviation of the system.

Implicit in the notion of feedback is the assumption of selective sensitivity to informational sources. The criteria for such sensitivity is normally assumed to be derived from the ascribed purpose of the system. Both types of feedback are important in this regard, but negative feedback is usually considered most critical since it alerts the system to the need to adapt itself to the contingencies of its environment consistent with its ascribed purpose.[41] At the same time positive feedback can be considered as significant for an understanding of system deviation in that, given a specifiable purpose, persistent system action apparently inconsistent with that purpose may well be a consequence of positive system feedback that literally reinforces the deviation.

In perceiving social organizations as open systems, an important part of the feedback process is the meaning of information related to organizational decision making. Thus, in social organizations, feedback can be viewed as the meaning associated with information obtained by the system about its previous output that is relevant to further action by the organization. Illustrative of the effects of positive feedback upon an organization's behavior is Harden's example of the development of monopolistic control of an economic market following organizational decisions consistent with the principle of laissez faire competition but oblivious to other environmental constraints. In this case organizational efforts are directed toward controlling as much of the market as possible, thereby in theory maximizing profits.[42] To the extent that the behavior of the organization is successful in producing that result, information about that success constitutes positive feedback and encourages the organization to continue its efforts. However, when the social environment places constraints upon such behavior, the organization must be sensitive to negative feedback. With no constraints, such organizational behavior would lead, according to Harden, to a single business organization controlling and monopolizing the total market. Constraints normally exist, however, and take at least two forms. One is environmental and extraneous to the purpose of the organization (for example, the requirements of competing businesses). The other derives from the limitations inherent in any human organization whereby erroneous decisions are made (that is, errors relative to the purpose of the organization). Negative feedback thus results when the organization fails to consider the effect of its behavior (beyond that associated with its purpose) upon the environment or as the result of behavior inappropriate to its purpose. Such negative feedback takes the form of information regarding potential or existing sanctions, or of product inadequacies relative to the purpose of the organization. In Harden's example, information regarding governmental sanctions of monopolistic practices, or the failure of the consumer to purchase the organization's product, informs the organization of corrections necessary in its subsequent behavior.[i]

HOMEOSTASIS. A system characteristically regulates inputs and internal system dynamics to insure a steady state called *homeostasis*.[43] On the physiological level, an example of homeostasis would be the body's ability to adjust to variable food or oxygen inputs (within limits) in order to sustain a particular level of operating effectiveness, or the ability of an organism to compensate for internal malfunctions in various organs in order to sustain itself. To achieve such an end, an open system uses a variety of means, which may proceed from differing original states.[44] It is important to note, of course, that homeostasis is not a static equilibrium. Rather it is a dynamic, continuous adaptation to a variety of internal and external pressures or tensions.

Considering the sociocultural system, Buckley argues that the homeostatic condition is best characterized in terms of ". . . its functioning *to maintain the given structure of the system within the pre-established limits.*"[45] He views societies as "complex adaptive systems" possessing not only self-regulation, but self-direction as a necessity for survival.[46] A slightly different interpretation of this system condition is offered by Katz and Kahn, who see the homeostatic state at a more complex system level as ". . . preserving the character of the system through growth and expansion."[47]

---

[i]It should be noted that "feedback" is seen as a "secondary regulatory mechanism." Such does not preclude "primary regulatory mechanisms," nor is it meant to suggest that information is the only type of feedback to the organization. See von Bertalanffy, *Robots,* pp. 66–69; and von Bertalanffy, "General Systems Theory—A Critical Review," in Buckley, *Modern Systems Research,* pp. 17–19.

The perspectives of both Buckley and Katz and Kahn regarding homeostasis can be interpreted as advancing what von Bertalanffy has described as the regulative and adaptive usage of the term,[48] and it is in this sense that we will use it. Thus, the *homeostasis* of a sociocultural organization at any given time *is the result of the environmental exchanges and internal organizational dynamics consistent with the organization's institutional role and environmental constraints.* Said in another way, as a purposive system, the organization must adapt its structural arrangements to both its internal system requirements and to the constraints imposed by its sociocultural environment and its institutional role.

STRUCTURAL DIFFERENTIATION.   An important processual characteristic of open systems is their tendency to evolve into more complex structural forms. The primary impetus for this tendency in open systems derives from the earlier noted "negative entropy" characteristic of the system, whereby surplus energy can be directed toward enhancing the system's position *vis à vis* its environment. A logical use of such surplus energy is for increased growth and specialization with attendant structural differentiation.[49]

Within sociocultural systems, Buckley refers to differentiation as a form of the more general characteristic of *morphogenesis,* which tends "to elaborate or change a system's given form, organization, state."[50] Following Maruyama,[51] he suggests that one can gain insight into the dynamics of structural differentiation by using the concept of positive feedback, previously discussed, wherein adaptive or nonadaptive organizational behavior leads to greater organizational complexity.[52] Katz and Kahn, on the other hand, ascribe a more evolutionary quality to the process, suggesting its inevitability.[53] Differentiation, according to them, is expressed through this process of growth and expansion, which they refer to as dynamic homeostasis.[54] Whether potential or inevitable, however, structural differentiation points to the nature of the response of the organization to environmental constraints as purposive.

The type of structural change associated with differentiation can be considered at various levels of abstraction. However, at any level there seem to be two primary forms. First, differentiation occurs *between* systems, such as institutions, often as a consequence of increased specialization.[55] Second, differentiation *within* a system can occur. Here, each subsystem of the larger system develops an increasing division of labor characterized by increasing specialization and complexity. Such increases in specialization and complexity have frequently been linked to increases in system size— the bigger the size of the organization, the more differentiated its internal structure. However, to some extent, a relationship between size and differentiation is dependent upon the type of organizational activity. A large industrial firm in one manufacturing area, for example, may be no more complex than a small industrial firm engaged in the same activity. On the other hand, in other types of manufacturing concerns, largeness may be associated with greater differentiation. Thus, the conditions that determine the presence or absence of such a relationship are somewhat unclear.[56]

MODERNIZATION AND THE EDUCATIONAL INSTITUTION

Having presented an introduction to the basic concepts of systems theory and to the characteristics and properties of open sociocultural systems, we turn our attention now to a consideration of how environmental modernity, as discussed in Chapter Two, influences education as a social institution. At the institutional level a sociocultural system can be defined in terms of structure or function. Structurally, it can be viewed as a pattern of standardized relationships organized around a particular aspect of cultural life. Functionally, it may be considered as the socially accepted and standardized manner in which an enduring collective problem is resolved by a society.[57] Both views are relevant to our considerations of modernity and education, for they are essentially complementary, and in the following discussion we shall use them in discussing the nature and role of formal education in modern society.

In the most general sense it may be said that the institutional role of formal education is that of socialization, and indeed this answer is frequently advanced both by educators and sociologists. Like most simple answers, however, it is correct only in the broadest terms, for the problem of socialization historically has been met and is still met to some degree by other social organizations, such as the family and the community. Further, unless a kind of socialization occurs in formal education that does not occur elsewhere, we must assume that family and community agencies could effectivelv educate the child without a need for formal education. Although schools have existed in one form or another for well over 2,000 years, an educational arrangement that systematically exposes the majority of each generation to a more or less standardized body of knowledge over a long period of time is a very recent phenomenon. Therefore, there is reason to argue that formal education in modern societies performs a distinctive socializing function not performed by other socializing agents.

To articulate the nature of this distinctive function in modern American society, we must consider the society's dominant cultural values, which can be derived logically from the dominant value configurations noted in Chapter Two. The "higher-order" values of industrial society generally, and of modern American society specifically, have been well expressed elsewhere.[58] They include, among other things, an emphasis upon achievement and material progress. Without these values, it is doubtful whether any society could motivate itself to industrialize.[j] On the "cultural-institutional" level, to use Parsons' term,[59] the values manifested by education should be congruent with those of the society and should be reflected in education's function as a socializing agent, as well as in the structural characteristics of the educational system.

The presence of these values in education, permitting an identification of its institutional function, is seen in the strong vocational preparatory emphasis in modern American education, which anticipates both individual occupational achievement in adult life and societal growth and development.[60] Given the accumulation of specialized knowledge in modern industrialized society, neither family nor community is knowledgeable enough to prepare the young for specific occupations, whether technological, economic, academic, or political. Instead, industrial societies develop an institution—that is, schooling—to transmit and expand the necessary knowledge. In so doing, the values placed by society on achievement and progress are expressed both on the individual and societal levels.

Beyond this rather obvious function of education as a transmitter of specialized knowledge is its less obvious function as a transmitter of an orientation[k] toward life appropriate for the culture of an industrialized society.[l] The nature of this orientation, derived in large part from the social structural peculiarities of modern society, has been well articulated by Weber and by Toennies[61] and was briefly touched upon in Chapter Two. Based upon a perception of others as means to an end rather than as ends in themselves, social relationships are predicated upon the individual's "rational pursuit of his self-interest." Such an orientation may be described as "instrumental." Of course, no preindustrial society completely lacks such a contractually specific form of social behavior, nor are all segments of modern industrial life so "rational" as to exclude ascriptive and emotional factors in social behavior. Still, within limits, the representation of an instrumental orientation as characteristic of modern industrial life seems valid.

---

[j]The indirect manner in which a society may adopt these values, contributing thereby to economic and industrial growth, has been well illustrated in Weber's classic study on the growth of capitalism in Western Europe. See Max Weber, *The Protestant Ethic and the Spirit of Capitalism*, trans. Talcott Parsons (London: George Allen and Unwin, Ltd., 1930).

[k]The term "orientation" used in this discussion was advanced by Merton and is ". . . the theme underlying the complex of social roles performed by an individual. It is the (tacit or explicit) theme which finds expression in each of the complex of social roles in which the individual is implicated." See Robert K. Merton, *Social Theory and Social Structure*, rev. ed. (New York: The Free Press, 1957), fn. p. 392.

[l]Dreeben makes a similar point in suggesting that an important part of school learning is the internalization of behavioral norms necessary for adult life. Such learning, according to Dreeben, is attributable to the social-structural character of the educational organization. See Robert Dreeben, *On What Is Learned in School* (Reading, Mass.: Addison-Wesley Publishing Co., 1968), chap. 5.

The need for developing such an outlook establishes what we view to be the second function of education.[m] In modern societies the only systematic attempt to instill in youth an instrumental orientation occurs in school. Such an orientation, as noted in Chapter Two, stresses the adoption in social contexts of behavior described by Parsons as universalistic, affectively neutral, achievement-oriented, and specific.[n] Thus in a modern society formal education is organized to encourage the young to act according to *universalistic* (that is, general) standards rather than standards limited to a particular situation. In their relationships with others the young are also encouraged to *neutralize* the immediate *affective* gratification of interpersonal relationships in favor of later gratification made possible by viewing others as means to an end. In addition, in principle if not always in fact, formal education encourages young people to evaluate others according to *achievement* rather than ascribed status, and to limit such evaluations to the *specific* situations in which they are most relevant. Institutionally, most formal education places the neophyte in a social context similar to that in which he will spend his adult life.[o] By "adjusting" to the school milieu over a period of years, the student

---

[m]Strictly speaking, the transmission of specific knowledge can be viewed as a *manifest* function (that is, as an intended and recognized consequence of the social institution), whereas the inculcation of an orientation would be a *latent* function (that is, unintended or unrecognized). Such a distinction is not crucial in our model, however, for we are not concerned with the participant's subjective evaluation, but rather with the contribution made by the institution to the larger society. For a discussion of manifest and latent functions, see Merton, *Social Theory and Social Structure,* pp. 1–84.

[n]Our description of this "instrumental orientation" is, of course, drawn from the pattern variables as developed by Parsons. See Talcott Parsons, *The Social System* (New York: The Free Press, 1951), esp. pp. 58–67. Along this same line, McClelland speaks of the importance of the "achievement motive" to industrialization. See David C. McClelland, *The Achieving Society* (Princeton, N. J.: D. Van Nostrand Co., Inc., 1961), esp. pp. 36–106.

[o]Dreeben, *On What is Learned in School,* chaps. 2 and 3. Also, Levy talks of the school as being the first situation in which the child is treated in a "universalistic" manner. See Marion J. Levy, Jr., *Modernization and the Structure of Societies,* Vol. I (Princeton, N.J.: Princeton University Press, 1966), 627.

It is important to note, of course, that the mere existence in a society of a formal system structured in this fashion does not necessarily lead to a "modern product." The content of the material will have some effect upon the student's orientation. Evidence of this is provided by a recent study conducted in Nigeria by Armer and Youtz. Unfortunately, a systematic analysis of the impact of the content of modern education upon the development of an instrumental orientation in modern societies has yet to be accomplished, although the studies of Litt on political indoctrination and Elson on the content of nineteenth-century American textbooks are suggestive of the value of this area of inquiry. See Michael Armer and Robert Youtz, "Formal Education and Individual Modernity in an African Society," *American Journal of Sociology,* 76 (1971), 604–26; Edgar Litt, "Civic Education, Community Norms and Political Indoctrination," *American Sociological Review,* 28 (1963), 69–75; and Ruth Miller Elson, *The Guardians of Tradition: American Schoolbooks of the 19th Century* (Lincoln, Nebr.: University of Nebraska Press, 1964).

learns ways to conduct social relationships necessary for successful performance as an adult in industrial society.[p]

In sum, the *institutional function* of the educational system can be seen as that of fulfilling the individual and social needs of modern industrialized society as reflected in modern values. Industrial development requires people with technical skills and the instrumental orientation necessary for them to use their knowledge effectively in the structural complexity of modern society. The inability of traditional socializing agencies to meet these particular needs has led, we have argued, to the institutional growth of education as the primary socializing agent.[q] For this reason, environmental modernization and educational system attributes covary.

From a larger perspective, it can be argued, as noted in Chapter One, that the advance of "rationalism" in modernizing societies brings increasing pressure to bear upon formal education to modify its structure so as to meet the new societal needs.[62] Thus formal education becomes increasingly defined as a resource of the society and evaluated as to whether it meets modern social requirements. These changes, of course, are not immediate but gradual, and reflect the uneven modernization within a particular society. Thus, a society may aspire to modernize, in the sense that it has access to the required technology and desires the material fruits of modernity, long before it is able to restructure uniformly its formal educational system in a rational fashion.

The insights of Max Weber on education as a bureaucracy seem particularly relevant to explain the dynamics of this structural relationship. Weber suggests that there is a close correspondence between the development of a society and the structure of its educational systems. As societies modernize, the importance of specialized training increases. Accompanying this change in the educational requirements of a society are changes in the educational system, for it becomes increasingly rational and bureaucratic in nature. According to Weber such "a rational and bureaucratic (modern)

---

[p]Although the importance of this internalization process has been generally ignored in educational research, its relevance for adult behavior in modern society has been observed. See, for example, David Riesman, *The Lonely Crowd: A Study of the Changing American Character* (New Haven: Yale University Press, 1950); William H. Whyte, *The Organization Man* (New York: Simon and Schuster, Inc., 1956); and Daniel R. Miller and Guy E. Swanson, *The Changing American Parent: A Study in the Detroit Area* (New York: John Wiley & Sons, Inc., 1958).

[q]To a larger degree, the inability of the family to meet these needs seems to lie in its structure and nature. Thus, families are effective socializing agencies in societies in which primary group relationships are emphasized, but not in societies in which secondary group relationships are emphasized. For a description of the declining function of the family in our society, see William F. Ogburn, "The Changing Family," *The Family*, 19 (1938), 139–43. For the role of technology in bringing about these changes, see William F. Ogburn and Meyer F. Nimkoff, *Technology and the Changing Family* (Boston: Houghton Mifflin Company, 1953).

structure" of education is best able to accomplish the "ideal" end of imparting specialized training.[63]

If we view the modern formal educational system as rational, it is relevant to ask how the educational system's inputs, structural characteristics, and outputs are related to modernization. Generally, following Weber's reasoning, to the extent that inputs and structural characteristics approach the bureaucratic ideal, the educational system may be defined as an "efficient" formal system.[64] To the extent that this efficiency results in outputs meeting modern societal requirements, the system can be viewed as "effective" with regard to those requirements. For example, both the number and type of students in societies at early stages of modernization are not usually consistent with modern social needs. The formal educational systems of such societies tend, in Weber's terms, to emphasize a "pedagogy of cultivation" for the elite and not the specialized training and orientation necessary for modern life.[65] Many contemporary ex-colonial African states are examples of this phenomenon. In such cases, the system may be very efficient in inputs and structural arrangements, but not effective in terms of the societies' actual needs. In contrast, a system of formal education that selects the number and type of students a modern society needs and orients and trains them according to the requirements of this society would be considered both a highly efficient and effective system within the framework of this discussion.

The perception of the institutional role of formal education as a highly specialized pattern of socialization is not inconsistent with a great deal of sociological literature on the general nature of modern society. However, it should not be construed as necessarily the "most desirable" state of affairs for individuals who are members of that society. In an insightful analysis of the impact of industrialization, with its bureaucratic functional specialization and segmented structure, upon the individual, Zijderveld concludes that "industrial society, losing more and more of its reality and meaning in the experience of man, tends to reduce him to a specialized expert and de-humanized functionary."[66] Nor do educators agree as to the long-run desirability of such educational "outputs" for the life of the society as a whole. Dewey's view of formal education's role in a modern society, for example, was in direct opposition to what has since occurred,[67] and many recent recommendations for reform aim at reversing the phenomena described above.[68] It is possible to suggest, in fact, that consistent with our discussion in Chapter One, the dialectical process of rationally incorporating the "needs of the individual" into current American education may result in the apparent structural anomaly of an institution specializing in a "nonspecialized" socialization process. The efficiency and effectiveness of such a system, however, would be contingent upon a major sociocultural redefinition of current meaning of education's directional state.

THE SCHOOL AS A SOCIAL ORGANIZATION

Because the school is the most concrete example of what we have been calling an educational system, it is heuristically desirable to apply our discussion of the educational system as a whole to the school itself.

Historically there has been little systematic sociological analysis of the school as an open system.[r] Some investigators have focused upon the school as a formal organization,[69] and others have treated it primarily as a closed social system,[70] but the fundamentally open nature of the American public school as a social system has not been explicitly investigated.[s] Several characteristics of open sociocultural systems can be applied to the school, but perhaps none are more crucial than inputs, throughputs, and outputs. Within the framework of the model previously discussed, inputs to the school may be identified as materials, personnel, and information. Materials include school plant, curricular supplies, and so on. Personnel consists of teachers, administrators, educational specialists, and such service employees as clerks and custodians. Information includes institutional and local environmental expectations, such as accreditation requirements and community values, and the knowledge and skills brought into the system that are to be taught to the students.

The organizational output of the school is the energy (both human and material) used in sustaining the school and in fulfilling its institutional role. The energies used for survival may be considered as a form of organizational output, similar to that energy used by the individual in meeting his physical or psychological needs. The school's energy, however, is not as readily apparent, for it is reflected in the energies expended by the organization in transforming its throughput (that is, the pupils) in ways consistent with both

---

[r]However, many studies of "school effectiveness" done largely by economists have implicitly adopted such an approach. See, for example, Jesse Burkhead *et al., Input and Output in Large-City High Schools* (Syracuse, N.Y.: Syracuse University Press, 1967); and J. A. Kershaw and R. N. McKean, "Systems Analysis of Education," unpublished research report (Santa Monica, Calif.: The Rand Corporation, 1959); Charles S. Benson *et al., State and Local Fiscal Relationships in Public Education in California* (Sacramento, Calif.: Senate of the State of California, 1965).

[s]Empirical studies in which particular attributes of the school's environment have been investigated implicitly include Neal Gross, *Who Runs Our Schools?* (New York: John Wiley & Sons, Inc., 1958), and Burton R. Clark, *The Open Door College: A Case Study* (New York: McGraw-Hill Book Company, 1960). For works that are speculative rather than empirical, see Albert J. Reiss, "An Introduction" in *Schools in a Changing Society,* ed. Albert J. Reiss (New York: The Free Press, 1965), pp. 1–19; Daniel E. Griffiths, "System Theory and School Districts," in *Readings on the School in Society,* ed. Patricia Cayo Sexton (Englewood Cliffs, N.J.: Prentice-Hall, Inc., 1967), pp. 175–84; Richard C. Lonsdale, "Maintaining the Organization in Dynamic Equilibrium," in Griffiths, *Behavioral Science,* pp. 142–77; and Bernard J. Siegal, "Models for the Analysis of the Educative Process in American Communities," in *Education and Anthropology,* ed. George D. Spindler (Stanford, Calif.: Stanford University Press, 1955), pp. 38–49.

institutional and local constraints. Thus, organizational output includes all energy directed toward changing the pupils. The production output of the school, consistent with our earlier discussion, is the knowledge, skills, and orientations required by the larger society and possessed by the pupils at the time they leave school. Thus, for example, a school's holding power and the proportion of graduates who go on to further education are indirectly indicative of production output.[71] Within an open systems perspective, production throughput as well as production output can be represented by pupil behavior. However, whereas the output is characteristic of some terminal state of pupil behavior, throughput is represented by all intermediate states.

An important characteristic of schools in comparison to other sociocultural systems is the lack of control the organization has over its production throughput. Pupils enter first grade with a variety of initial behavior. They are returned by the organization to the environment each evening, on weekends, and during vacations. In the environment, they are susceptible to many influences counter to the purpose of the organization. In addition, owing to parental mobility, pupils may be transferred from one school to another. When these changes are widespread (as when many Blacks moved from rural areas of the South to urban areas of the North) their effects upon the throughput of both the sending and receiving schools can be dramatic. Thus "quality control" problems with respect to production throughputs are particularly severe in the case of American public schools as open sociocultural systems.

Implicit in this discussion of production outputs and throughputs is the assumption that the pupils are not part of the structure of the school as a social organization. This may seem strange to those accustomed to viewing pupils as "members" of the school, but it is quite consistent with a general systems approach to sociocultural systems. Although the school's purpose is socialization and its production throughput is human, *from the standpoint of the organization as an open sociocultural system,* pupils can be identified as outside its structure much like patients in a hospital. They are the raw materials being acted upon by the organization and, therefore, are not necessarily a part of its formal structure.[t]

An understanding of the inputs, throughputs, and outputs of the school as an open sociocultural system is important for an understanding of homeostasis, negative entropy, differentiation, and feedback. The homeostasis of the school may be viewed as its ongoing effort to meet its negative entropic requirements expressed as internal needs consistent with the constraints im-

---

[t]Actually there is considerable support in the conventional literature for our view of pupils as the "material" processed by the school. See, for example, Stanton Wheeler, "The Structure of Formally Organized Socialization Settings," in *Socialization After Childhood: Two Essays,* ed. Orville G. Brim and Stanton Wheeler (New York: John Wiley & Sons, Inc., 1966), esp. p. 57; Katz, "The School as a Complex Social Organization," p. 440; and Fraser, "Schools as Organizations," p. 26.

posed by institutional and other environmental requirements. The school must concern itself, in other words, not only with adequate inputs and their efficient use (which we may regard as a form of internal homeostasis), but with institutional requirements and local needs in maintaining a steady state.[u] For example, the organization, in attempting to fulfill its institutional function, may wish to allocate energy to the use of new technological innovations consistent with the adaptive process. At the same time, however, the local environment may be indifferent or opposed to such a change and require the organization to allocate energy to other developments (for example, a stronger football team). Simultaneously, institutional changes can require the introduction of a new curriculum. How the school responds to these requirements will undoubtedly vary with important aspects of its environment.[v] As an open system, however, its guiding consideration will be to maintain itself in a viable state—to maintain homeostasis.

The school maintains itself partly through its tendency to evolve into a more complex form, by specialization in production, in its role requirements, or in production throughput. Differentiation occurs in production as teachers specialize in the teaching of fewer grades and subjects. Role differentiation occurs with the development of a hierarchy of administrative, service, and teaching roles. The third form of differentiation occurs when the organization limits its throughputs by age, for example, by the separation of rural 1–12 schools into 1–6 elementary schools and 7–12 secondary schools. (Other variations are possible, of course.)

The final characteristic in need of consideration is feedback. Feedback is made up of information. In schools, such information concerns the academic performance of the school's graduates, the nature and extent of dropouts, reaction to various changes or lack of change in school curriculum, teacher recruitment, subject matter content, physical facilities, and the like. Such information can come from a number of sources. For schools, the most important of these seem to be the local environment, educational agencies, and other organizations that receive the school's output. However, since the school is a contrived purposive system, with the meaning of formal education dependent in part upon its local sociocultural context, whether feedback is negative or positive is a function of the directional state of the organization within that context.

---

[u]For a description of some of the processes operating in such situations, see Lonsdale, "Dynamic Equilibrium."

[v]Along this same line, Cocking found differences, by cosmopolitanism of the school, concerning the adoption of new educational ideas. See Willard R. Lane, Ronald G. Corwin, and William G. Monahan, *Foundations of Educational Administration* (New York: The Macmillan Company, 1966), p. 97. For an interesting analysis of some of the problems of initiating change in schools, see Seymour B. Sarason, *The Culture of the School and the Problems of Change* (Boston: Allyn and Bacon, Inc., 1971).

In an "ideal" socially homogeneous setting, everyone would agree about the purpose of the school and the school would use negative feedback simply to correct output deviations from its socially agreed-upon purpose. Positive feedback would then be defined as erroneous information about matters concerning the attainment of that purpose. But usually, schools confront heterogeneous sources of information. Accordingly, whether specific information is considered negative or positive is in part a function of the importance of the source of the feedback to the school and in part a function of the meaning assigned to that feedback by the school. The school is selectively "open" to feedback, and its interpretation of it as negative or positive is guided by its basic homeostatic requirement to maintain its viability on the one hand, and by its need to maintain a negative entropic state through growth and increasing complexity on the other. Thus feedback from universities, colleges, teacher organizations, or powerful political groups in the community could influence the school to change. On the other hand, feedback from politically weak groups in the community or from educational organizations peripheral to the organization's institutional role (for example, certain vocational schools, some education interest groups) would have little effect upon the organization's behavior.[72]

This feedback process is further complicated by the transitional and relative nature of the importance of various sources. For example, in some circumstances, local environmental support may be far more critical to the viability of the system than in other circumstances. Accordingly, schools would vary in their susceptibility at a given point in time to local constraints and pressures.[w] Public and private schools may be distinguished in this respect, as can public schools in different environments. Or, in an example of another type, given the unqualified support of the local environment, a school's sensitivity to negative feedback from other environmental sources could be appreciably less than it would be without this support. This can be observed when schools in rural areas suffer disaccreditation rather than improve their plant or staff.

MODERNIZATION AND THE SCHOOL

One of the most important change processes for social systems associated with modernization is "enhancement of adaptive capacity," which

---

[w]Also, Lane, Corwin, and Monahan assert that early studies in education indicate that local control of the school produces greater adaptability. See Lane, Corwin, and Monahan, *Educational Administration,* p. 16. For further discussion on this topic, see Henry M. Levin, ed., *Community Control of Schools* (Washington, D. C.: The Brookings Institution, 1970).

is achieved by structural differentiation, and the establishment of a more general "value pattern" consistent with the specialization of subunit functions.[73] In schools, this may be interpreted to mean that structurally, as the environment of the school becomes increasingly modern, there is a growing emphasis upon adaptation to external constraints as opposed to internal dynamics.[x] Thus, we would expect schools in such social settings to devote much energy to those relationships whose primary concern is with the nature of environmental relations. Such things as increased attention to educational innovations in technology, curriculum, and the like would tend to assume more relevance. So, also, organizational activities concerned with production, such as the number and quality of outputs, would tend to become more important. In other words, this change, frequently manifest in organizational differentiation, finds substantive expression in the increasing concern of modern schools with student population growth, curriculum innovation and development, and postgraduate training for faculty and administrators.[74] Further, the development of local environmental support through school-sponsored social events, publicity about students' academic or athletic achievement, and adult education programs increases the social and financial involvement of the community in the school. So, also, modernization would bring increased emphasis upon classroom efficiency, audio-visual aids, the number of graduating pupils going on to higher education, and the like.[y]

Although these developmental tendencies lead to the stressing of adaptation to environmental constraints, other organizational imperatives are not necessarily ignored. The question is one of emphasis. Perhaps the early emphasis of an organization must be upon insuring its survival and upon meeting its needs. Such an emphasis would find strong environmental support in a traditional setting, where community expectations are firmly established and social change is resisted, if not rejected. Thus, the "reactionary's" cry for a return to the "3 R's" and a tradition of general education presupposes a clearly defined organizational role not entirely consistent with the social complexities of modern life.

Whereas in the more traditional setting community values and ideology

---

[x]Parsons differentiates the emphasis in terms of an external-internal dimension of the major focus of the system. This distinction, along with an instrumental-consummatory dimension, forms the basis for his well-known fourfold table within which functional prerequisites may be distinguished. [See Talcott Parsons, "Pattern Variables Revisited: A Response to Robert Dubin," *American Sociological Review* (1960), 467–82.] In this instance, consistent with Parsons, structurally organizations in more modern contexts become both more highly differentiated and specialized, thereby increasing their dependence upon the environmental context.

[y]Reiss asserts that today most changes in schools come "largely as a response to external crises and organized efforts rather than as a response to definitions of problems generated within school systems." *Ibid.,* p. 2.

are attuned to local tradition and needs, more modern settings increasingly reflect ideology and values consistent with the requirements of the larger society. This propensity toward change is further reinforced structurally by increasing specialization within institutions, which promotes organizational sensitivity to larger societal needs, often at the expense of local community needs. Such a distinction can be seen in Figure 3–1, which portrays the school as being faced with conflicting pressures from its institutional and local environments in the traditional setting and compatible pressures in the modern setting.[z] As traditional settings become modern, ideology

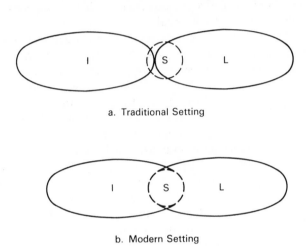

a. Traditional Setting

b. Modern Setting

FIGURE 3–1 *Schematic representation of institutional (I) and local (L) environmental influences on American public schools (S) as open sociocultural systems, in traditional and modern settings.*

and values dominant at the societal level diffuse to the local environment, and organizational rationality is given increasing priority over the locally perceived needs of the community. Interpreting such a development within the context of our earlier discussion, in effect the school becomes increasingly sensitive to feedback from more inclusive environmental layers at the expense of the local environment, leading to a greater probability of contradictory feedback for those schools located in local settings with values and ideology at variance with those dominant in the larger society. Exemplary of this

[z]Warren provides an interesting discussion of the relations of community "subsystems" to one another and to the larger society. For his discussion of the school in this regard, see Roland T. Warren, *The Community in America* (Skokie, Ill.: Rand McNally & Company, 1963), pp. 175–77.

conflict are those schools in less modern regions caught between the demands of an industrial society and the local constraints of keeping the "frills" out of the system, "frills" frequently referring to any deviations from the basic curriculum. On the other hand, ghetto schools in modern settings may suffer similar conflicts constituting an exception to the generalization regarding organizational rationality in modern settings—a point to which we shall return.

The effect of sociocultural change upon the school is also reflected in the criteria upon which schools operate. Thus, as a setting is modernizing, the consequences of a negative entropy balance, that is, excess energy inputs, is increasingly expressed by internal differentiation, which in turn is consistent with the institutional requirements of the larger society rather than with those of the local community. Accordingly, schools in more modern environments would tend to be more responsive to accreditation agencies, professional norms, and so on than would those in less modern environments. This difference can be explained in part by information feedback changes; for by displacing local criteria for decision making with criteria derived from societal sources, the organization reduces its sensitivity to local pressure. In part, also, such a change in organizational sensitivity may be explained by the structural incompatibility of various parts of the organization with the local environment. Thus, vocational guidance programs in a rural consolidated school may have little relevance to the occupational positions available to high school graduates in that type of community.

The likelihood of problems developing in the course of such change is partly a function of the openness of the system to feedback. And that openness, in turn, is related to the source of the organization's major inputs, and to the compatibility of local and institutional constraints. Openness of the school to institutional pressures is more likely in modern settings, by virtue of the greater likelihood of a diversity of inputs and of a compatibility of the local environments with the larger American society. At the same time, however, the openness of the school is often inhibited in a modern setting when local and institutional constraints become incompatible. Thus, the urban slum school, by virtue of its being in a modern community, is attuned to institutional feedback regarding productivity, but given the nature of its throughput finds itself dealing extensively with problems of internal control and maintenance, thereby reducing its ability to respond to institutional feedback.

The above adaptation may be inferred, as well, in considering the substantive value and ideological grounds upon which objective rationality leads to organizational action in a modern setting. To the extent that a modern setting places value upon pluralistic goals and individual achievement and development, system maintenance becomes of secondary importance to the organization. The organization in a very special sense becomes "other-directed," the "other" being the larger society. By way of contrast, the legitimacy of organizations in more traditional settings is in some respects antithetical to the rationalization process associated with modern life, in that it rests upon the mores and customs of the past. Thus organizations in traditional settings have less need to be sensitive to societal demands. Accordingly, organizational efforts are much more directed toward maintaining existing organizational relationships within the school.

Turning to the productive aspects of the school as an open social system, the modification of existing organizational emphases toward societal requirements can be exemplified in modern environments by the explicit or implicit tracking of students according to institutionally approved "objective" criteria such as age, course grades, and ability test scores. Other examples of such concern are the school's acquiescence to the attempts of regional or national accreditation organizations to define "adequate education" in terms of societal norms rather than local requirements; or to legislatively imposed qualifications for teachers and administrators, or to nationally imposed standardized testing programs to determine both ability and achievement among local students. In contrast, traditional social contexts, although in some instances paying lip service to such institutional priorities, tend to separate students on socially ascriptive bases (for example, by social class or race) within the organization, circumvent or ignore the accreditation requirements, use informal and local standards for teachers and administrator qualifications, and minimize the value of standardized test results in appraising student ability and achievement.

Openness of schools to institutional constraints in the more modern setting, though likely, is not inevitable. The urban slum school would certainly be an exception. However, schools in modern settings by and large tend to stress preparing their pupils for adult roles. Thus, such schools show a greater concern with instructional arrangements that emphasize new curricula, as well as such technical skills as typing and driver education that are indicative of changing adult roles in modernizing societies. The relative success of the progressive education movement in the first half of the twentieth century, for example, was greater in the more modern segments of American society than in the more traditional segments.[75] Conversely, schools in traditional environments have tended to perpetuate an emphasis upon achievement in conventional subject matter that is not necessarily related to adult occupations. Accordingly, a great deal of emphasis is placed upon assuring minimal competence in reading, writing, arithmetic, and history. Though for individuals both approaches may in one sense produce equal results (that is, graduation from school), for schools a differential expenditure of organizational effort is required and is reflected in a different structure. Thus, whereas schools in more modern areas tend to stress the importance of "relevance" in their relationships with the community, schools in more traditional areas emphasize internal control and order consistent with the traditional mores and norms of the community. Before presenting a formal model for a portion of the preceding discussion, it may be useful to reiterate an important point. The structural hallmark of a modern industrial state is basically the interdependence of its various specialized institutional arrangements, an interdependence necessitated by the requirements of a complex division of labor and the cultural diversity of its people. In contrast, a traditional society, with a relatively homogeneous culture and simple division of labor does not require a high degree of rational interdependence in its structural arrangements.[76] Accordingly, the increased "sensitivity" and "other-directedness" of the school in a modern social context is a rational response to a changing social environment. What is sometimes difficult to grasp regarding the nature of this school-environment relationship is that this "rationality" is basically that of bureaucratic principles, previously discussed in terms of the purposive nature of the system as a symbolically contrived open system, rather than the subjective rationality ascribed to its membership or those members of the society who seek to influence the school. It is this social anomaly that explains in part the psychological estrangement of many individuals from the school, leading to charges against "the system" or "the education establishment" at the same time as the American school has become more sensitive and open to environmental influences than ever before in its history. The social-psychological ramifications of such sociocultural developments constitute, perhaps, one of the most significant problems faced by formal education today. We shall return to a consideration of these ramifications in Chapter Seven, after an empirical analysis of the school as an open system.

A FORMAL MODEL

Here we will present a model of part of the system-environment relationships of American educational systems. This model summarizes much of our previous reasoning, and should prove useful in understanding Chapters Four, Five, and Six.

In offering this model we make no claims regarding its exhaustiveness. We have selected only a few of the many elements of systems and environments introduced above. Other models could be constructed to show more generally the relationship between an educational system and its environment. Several important considerations that our model does not include are the following.

1) Most notably our *formal* model ignores the dynamic nature of system-environment relationships. It lacks a time parameter and thus is not a model of educational change, but rather one of covariation at given points in time. Clearly this is an oversimplification, for a system at a particular point in time is likely to vary as a function of its environment both at that time and at many previous times.

2) The model focuses exclusively upon the impact of environments upon systems and not vice versa. As we suggested earlier, system-environment relationships are reciprocal.

3) Further, our model ignores the possible presence of interactive properties *within educational systems* that can play a role in educational change independent of that produced by the environment.

4) Finally, the model focuses exclusively upon the additive effects of various dimensions of sociocultural environments upon educational systems. This too is an oversimplification for it is quite likely that environmental effects interact in producing change in educational systems. But in the name of parsimony we have chosen to ignore all forms of interaction *within environments* for the time being.

Before presenting our formal analytic model of the relationship of educational systems to their environments, let us review some of the basic definitions and assumptions introduced previously.

1) The basic phenomenon with which we are concerned is the *degree of modernity* of educational systems and of their environments.

2) Educational *systems* are open social systems with at least four major *properties:* input, throughput, output, and structure.

3) Educational *environments* are sociocultural environments with at least three major *dimensions:* the cultural, the ecological, and the structural.

4) Educational systems exist at at least six distinct *levels:* school, school district, state, region, nation, and civilization.

5) Educational environments exist at at least six distinct *layers:* neighborhood, community, state, region, society, and civilization.

6) The environment of an educational system cannot exist at a layer below the corresponding level of the system. (Thus one can speak of the neighborhood environment of a school or the state environment of a school district, but not the neighborhood environment of a school district nor the community environment of a state educational system.)

Given these definitions and assumptions, our model can be summarized by the general hypothesis that:

The degree of modernity of an educational system **(S)** *varies as a function* **(F)** *of the degree of modernity of its sociocultural environment* **(E),** given certain constraints **(C).**

Using matrix notation[aa] this general hypothesis can be expressed as:

$$S = F(EC)$$ (Equation 3.1)

where, given the assumptions and definitions noted above:

1) S is a $p \times v$ matrix of 4 rows representing the four major system properties (p) [input (i), throughput (t), output (o), and structure (s)] and 6 columns representing the six system levels (v) [school (s), school district (d), state (a), region (r), nation (n), and civilization (z)].

2) E is a $d \times y$ matrix of 3 rows representing the 3 environmental dimensions (d) [the cultural (c), the ecological (e), and the structural (s)] and 6 columns representing the 6 environmental layers (y) [neighborhood (n), community (c), state (a), region (r), society (o) and civilization (z)].

3) F is a $p \times d$ matrix of 4 rows and 3 columns which relates the dimensions (d) of E to the properties (p) of S.

4) C is a $y \times v$ lower triangular design matrix of 6 rows representing the six environmental layers (y) and 6 columns representing the six system levels (v), which constrains the coexistence of levels and layers such that all layers must be equal to or greater than their corresponding level.

The meaning of Equation 3.1 may be clearer if it is written in extended matrix form as follows:

$$
\begin{bmatrix}
s_{is} & s_{id} & s_{ia} & s_{ir} & s_{in} & s_{iz} \\
s_{ts} & s_{td} & s_{ta} & s_{tr} & s_{tn} & s_{tz} \\
s_{os} & s_{od} & s_{oa} & s_{or} & s_{on} & s_{oz} \\
s_{ss} & s_{sd} & s_{sa} & s_{sr} & s_{sn} & s_{sz}
\end{bmatrix}
=
\begin{bmatrix}
f_{ic} & f_{ie} & f_{is} \\
f_{tc} & f_{te} & f_{ts} \\
f_{oc} & f_{oe} & f_{os} \\
f_{sc} & f_{se} & f_{ss}
\end{bmatrix}
\cdot
\begin{bmatrix}
e_{cn} & e_{cc} & e_{ca} & e_{cr} & e_{co} & e_{cz} \\
e_{en} & e_{ec} & e_{ea} & e_{er} & e_{eo} & e_{ez} \\
e_{sn} & e_{sc} & e_{sa} & e_{sr} & e_{so} & e_{sz}
\end{bmatrix}
\cdot
\begin{bmatrix}
1 & 0 & 0 & 0 & 0 & 0 \\
1 & 1 & 0 & 0 & 0 & 0 \\
1 & 1 & 1 & 0 & 0 & 0 \\
1 & 1 & 1 & 1 & 0 & 0 \\
1 & 1 & 1 & 1 & 1 & 0 \\
1 & 1 & 1 & 1 & 1 & 1
\end{bmatrix}
$$

(Equation 3.2)

To understand the meaning of Equation 3.1, note that the general hypothesis expressed therein contains many subsidiary hypotheses, which are represented by various combinations of the elements of the matrices S, F, E, and C as portrayed in Equation 3.2. For example, the subsidiary hypothesis that "the more modern the social structure (s) of the community (c) environment of a school district (d), the more modern its input (i)," can be expressed as:

[aa]The reader unfamiliar with matrix algebra and notation may want to consult one of the standard social science references. See, for example, Paul Horst, *Matrix Algebra for Social Scientists* (New York: Holt, Rinehart and Winston, Inc., 1963); or Robert McGinnis, *Mathematical Foundations for Social Analysis* (Indianapolis: The Bobbs-Merrill Company, Inc., 1965), chap. 8.

$$\begin{bmatrix} 0 & s_{id} & 0 & 0 & 0 & 0 \\ 0 & 0 & 0 & 0 & 0 & 0 \\ 0 & 0 & 0 & 0 & 0 & 0 \\ 0 & 0 & 0 & 0 & 0 & 0 \end{bmatrix} = \begin{bmatrix} 0 & 0 & f_{is} \\ 0 & 0 & 0 \\ 0 & 0 & 0 \\ 0 & 0 & 0 \end{bmatrix} \cdot \begin{bmatrix} 0 & 0 & 0 & 0 & 0 & 0 \\ 0 & 0 & 0 & 0 & 0 & 0 \\ 0 & e_{sc} & 0 & 0 & 0 & 0 \end{bmatrix} \cdot \begin{bmatrix} 0 & 0 & 0 & 0 & 0 & 0 \\ 0 & 1 & 0 & 0 & 0 & 0 \\ 0 & 0 & 0 & 0 & 0 & 0 \\ 0 & 0 & 0 & 0 & 0 & 0 \\ 0 & 0 & 0 & 0 & 0 & 0 \\ 0 & 0 & 0 & 0 & 0 & 0 \end{bmatrix}$$ (Equation 3.211)

which, in scalar form becomes:

$$s_{id} = f_{is}(e_{sc}).$$ (Equation 3.212)

The subsidiary hypothesis that "the more modern the ecology (e) of the neighborhood (n) environment of a school (s), the more modern its output (o)," can be expressed as:

$$\begin{bmatrix} 0 & 0 & 0 & 0 & 0 & 0 \\ 0 & 0 & 0 & 0 & 0 & 0 \\ s_{os} & 0 & 0 & 0 & 0 & 0 \\ 0 & 0 & 0 & 0 & 0 & 0 \end{bmatrix} = \begin{bmatrix} 0 & 0 & 0 \\ 0 & 0 & 0 \\ 0 & f_{oe} & 0 \\ 0 & 0 & 0 \end{bmatrix} \cdot \begin{bmatrix} 0 & 0 & 0 & 0 & 0 & 0 \\ e_{en} & 0 & 0 & 0 & 0 & 0 \\ 0 & 0 & 0 & 0 & 0 & 0 \end{bmatrix} \cdot \begin{bmatrix} 1 & 0 & 0 & 0 & 0 & 0 \\ 0 & 0 & 0 & 0 & 0 & 0 \\ 0 & 0 & 0 & 0 & 0 & 0 \\ 0 & 0 & 0 & 0 & 0 & 0 \\ 0 & 0 & 0 & 0 & 0 & 0 \\ 0 & 0 & 0 & 0 & 0 & 0 \end{bmatrix}$$ (Equation 3.221)

or

$$s_{os} = f_{oe}(e_{en}).$$ (Equation 3.222)

A more complex subsidiary hypothesis, such as that which will be tested in Chapter Six, of the form "the more modern the culture of the region environment and the ecology of the community environment and the structure of the neighborhood environment of a school, the more modern its structure," can be expressed as:

$$\begin{bmatrix} 0 & 0 & 0 & 0 & 0 & 0 \\ 0 & 0 & 0 & 0 & 0 & 0 \\ 0 & 0 & 0 & 0 & 0 & 0 \\ s_{ss} & 0 & 0 & 0 & 0 & 0 \end{bmatrix} = \begin{bmatrix} 0 & 0 & 0 \\ 0 & 0 & 0 \\ 0 & 0 & 0 \\ f_{sc} & f_{se} & f_{ss} \end{bmatrix} \cdot \begin{bmatrix} 0 & 0 & 0 & e_{cr} & 0 & 0 \\ 0 & e_{ec} & 0 & 0 & 0 & 0 \\ e_{sn} & 0 & 0 & 0 & 0 & 0 \end{bmatrix} \cdot \begin{bmatrix} 1 & 0 & 0 & 0 & 0 & 0 \\ 1 & 0 & 0 & 0 & 0 & 0 \\ 0 & 0 & 0 & 0 & 0 & 0 \\ 1 & 0 & 0 & 0 & 0 & 0 \\ 0 & 0 & 0 & 0 & 0 & 0 \\ 0 & 0 & 0 & 0 & 0 & 0 \end{bmatrix}$$ (Equation 3.231)

or

$$s_{ss} = f_{sc}(e_{cr}) + f_{se}(e_{ec}) + f_{ss}(e_{sn}).$$ (Equation 3.232)

Some understanding of these forms of expressing subsidiary hypotheses will be important in interpreting the hypotheses to be tested in Chapters Four, Five, and Six.

SUMMARY

In this chapter a view of the nature of social reality as an emergent phenomenon whose characteristics are distinguishable at different systemic levels was presented as a conceptual tool for the analysis of the complex nature of system-environment relationships, which is the focus of our study. The general nature of a social system as a set of lawfully related complex social relationships, as well as several properties of that system (for example, input, throughput, output, negative entropy, feedback, homeostasis, and differentiation) was discussed.

Throughout this discussion we have attempted to relate two central ideas of importance. Most important is the dynamic, reciprocal nature of the relationship between a social system and its environment. System characteristics such as feedback, homeostasis, and structural differentiation are, in effect, mechanisms by which a system both adapts to environmental contingencies and, in turn, has an effect upon its environment. Because, however, our subsequent analysis focuses upon the system as it is influenced by the environment, we have chosen to accentuate that aspect of what is obviously a reciprocal relationship.

A second central idea is the fundamentally symbolic nature of social systems as represented by the *meaning* associated with their development and purpose. "Purpose" here means simply a directional state that is determined by a social organism's relationship to the larger society. By distinguishing between the "subjective" rationality of the organization's members and the "objective" rationality of the organization itself, we hoped to communicate a view of social organizations as emergent phenomena with immanent characteristics and a logic of their own. To advance such reasoning presupposes that the meaning humans associate with their organizational relationships transcends their immediate involvement and is related to the total configuration of the cultural pattern of meaning in a society, a meaning they may not totally comprehend.

Given this background, we have discussed formal education as an open sociocultural system at the level of both the society and the school. This discussion, in turn, was related to the effect of modernization on a variety of system properties. Then we set forth a formal model of the system-environment relationship in American public education to summarize that discussion and to offer the general hypothesis to be tested in Chapters Four, Five, and Six. Throughout this discussion it has been noted that our analysis, of course, is not exhaustive of the nature of either open systems or of the effect of modernization upon them.

REFERENCES

[1]May Brodbeck, "Models, Meaning, and Theories," in *Symposium on Sociological*

Theory, ed. Llewellyn Gross (New York: Harper and Row, Publishers, 1959), pp. 373–403.

²Charles K. Warriner, *The Emergence of Society* (Homewood, Ill.: The Dorsey Press, 1970).

³Jay Rumney, *Herbert Spencer's Sociology* (New York: Atherton Press, 1966).

⁴For a particularly lucid account of this process, see S. N. Eisenstadt, "Social Change, Differentiation and Evolution," *American Sociological Review,* 29 (1964), 375–86.

⁵Wilbert Moore, *Social Change* (Englewood Cliffs, N.J.: Prentice-Hall, Inc., 1963), pp. 116–17; and Raymond Aron, *The Industrial Society* (New York: Frederick A. Praeger, Inc., 1967).

⁶Abraham Edel, "The Concept of Levels in Social Theory," in Gross, *Symposium on Sociological Theory,* p. 167.

⁷Edel, "Concept of Levels in Social Theory," p. 179.

⁸Walter Buckley, *Sociology and Modern Systems Theory* (Englewood Cliffs, N.J.: Prentice-Hall, Inc., 1967); Walter Buckley, ed., *Modern Systems Research for the Behavioral Scientist* (Chicago: Aldine Publishing Co., 1968); Daniel Katz and Robert L. Kahn, *The Social Psychology of Organizations* (New York: John Wiley & Sons, Inc., 1966); Talcott Parsons, *Essays in Sociological Theory,* rev. ed. (New York: The Free Press, 1954); Talcott Parsons, *The Social System* (New York: The Free Press, 1951); Ludwig von Bertalanffy, *Robots, Men and Minds* (New York: George Braziller, Inc., 1967); and Ludwig von Bertalanffy and Anatol Rappoport, eds., *General Systems,* Vols. I–III, Yearbook of the Society for the Advancement of General Systems Theory (Ann Arbor, Michigan: SAGST, 1956).

⁹Ludwig von Bertalanffy, "General Systems Theory," in von Bertalanffy and Rappoport, *General Systems,* p. 2.

¹⁰A. D. Hall and R. E. Fagen, "Definition of System," in Buckley, *Modern Systems Research,* p. 8.

¹¹*Ibid.,*

¹²*Ibid.,* p. 82.

¹³*Ibid.*

¹⁴Mario Augusto Bunge, *Causality: the Place of the Causal Principle in Modern Science* (Cambridge, Mass.: Harvard University Press, 1959), p. 199.

¹⁵*Ibid.,* pp. 146–47.

¹⁶*Ibid.,* p. 26.

¹⁷Hall and Fagen, "Definition of System," p. 83.

¹⁸Heinz von Foerster, "From Stimulus to Symbol: The Economy of Biological Computation," in Buckley, *Modern Systems Research,* p. 171.

¹⁹*Encyclopaedia Britannica,* Vol. VIII (Chicago: Encyclopedia Britannica, Inc., 1969), 383.

²⁰*Ibid.,* pp. 384–86.

²¹Hall and Fagen, "Definition of System," p. 2.

²²von Bertalanffy, *Robots,* p. 74.

²³Robert K. Merton, *Social Theory and Social Structure,* rev. ed. (New York: The Free Press, 1957), p. 51.

²⁴von Bertalanffy, *General Systems Theory,* pp. 80–84; Berrien, *General and Social Systems,* chap. 2.

²⁵Cf. Bunge, *Causality.*

²⁶Parsons, *The Social System,* p. 24.

²⁷*Ibid.,* p. 25.

²⁸Katz and Kahn, *Social Psychology of Organizations,* p. 17.

²⁹*Ibid.,* p. 33.

³⁰See Raymond Aron, *Main Currents in Sociological Thought,* Vol. II, trans. Richard Howard and Helen Weaver (New York: Basic Books, Inc., 1967), 227–32.

³¹Max Weber, *The Theory of Social and Economic Organization,* trans. A. M. Hender-

102 AMERICAN PUBLIC EDUCATION AS AN OPEN SOCIOCULTURAL SYSTEM

son and Talcott Parsons (New York: Oxford University Press, 1947), p. 333.

[32]Aron, *Main Currents in Sociological Thought*, p. 214.

[33]Weber, *Theory of Social and Economic Organization*; Aron, *Main Currents in Sociological Thought*; Jacques Ellul, *The Technological Society* (New York: Vintage Books, 1967).

[34]Gunnar Myrdal, *Beyond the Welfare State* (New Haven, Conn.: Yale University Press, 1960); John Kenneth Galbraith, *The New Industrial State* (Boston: Houghton Mifflin Company, 1967).

[35]von Bertalanffy, *General Systems Theory*, p. 215–18.

[36]Katz and Kahn, *Social Psychology of Organizations*, p. 33.

[37]Walter Buckley, "Social as a Complex Adaptive System," in Buckley, *Modern Systems Research*, p. 490.

[38]Katz and Kahn, *Social Psychology of Organizations*, p. 32.

[39]*Ibid.*, p. 21.

[40]*Ibid.*

[41]Buckley, *Sociology*, pp. 52–53.

[42]Garrett Harden, "The Cybernetics of Competition: A Biologist's View of Society," in Buckley, *Modern Systems Research*, pp. 452–54.

[43]Hall and Fagen, "Definition of System," p. 18.

[44]von Bertalanffy, "General Systems Theory: A Critical Review," p. 4. See also Arthur L. Stinchcombe, *Constructing Social Theories* (New York: Harcourt, Brace Jovanovich, Inc., 1968), pp. 80–82.

[45]Buckley, "Society," p. 490. (Italics those of the author.)

[46]*Ibid.*

[47]Katz and Kahn, *Social Psychology of Organizations*, p. 24.

[48]von Bertalanffy, "General Systems Theory: A Critical Review," p. 18.

[49]von Bertalanffy, *Robots*, p. 76.

[50]Buckley, *Sociology*, pp. 58–59.

[51]See Margoroh Maruyama, "The Second Cybernetics: Deviation-Amplifying Mutual Causal Processes," in Buckley, *Modern Systems Research*, pp. 304–13.

[52]Buckley, *Sociology*, pp. 59–60.

[53]Katz and Kahn, *Social Psychology of Organizations*, p. 25.

[54]*Ibid.*, p. 25.

[55]For a discussion of institutional differentiation, see S. N. Eisenstadt, "Social Change."

[56]For examples of research on this subject, see Frederick W. Terrien and Donald L. Mills, "The Effects of Changing Size upon the Internal Structure of an Organization," *American Sociological Review*, 20 (1955), 11–14; Theodore R. Anderson and Seymour Warkov, "Organizational Size and Functional Complexity: A Study of Administration in Hospitals," *American Sociological Review*, 26 (1961), 23–38; D. S. Pugh, D. F. Hickerson, C. R. Hinings, K. M. MacDonald, C. Turner, and T. Lupton, "A Conceptual Scheme for Organizational Analysis," *Administrative Science Quarterly*, 8 (1963–1964), 289–315; Bernard P. Indik, "The Relationship between Organizational Size and Supervision Ratio," *Administrative Science Quarterly*, 9 (1964), 301–12; and William A. Rushing, "Organizational Size and Administration: The Problems of Causal Homogeneity and a Heterogeneous Category," *Pacific Sociological Review*, 9 (1966), 100–108.

[57]Don Martindale, *Social Life and Cultural Change* (Princeton, N. J.: D. Van Nostrand Co., Inc., 1962), pp. 39–40.

[58]Among many works in this area, see Reinhard Bendix, "Industrialization, Ideologies, and Social Structure," *American Sociological Review*, 24 (1959), 613–23; Seymour Martin Lipset, *The First New Nation: The United States in Historical and Comparative Perspective* (New York: Basic Books, Inc., 1963), esp. pp. 1–11 and chap. 3; Robin M. Williams, Jr., *American Society; A Sociological Interpretation*, 2d ed. (New York: Alfred

A. Knopf, Inc., 1963), esp. chap. 11.

[59]Talcott Parsons, "Suggestions for a Sociological Approach to the Theory of Organizations," in *Complex Organizations,* ed. Amitai Etzioni (New York: Holt, Rinehart and Winston, Inc., 1961), p. 36.

[60]For example, see A. H. Halsey, Jean Floud, and C. Arnold Anderson, eds., *Education, Economy and Society: A Reader in the Sociology of Education* (New York: The Free Press, 1961); Campbell Steward, "The Place of Higher Education in a Changing Society," in *The American College: A Psychological and Social Interpretation of the Higher Learning,* ed. Nevitt Sanford (New York: John Wiley & Sons, Inc., 1962), pp. 894–939; and S. N. Eisenstadt, *From Generation to Generation,* paperback ed. (New York: The Free Press, 1964), pp. 163–66.

[61]Max Weber, *The Theory of Social and Economic Organization,* trans. A. M. Henderson and Talcott Parsons (New York: Oxford University Press, 1947); Ferdinand Toennies, *Community and Society: Gemeinschaft and Gesellschaft,* trans. Charles P. Loomis (East Lansing, Mich.: Michigan State University Press, 1957).

[62]Max Weber, *The Theory of Economic Organizations,* p. 244.

[63]H. Gerth and C. Wright Mills, trans. and eds., *From Max Weber: Essays in Sociology* (New York: Oxford University Press, 1946).

[64]James Price, *Organizational Effectiveness* (Homewood, Ill.: Richard D. Irwin, Inc., 1968).

[65]Gerth and Mills, *From Max Weber, op. cit.,* p. 426.

[66]Anton C. Zijderveld, *The Abstract Society: A Cultural Analysis of Our Time* (Garden City, N. Y.: Doubleday and Co., Inc., 1971), p. 81.

[67]John Dewey, *Democracy and Education* (New York: The Macmillan Company, 1916).

[68]See, for example, Shelley Umans, *The Management of Education: A Systematic Design for Educational Revolution* (Garden City, N. Y.: Doubleday and Co., Inc., 1971); Charles E. Silberman, *Crisis in the Classroom: The Remaking of America* (New York: Random House, Inc., 1970); Seymour W. Itzkoff, *Cultural Pluralism and American Education* (Scranton, Pa.: International Textbook Co., 1969); Brendan Sexton, "Realistic Vistas for the Poor," in *Readings on the School in Society,* ed. Patricia Cayo Sexton (Englewood Cliffs, N.J.: Prentice-Hall, Inc., 1967).

[69]See, for example, Charles E. Bidwell, "The School as a Formal Organization," in *Handbook of Organizations,* ed. James G. March (Skokie, Ill.: Rand McNally & Company, 1965), pp. 972–1022; W. W. Charters, Jr., "An Approach to the Formal Organization of the School," in *Behavioral Science and Educational Administration,* Yearbook of National Society for the Study of Education, Vol. 63, Part II, ed. D. E. Griffiths (1964), 243–61; Ronald G. Corwin, "Education and the Sociology of Complex Organizations," in *On Education: Sociological Perspectives,* ed. Donald A. Hansen and Joel E. Gerstl (New York: John Wiley & Sons, Inc., 1966), pp. 156–223; Amitai Etzioni, "The Organizational Structure of 'Closed' Educational Institutions in Israel," *Harvard Educational Review,* 27 (1957), 107–25; Graeme Fraser, "Some Properties of Schools as Organizations," *Delta One* (August 1967), pp. 23–30; and Fred E. Katz, "The School as a Complex Social Organization," *Harvard Educational Review,* 34 (1964), 428–55.

[70]See, for example, James Coleman, *The Adolescent Society* (New York: The Free Press, 1961); C. Wayne Gordon, *The Social System of the High School* (New York: The Free Press, 1957); David A. Goslin, *The School in Contemporary Society* (Glenview, Ill.: Scott, Foresman and Company, 1965), pp. 19–41; W. W. Charters, Jr., "The School as a Social System," *Review of Educational Research,* 22 (1952), 41–50; and Talcott Parsons, "The School Class as a Social System," *Harvard Educational Review,* 29 (1959), 297–318.

[71]See, for example, Burkhead *et al., Input and Output.*

[72]Reiss asserts that generally the strongest "pressure groups" tend to reside partly within the immediate environment of the schools. See Reiss, "Introduction," *Schools in a Changing Society,* p. 3.

[73]Talcott Parsons, *Societies: Evolutionary and Comparative Perspectives* (Englewood

Cliffs, N.J.: Prentice-Hall, Inc., 1966), pp. 21–24.

[74]Reiss, "Introduction," *Schools in a Changing Society,* pp. 8–9.

[75]Lawrence A. Cremin, *The Transformation of the School* (New York: Vintage Books, 1961).

[76]Emile Durkheim, *The Division of Labor,* trans. George Simpson (New York: The Free Press, 1964); Zijderveld, *The Abstract Society.*

four

The State, Region, and Nation as Open Educational Systems

In the introductory chapter of this book we suggested that an understanding of contemporary American public education can be greatly facilitated by a systematic and historical view of the relationship of schooling to both the individual and the society, a view that focuses on the interaction of educational systems and their sociocultural environments. We extended this view, first by describing the sociocultural environment of educational systems and considering some of the available evidence on the effects of various sociocultural environments on educational phenomena (Chapter Two). Then we spoke of educational systems as open sociocultural systems and offered a theoretical model of how the degree of modernity of the properties and levels of educational systems can vary as a direct function of the degree of modernity of the dimensions and layers of their sociocultural environments (Chapter Three).

A thorough empirical test of the conceptual model presented in Chapter Three would require systematic data on both American educational systems and their sociocultural environments over an extended time. Such data would need to be analyzable as to school-neighborhood relationships, school district-community relationships, state educational system-state relationships, regional ¦educational system-region relationships, and national educational system-societal relationships. Unfortunately, the data necessary to conduct such a thorough test are currently unavailable. Because of the strong emphasis on local control of education in the United States, *compara-*

ble data across all schools and school districts have not been collected and published. Some comparable data have been reported at the state level, but these data are often unreliable across states and years, even when they are tabulated by a single federal agency. Further, such data tend to describe primarily the pupil or teacher rather than properties of educational systems. Thus any analysis of American education from a systems perspective, such as that explicated in Chapter Three, faces a mosaic of data of questionable validity and reliability.

Therefore, the empirical analyses that follow in this and the two subsequent chapters can offer only a very limited examination of a few of the predictions implicit in the general hypothesis presented in Chapter Three. In general, the hypotheses to be proposed and tested must rely upon "proxy variables" within data collected by the U.S. Office of Education for administrative rather than research purposes. Accordingly, although possible implications for the nature of educational system-environment relationships will be evident, and will be discussed in Chapter Seven, our empirical analysis can best be considered merely *suggestive* of the type of research that must be carried out if our conceptual model is to be fully validated. Further, since the variables available to us are merely illustrative of the concepts elaborated in our theoretical model, we have not attempted to feature specific variables in our discussion of results. Instead we emphasize the consistency of trends.

In this chapter we analyze the relationship of the degree of modernity of the sociocultural environments of *national, state,* and *regional* educational systems to their inputs, outputs, and structure. Subsequently we will examine similar relationships for *school districts* (Chapter Five) and *schools* (Chapter Six). Thus, our empirical analyses of system-environment relationships will consider evidence with respect to the American educational system at five distinct levels: nation, region, state, school district, and school.

THE FORMAL ORGANIZATION
OF AMERICAN PUBLIC EDUCATION

A primary distinguishing feature of education in the United States is the absence of any centralized national agency for the administration of formal education. Thus, education is primarily the responsibility of the several states.

Historically, the first systematic legislative action to create or control education in America was the "Old Deluder Satan Act" enacted by the General Court (legislature) of Massachusetts in 1647. It required communities with at least fifty families to appoint a teacher of reading and writing supported from public funds. Although in 1812 New York State created the first state "superintendency of common schools," the first permanent organization for the state administration of education was established in Massachusetts in 1837.

Today, each of the 50 state educational systems is under the jurisdiction of a policy-making body, usually known as the state board of education. This board is created by the state legislature, and although its members may be elected directly by the people or by the legislature, generally they are appointed by the governor. The typical board contains 10 members.

All elementary and secondary education within a state—public and nonpublic—generally comes under the jurisdiction of the state board of education. Although compulsory attendance laws, now operative in all 50 states, require that all school-age children (generally those between the ages of 7 and 16) be sent to "a school," the state board of education has the authority to certify schools that meet minimum standards and can close those that do not by denying certification.[a] Although historically the raising of funds to conduct public education has largely been the responsibility of the city, county, or school district, all states make some provision for the general support of education, often with the intent of making educational opportunity more equal across school districts within the state.[b]

We begin our analysis with the state because of its historical and contemporary importance to education, because statistical data are more complete for states than for any other level, and because analysis at the state level will permit us to document many of our assumptions about variations in modernity within the United States. As noted in Chapter Two, regional differences have also been important in American society. Although in a formal sense the United States does not have regional educational systems, it is relevant to speak of an informal regional educational system owing to regional associations and commissions that influence education primarily through the accreditation of schools and colleges.[1] Therefore, we will group state data according to the five American regions discussed in Chapter Two. Finally, to characterize the United States as a whole, we aggregate state data to the level of the nation.

---

[a]The preceding discussion has been drawn largely from the fine summary by William W. Brickman, *Educational Systems in the United States* (New York: The Center for Applied Research in Education, Inc., 1964), pp. 1–38. A most comprehensive survey of policies and practices within American state school systems was conducted in 1947–1948 by the Council of State Governments. See *The Forty-Eight State School Systems* (Chicago: The Council of State Governments, 1949).

[b]For the 1967–1968 school year the national breakdown of revenue receipts for public elementary and secondary education was as follows: local, 52.7 percent; state, 38.5 percent; federal, 8.8 percent. [See Kenneth A. Simon and W. Vance Grant, *Digest of Educational Statistics, 1970 Edition* (Washington, D.C.: Government Printing Office, 1970), Table 70.]

RESEARCH DESIGN

The specific hypotheses to be tested in this chapter are derived from the general hypotheses presented in Chapter Three. At that time we stated

$$S = F(EC),$$

which hypothesized that "the degree of modernity of an educational system (S) varies as a function (F) of the degree of modernity of its sociocultural environment (E), given certain constraints (C)."[c]

The constraints to be imposed in this chapter are that the educational system will be considered only at the levels of the state, region, and nation and the sociocultural environment only at the layers of the state, region, and society. In using published state data the system properties will take on only the values of input, output, and structure. Owing to limitations (to be noted in the following section) in available data for the state, and thus the region and nation as well, we have not attempted to examine individually these environments' cultural, ecological, and structural dimensions. Instead a single measure of the general modernity of state, regional, and societal environments will be used.

Such a specification of the general hypothesis produces the following nine subsidiary hypotheses:

Hypothesis 4.11: $s_{in} = f_{ig}(e_{go})$.
The degree of modernity of the input (i) of a national (n) education system (s) varies over time as a direct function of the degree of general (g) modernity of its societal (o) environment (e).

Hypothesis 4.12: $s_{ir} = f_{ig}(e_{gr})$.
The degree of modernity of the input (i) of a regional (r) educational system (s) varies as a direct function of the degree of general (g) modernity of its regional (r) environment (e).

Hypothesis 4.13: $s_{ia} = f_{ig}(e_{ga})$.
The degree of modernity of the input (i) of a state (a) educational system (s) varies as a direct function of the degree of general (g) modernity of its state (a) environment (e).

Hypothesis 4.21: $s_{on} = f_{og}(e_{go})$.
The degree of modernity of the output (o) of a national (n) educational system

---

[c]The reader unfamiliar with the symbolic notation presented in this chapter is referred to the final section of Chapter Three.

(s) varies over time as a direct function of the degree of general (g) modernity of its societal (o) environment (e).

Hypothesis 4.22: $s_{or} = f_{og}(e_{gr})$.
The degree of modernity of the output (o) of a regional (r) educational system (s) varies as a direct function of the degree of general (g) modernity of its regional (r) environment (e).

Hypothesis 4.23: $s_{oa} = f_{og}(e_{ga})$.
The degree of modernity of the output (o) of a state (a) educational system (s) varies as a direct function of the degree of general (g) modernity of its state (a) environment (e).

Hypothesis 4.31: $s_{sn} = f_{sg}(e_{go})$.
The degree of modernity of the structure (s) of a national (n) educational system (s) varies over time as a direct function of the degree of general (g) modernity of its societal (o) environment (e).

Hypothesis 4.32: $s_{sr} = f_{sg}(e_{gr})$.
The degree of modernity of the structure (s) of a regional (r) educational system (s) varies as a direct function of the degree of general (g) modernity of its regional (r) educational environment (e).

Hypothesis 4.33: $s_{sa} = f_{sg}(e_{ga})$.
The degree of modernity of the structure (s) of a state (a) educational system (s) varies as a direct function of the degree of general (g) modernity of its state (a) educational environment (e).

MEASURING THE MODERNITY
OF STATES, REGIONS, AND NATIONS

Since, as noted earlier, most data for characterizing the sociocultural environments of American educational systems come from the state, we first measured the modernity of states. Ideally, one should have many objective measures of each state's position as to the cultural, ecological, and structural phenomena identified in Chapter Two. Given such multiple indicators of each dimension one could apply a mathematical model to data from all American states in order to reduce the many indicators to scores on the three hypothesized dimensions.[d] In this way the culture, ecology, and structure of American states could be assessed. Further, given the availability of such indicators at many different points in time, the historical development of modernization in America could be portrayed.

Unfortunately, such broad data are not available for all American states. Although compilations of contemporary and historical social and economic data tapping many important ecological indicators of modernity are available through the decennial census of the U.S. Bureau of the Census, appropriate data for assessing cultural and structural phenomena are extremely limited. In particular, little systematic data describe variations in values and ideology characteristic of what we termed "culture" in Chapter Two.

Rather than attempt to measure each of the three sociocultural dimensions of modernity through the use of "proxy" variables that bear only indirect relevance to the view offered in Chapter Two, in this chapter we simply measure "general modernity" (g) through a single index composed of five indicators measured at each of five points in time. Although the index we introduce below relies heavily upon variables that have often been used in cross-cultural studies to characterize solely "economic" or "technological" development, our use of them is in no sense intended to suggest that to be "modern" is simply to be rich or to have available an advanced technology. As we noted in Chapter Two, modernity implies both such technology *and* the restructuring of social life in order to use that technology most efficiently. Unfortunately, because data are limited, economic variables must be used both to measure directly the relative availability of technology and to measure indirectly the restructuring of social life. Hopefully, in the future, as the United States develops nationwide "social indicators," noneconomic data will be available for the more direct measurement of each of the three sociocultural dimensions of modernity as presented in Chapter Two.[2]

Interstate Variation in Modernity

The technical details of our "modernity index" for the 48 coterminous American states during the period 1930–1970 are presented in Appendix A. Basically, we began by considering carefully the primary cultural, ecological, and structural components of modernity identified in Chapter Two. From an extensive review of the numerous indicators used in cross-cultural research we selected five as; a) particularly relevant to the concept of moder-

---

[d]There are a variety of mathematical models available for such a data reduction process. Perhaps the most widely used is principal components analysis. [See Harry H. Harman, *Modern Factor Analysis* (Chicago: University of Chicago Press, 1960), or Mattei Dogan and Stein Rokkan (eds.), *Quantitative Ecological Analysis in the Social Sciences* (Cambridge, Mass.: MIT Press, 1969), especially Part IV, "Factor Analysis and Ecological Typologies."]

nity at a general level, b) sensitive to differences within a relatively modern society, and c) available during the 1930–1970 time period for all the American states. The selected indicators are: 1) percent of males in the labor force engaged in nonagricultural work, 2) percent of the population located in urban areas, 3) per capita annual income, 4) number of physicians per 100,000 people, and 5) number of telephones per 100 people.

As noted in Figure 4–1, the first indicator (percent of males in non-agricultural work) directly reflects the structural dimension of modernity, whereas the second (percent urban) directly reflects the ecological dimen-

Indicator	*Rationale for Selection*
1. Percent of males in the labor force engaged in non-agricultural work.	Directly reflects the structural dimension of modernity. Indirectly taps the ecological dimension of modernity. Widely used in cross-cultural studies to tap technological development.
2. Percent of the population in urbanized area.	Directly reflects the ecological dimension of modernity. Indirectly taps the structural dimension of modernity.
3. Per capita annual income	Indirectly taps the cultural and structural dimensions of modernity. Frequently used in cross-cultural studies to tap technological development.
4. Number of physicians per 100,000 of population.	Indirectly taps the structural dimension of modernity. Frequently used in cross-cultural studies to tap technological development.
5. Number of telephones per 100 of population.	Indirectly taps the ecological and structural dimensions of modernity. Widely used in cross-cultural studies to tap technological development.

FIGURE 4–1. *Five selected indicators of modernity within contemporary American society.*

sion of modernity. The third (per capita income) indirectly taps the cultural and structural dimensions and is the most common single indicator of modernity used in cross-cultural research. The fourth (physicians per capita) indirectly taps the structural dimension of modernity, and the fifth (tele-phones per capita) taps indirectly both the structural and ecological dimensions. Although, as suggested earlier, these five indicators are only a sample of a larger set of indicators which ideally should be used to characterize the relative degree of general modernity of American states during the 1930–

70 time period, they seem particularly representative, and we strongly doubt that any other *carefully justified* set of indicators would lead to a drastically different ranking of the states *during this time period.*[e]

A detailed roster of the 48 coterminous American states in terms of each of these five indicators of modernity in each of the five census years is presented in Appendix A (Tables A–1 through A–5). Table 4–1 presents a brief roster of eight of those states (New York, New Hampshire, Utah, Minnesota, Florida, Nebraska, New Mexico, and Mississippi) selected for their representation of different patterns of change over the 40-year period. In comparing all states in the different years one notes that New York has been consistently the highest of the 48 on all five indicators, and Mississippi the lowest (Tables A–1 through A–5). Florida and Minnesota have rather consistently been in the middle. New Hampshire and Nebraska have regressed relative to the other six states during the 40-year period, whereas Utah and New Mexico have progressed.

To combine basic data of the type presented in Table 4–1 into a single index the statistical technique of principal components analysis was applied to the 1950 data, and component scores computed for each state in each of the five years (see Appendix A for details). Table 4–2 presents a roster of the 48 states ranked as to average modernity score over the 40-year period and also in each of the five census years.

Figure 4–2 portrays graphically four different patterns apparent for the individual states in Table 4–2. There the modernity scores for New York, New Hampshire, New Mexico, and Mississippi are plotted across the 1930–1970 period. New York, the highest of the 48 states in modernity over the 40-year period, rose consistently during this period. Mississippi, the lowest of the 48 states, changed very little between 1930 and 1940, but then rose at a rate that appears to be more rapid than that of New York.[f] New Hamp-

---

[e]The emphases on "carefully justified" and "during this time period" are particularly crucial to an understanding of the measurement of modernity for, as we noted in Chapter Two, modernization is a dynamic process and what is highly "modern" in one time period may not be so in others. Clearly in studying trends between 1800 and 1950, it would make little sense to build an index of modernity that includes a measure of telephones per capita (one of our indicators), for the telephone was not perfected for practical use until 1896. Similarly, the use of percent of nonagricultural workers (another of our indicators) is not likely to be very useful beyond 1970, when almost all states will contain over 95 percent males in this category, thus producing a "ceiling effect."

The important point is that the indicators used to measure modernity during any time period must be relevant both conceptually and to the time period under study. If one is studying modernity in widely different time periods, it follows that different indicators may be required. The major consideration is always that the indicators used tap the adaptation and restructuring of the society, or its social elements, to the maximum utilization of *available* technology.

[f]Because of the "ceiling effect" discussed in footnote e, one must be careful in comparing states that are extremely high in modernity with those that are extremely low. The increase in modernity of New York between 1960 and 1970 would no doubt be

TABLE 4–1   Roster of Eight American States on Five Indicators of Modernity by Census Year, 1930–1970

State	Year	Percent Nonagricultural	Percent Urban	Per Capita Income (1970 Dollars)	Physicians Per 100,000 Population	Telephones Per 100 Population
New York	1930	93.7%	83.6%	$ 2688	160	21
New Hampshire	1930	84.9	58.7	1600	117	17
Utah	1930	71.4	52.4	1296	100	12
Minnesota	1930	62.8	49.0	1387	125	17
Florida	1930	74.2	51.7	1208	123	10
Nebraska	1930	53.7	35.3	1368	129	18
New Mexico	1930	52.9	25.2	944	90	5
Mississippi	1930	32.3	16.9	661	76	3
New York	1940	94.8	82.8	2411	196	22
New Hampshire	1940	88.8	57.6	1604	114	19
Utah	1940	77.7	55.5	1349	100	18
Minnesota	1940	64.6	49.8	1458	122	16
Florida	1940	80.6	55.1	1422	108	10
Nebraska	1940	55.8	39.1	1216	120	15
New Mexico	1940	62.4	33.2	1039	80	8
Mississippi	1940	38.0	19.8	604	61	5
New York	1950	96.5	80.3	3036	207	36
New Hampshire	1950	92.0	58.6	2123	121	27
Utah	1950	85.2	62.9	2068	116	28
Minnesota	1950	73.0	53.9	2253	135	23
Florida	1950	87.6	56.5	2076	107	16
Nebraska	1950	64.9	45.8	2374	111	23
New Mexico	1950	81.4	46.2	1874	83	16
Mississippi	1950	52.9	27.6	1182	63	10
New York	1960	97.8	72.8	3645	194	49
New Hampshire	1960	96.4	59.8	2726	103	36
Utah	1960	92.5	66.5	2518	118	38
Minnesota	1960	81.5	61.0	2709	138	33
Florida	1960	93.9	62.2	2577	115	28
Nebraska	1960	72.0	52.0	2802	116	24
New Mexico	1960	91.0	61.8	2369	87	29
Mississippi	1960	73.7	36.2	1533	68	20
New York	1970	98.4	85.5	4797	236	64
New Hampshire	1970	97.9	54.2	3608	140	50
Utah	1970	95.1	80.5	3210	138	51
Minnesota	1970	88.4	66.4	3793	151	53
Florida	1970	94.7	80.5	3584	154	52
Nebraska	1970	79.3	61.5	3700	115	54
New Mexico	1970	94.0	69.9	3044	112	44
Mississippi	1970	89.4	44.5	2561	83	35

revealed as greater than that shown in Figure 4–2 if modernity were not measured by such "bounded" indicators as percent of nonagricultural workers and percent of urban population.

TABLE 4-2   Degree of Modernity[a] of the 48 Coterminous American States, 1930-1970

State[b]	1930-1970 Average Rank	Score	1930 Rank	Score	1940 Rank	Score	1950 Rank	Score	1960 Rank	Score	1970 Rank	Score
New York	1	9.10	1	4.70	1	5.46	1	8.56	1	10.47	1	16.30
Massachusetts	2	7.90	2	3.80	2	4.91	2	7.33	2	9.75	4	13.69
Connecticut	3	7.42	6	2.09	3	3.95	3	7.02	3	9.64	2	14.42
California	4	6.90	3	3.36	4	3.62	5	5.34	5	7.81	3	14.35
New Jersey	5	6.80	7	1.85	5	3.56	4	6.35	4	9.20	5	13.05
Rhode Island	6	5.87	5	2.26	6	3.51	6	5.28	6	7.37	9	10.92
Illinois	7	5.64	4	2.37	7	2.42	8	4.92	9	6.48	7	12.00
Maryland	8	4.96	10	-.03	9	1.60	9	4.14	7	6.88	6	12.19
Delaware	9	4.67	13	-.83	8	1.65	7	4.94	8	6.54	8	11.03
Pennsylvania	10	4.18	8	.29	10	.81	10	3.36	11	5.76	12	10.68
Ohio	11	3.79	9	-.02	11	.58	12	3.13	13	5.32	13	9.94
Michigan	12	3.71	11	-.64	12	.52	11	3.32	12	5.73	16	9.62
Colorado	13	3.53	17	-1.42	16	-.81	13	2.76	10	6.24	10	10.89
Washington	14	3.29	12	-.66	13	-.18	14	2.42	14	4.96	14	9.91
Nevada	15	3.13	14	-.91	15	-.64	15	1.80	15	4.55	11	10.84
Oregon	16	2.41	16	-1.25	17	-1.16	17	1.44	16	4.30	18	8.71
New Hampshire	17	2.37	15	-.95	14	-.58	16	1.78	19	3.76	23	7.86
Missouri	18	1.87	18	-1.82	19	-2.22	19	1.01	20	3.75	19	8.64
Utah	19	1.58	26	-3.90	20	-2.44	17	1.44	17	4.22	20	8.60
Indiana	20	1.29	19	-2.20	18	-2.06	20	.75	27	2.49	25	7.45
Minnesota	21	1.28	22	-3.18	24	-3.10	21	.32	21	3.42	17	8.92
Florida	22	1.15	23	-3.46	22	-2.90	26	-.52	23	2.83	15	9.79
Arizona	23	.49	29	-4.91	26	-3.96	28	-1.07	18	3.88	21	8.51
Wisconsin	24	.45	21	-2.95	23	-3.02	22	-.05	32	1.21	27	7.04
Kansas	25	.30	27	-4.27	28	-4.45	25	-.40	23	2.83	24	7.78
Texas	26	.09	32	-5.94	32	-4.93	23	-.10	22	3.25	22	8.19
Vermont	27	.05	24	-3.65	25	-3.61	29	-1.14	28	1.82	29	6.82
Maine	28	-.07	20	-2.86	21	-2.84	27	-.75	34	.85	37	5.25
Wyoming	29	-.23	30	-5.35	27	-4.42	24	-.36	26	2.57	31	6.41
Nebraska	30	-.60	28	-4.40	31	-4.92	31	-1.23	36	.62	28	6.91
Iowa	31	-.68	25	-3.83	30	-4.78	34	-1.77	35	.70	32	6.28
Oklahoma	32	-.91	34	-6.36	36	-6.12	33	-1.66	25	2.76	30	6.81
Virginia	33	-.93	35	-6.57	33	-4.97	35	-1.80	31	1.47	26	7.20
Louisiana	34	-1.24	36	-6.81	35	-5.82	32	-1.34	29	1.58	33	6.20
Montana	35	-1.35	33	-6.23	29	-4.77	30	-1.19	37	.54	38	4.91
West Virginia	36	-1.80	31	-5.73	34	-5.45	38	-3.04	33	1.14	40	4.09
New Mexico	37	-2.15	41	-8.53	39	-7.16	36	-2.60	30	1.55	34	5.98
Tennessee	38	-2.25	37	-6.98	38	-6.69	39	-3.50	38	.39	36	5.53
Idaho	39	-2.54	38	-7.21	37	-6.30	37	-2.77	40	-.57	39	4.14
Georgia	40	-2.69	40	-8.29	40	-7.39	40	-3.85	39	.32	35	5.76
Kentucky	41	-3.70	39	-7.33	41	-7.73	42	-5.20	43	-2.11	43	3.89
Alabama	42	-4.16	43	-9.27	44	-8.87	43	-5.33	41	-1.28	42	3.95
North Carolina	43	-4.31	44	-9.46	42	-8.53	44	-5.62	42	-1.97	41	4.05
South Dakota	44	-4.62	42	-8.91	45	-8.91	41	-5.06	44	-2.39	47	2.15
South Carolina	45	-5.02	47	-10.47	43	-8.63	46	-6.33	46	-2.87	44	3.20
Arkansas	46	-5.16	45	-9.59	47	-9.84	47	-6.56	45	-2.52	45	2.70
North Dakota	47	-5.39	46	-10.16	46	-9.76	45	-6.02	47	-3.62	46	2.62
Mississippi	48	-6.78	48	-11.58	48	-11.31	48	-8.16	48	-4.23	48	1.39

[a] See Appendix A for the operational definition of modernity.
[b] States listed in descending order of *average* modernity during the period 1930-1970.

114

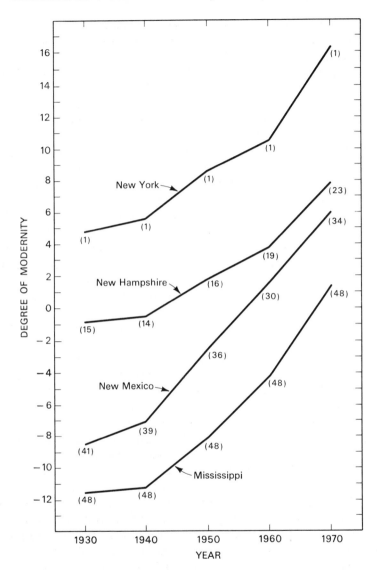

FIGURE 4-2. Degree of modernity of four selected American states, by census year: 1930–70. [National rank in parentheses.]

shire, fifteenth in modernity in 1930, increased slightly between 1930 and 1940 and then increased more markedly between 1940 and 1970, but at a rate of increase well below that of New Mexico, which was ranked 41st in 1930 (Figure 4–2). However, in spite of such variation in state rankings in the different years, their overall similarity is rather striking. For example, the Pearsonian correlation between the modernity scores for the 48 states for each pair of the five different years is always in excess of .93, demonstrating persistence in the rank ordering of the states in modernity between 1930 and 1970. (See Appendix A, Table A–8 for details).

The analysis presented above demonstrates that variation in modernity *within* American society can be documented empirically at several points in time. Further, the longitudinal analysis of modernity during the period 1930–1970 points to both the consistency and variation in development among states. A more intensive analysis of social, political, and economic factors associated with both the continuity and variability of the modernity scores for the states could help greatly to reveal the specific dynamics of this process. However, empirical demonstration of the existence of such variation in modernity, and the overall developmental changes of the states, provides the necessary basis for our analysis of regional and national variation in modernity and its consequences for the American educational system.

Regional Variation in Modernity

To develop an ideal set of American regions reflecting the ideology and values that underlie modernization and that in turn can be associated with differences in educational structure and functioning, we weighed carefully the alternatives presented by the Bureau of the Census, the Office of Education, the educational accrediting associations, and Odum and Moore, which are presented in Figure 4–3. After comparing each available alternative with the modernization scores for each state presented in Table 4–2, we selected a slight modification of the Odum-Moore approach. Figure 4–4 presents a characterization of our five major regions of the United States, along with the 1930–1970 average modernity score for each state. We have identified the five regions as Northeast, Southeast, Great Lakes, Plains, and Far West. The major distinction between the Odum-Moore approach and ours is with respect to the Plains areas and West Virginia. Odum and Moore characterize our Plains area as two distinct regions (Southwest and Northwest), and they place West Virginia in the Northeast rather than in the Southeast. We feel justified in combining their Southwest and Northwest because the two areas are similar culturally, share a similar historical heritage, and would have roughly identical modernity scores. West Virginia's modernity score is far more similar to those of bordering states in the Southeast than it is to scores for bordering states in the Northeast. Furthermore, our decision with respect to West Virginia conforms to the regional definitions of the Bureau of the Census and the Office of Education (see Figures 4–3A, 4–3B, 4–4).

Figure 4–5 is a graphic representation of the degree of modernity of

B. U.S. Office of Education

D. Regional Delineations of Odum & Moore

A. U.S. Bureau of the Census

C. Educational Accrediting Associations

FIGURE 4–3. *Four conventional regional distinctions relevant to the study of American public education.*

117

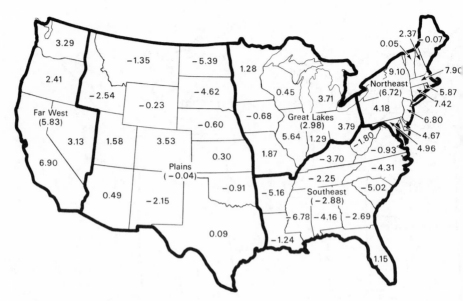

FIGURE 4–4. *Five "ideal" sociocultural regions of the United States. (Open figures indicate state average modernity index, 1930–70. Figures in parenthesis indicate region average modernity.)*

our five proposed sociocultural regions between 1930 and 1970. These regional modernity scores were computed for each census year by weighting each state's modernity score (as presented in Table 4–2) by the state's population in that year and then summing across all states within each region. It is apparent from Figure 4–5 that the Northeast region was the most modern in each of the five time periods, followed closely by the Far West, and then by the Great Lakes, Plains, and the Southeast in that order. Considering the ecological and structural indicators that make up the modernization score, variations among regions are considerable, and these have previously been well documented.[g] Less apparent, but of equal relevance to any discussion of the influence of the sociocultural context upon an educational system, are the ideological and value (that is, cultural) differences implied by our conception of modernity. For, as we have suggested in our general discussion of modernity (Chapter Two) and of modernity and education (Chapter Three), the beliefs and values dominant in regions are likely to be instrumental in determining the importance an educational system

---

[g]One of the best summaries of such variations among census regions is found in the work of Harvey S. Perloff *et al.*, *Regions, Resources, and Economic Growth* (Baltimore: The Johns Hopkins Press, 1960).

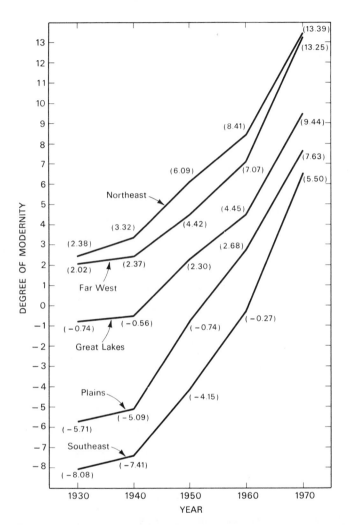

FIGURE 4–5. *Degree of regional modernity by census year, 1930-70.*

gives to internal and external elements, its sensitivity to environmental demands, the quality of its input, and the type of output it seeks to produce.

National Variation in Modernity

Figure 4–6 portrays the degree of modernity of the United States as a whole during the period between 1930 and 1970. As with each region the rise in modernity during this period has been a consistent one. The increase during the depression years (1930–1940) was slight, but since 1940 the

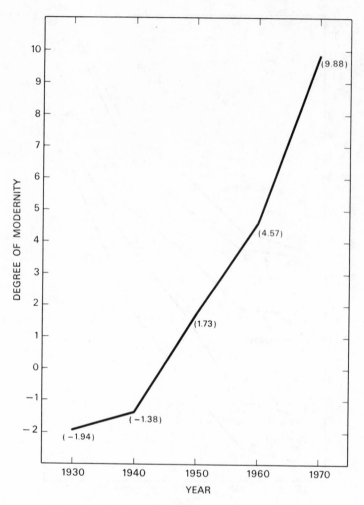

FIGURE 4–6. Degree of modernity of the United States by census year: 1930–70.

degree of modernity of the United States appears to be increasing at an increasing rate. However, one must guard against the temptation to make precise generalizations from our data about modernity over time. As was noted earlier, there are great difficulties in finding a common set of indicators of general modernity that can span long time periods. The five indicators that compose our modernity index were chosen primarily because of their relevance in 1950 and then extrapolated both backwards and forwards for 20 years. Several of these indicators (particularly percent of nonagricultural workers and percent of urban population) were approaching their mathematical ceilings of 100 percent in 1970 for many states and thus are unlikely to be fully discriminating in that year. Although such problems make a comparison of the precise *rate* of increase in modernity between various decades rather hazardous, they do not inhibit the generalization apparent from the data presented in Figure 4–6 that the degree of modernity of the United States as a whole has been increasing monotonically between 1930 and 1970.

VARIATION IN EDUCATIONAL SYSTEMS

We turn now to an examination of variations in modernity of educational environments related to variation in their systemic properties. After discussing how we have operationalized the properties of educational input, output, and structure we will offer empirical data in support of the system-environment hypothesis at the levels of the nation, region, and state.

Measures of Educational Input, Output, and Structure

INPUT.   In Chapter Three we defined input as the energy and meaning an open sociocultural system receives from its environment: materials, personnel, or information. The longitudinal data currently available from governmental sources are far too limited for a test using many indicators of each component of input, but data are available for each of the five time points on one variable that serves as an excellent summary for the three types of input, the current expenditure on the "average pupil."[h] In addition we will present data on average annual salary of instructional personnel (teachers, counselors, librarians, etc.) and the proportion of teachers who hold at least a master's degree—two important proxy variables for the quality of personnel.

OUTPUT.   Our discussion of outputs of educational systems in Chapter Three stressed the production of students with cognitive and social skills required by the economic system or desired by institutions of higher educa-

---

[h]In order to make dollar amounts comparable across census years, the actual current expenditure per pupil in each year was adjusted via the Consumer Price Index to reflect 1970 dollars, using 1967 as the standardization year. The weights used to make these adjustments were as follows: 1930, 2.319; 1940, 2.771; 1950, 1.613; 1960, 1.311; 1970, 1.000. These same adjustments were made in the case of the salary per instructional staff member.

Ideally, it would be desirable to make similar adjustments for interstate and interregional variation in the cost of living at the five time points, but the trend data necessary for such adjustments are simply not available. However, we suspect that only a small portion of the variation in expenditures reported in Tables 4–4 and 4–7 among the various regions and states, would be explained away if such adjustments were possible.

tion. Unfortunately, no historical assessment of such competencies is possible, for the necessary data have not been collected by any agencies for either the United States as a whole or for any state. The first systematic attempt at national assessment of educational progress began in 1964 with the formation of The Committee on Assessing the Progress of Education. With initial grants from the Carnegie Corporation and the Fund for the Advancement of Education of the Ford Foundation, the committee began to design a longitudinal program of national assessment, which collected its first data in 1970. Although the results of this first assessment are not analyzable by state, the regional and national tabulations that will be produced can provide a useful opportunity to test in considerable detail the system-environment hypothesis at those levels.[3]

However, longitudinal data are available from the U.S. Office of Education and the U.S. Bureau of the Census that can be recomputed to serve as proxies for measures of cognitive and social competence. We refer to the median years of schooling completed by persons 25 years or older, the percentage of such persons having completed four or more years of college, and the percentage of high school students and graduates per appropriate cohort. None of these indicators of educational outputs is without limitations,[1] but all are clearly indicative of important educational outcomes in a modern society.

STRUCTURE. Many characteristics of the structure of national, regional, and state educational systems, if the model presented in Chapter Three is correct, are likely to be influenced by the degree of modernity of their sociocultural environment. Of particular importance are size, differentiation, and boundaries of the schools. To measure all three variables we have performed some simple computations on published data from the U.S. Office of Education. Our indicator of school size for the educational system is the number of teachers per school. To tap differentiation we have computed the proportion of schools with more than one teacher, on the assumption that this is the point at which a division of labor will begin. As a measure of variation in school boundary we have computed the kindergarten full-time equivalent (FTE) enrollment as a proportion of the total kindergarten and elementary FTE enrollment. Such a measure gets at the degree to which the boundary of an educational system has been extended

---

[1]For example, the median years of schooling completed might be biased by the fact that not all persons 25 years or older received their schooling in the state in which they reside at the time of a census. However, the best available evidence on the effects of geographical mobility upon this variable suggests that although the actual mobility may be considerable, its net effects on median years of schooling completed is minor. [See John K. Folger and Charles B. Nam, *Education of the American Population* (Washington, D.C.: Government Printing Office, 1967), pp. 178–86.]

to encompass pre-primary socialization traditionally under the control of the family.[j]

The sources from which each measure of educational input, output, or structure were obtained are considered in Appendix C, as well as any computations that were performed upon such "original" variables in order to obtain "derived" variables, at the level of the state, region, and nation.

National Variation in Education

When the various measures of educational input, output, and structure for the 48 coterminous American states are aggregated to the level of the nation as a whole, it is readily apparent that Hypotheses 4.11, 4.21, and 4.31 receive strong support. Although complete data are not available for all measures at each of the five time points, data that are available show a very consistent trend for the degree of modernity of educational input, output, and structure (Table 4–3) to increase in association with the increasing modernity of American society (Figure 4–6). Particularly noteworthy is a tendency for the percent of increase in educational outputs to be somewhat less than that for educational inputs, suggesting a lag at the national level between inputs into the educational system and those outputs reported in Table 4–3.

Structural changes have also been pronounced between 1930 and 1970. Particularly dramatic is the trend with respect to the number of teachers per public school, our measure of school size. As can be seen in Figure 4–7, in 1930 the average public school contained 3.4 teachers. By 1940 this number had risen only slightly to 4.2, and by 1950 to 6.0. However, since 1950 the increase has been dramatic, with a doubling every decade, to the point where in 1970 the average public school contained 22.2 teachers. Thus not only, as was shown in Chapter One, are proportionally more young persons in school, and for more years, in a more complex educational system, but school size has been increasing dramatically as well, a point to which we will return in Chapter Seven.

When viewed within the context of the modernization process discussed in Chapters Two and Three, there seems little doubt that the overall development of American education is consistent with our theoretical expectations. At the same time, however, we emphasized the differential rates such development is likely to exhibit across lower levels of the American educational

---

[j]One must be careful not to confuse this measure with the proportion of the age-eligible group enrolled in kindergarten, a frequent indicator of educational opportunity. Our measure taps the proportion of an educational system's energy devoted to pre-primary socialization. Its range is most likely to be from zero percent (no kindergarten instruction in the elementary educational system) to 14 percent (one-seventh of the instruction in the elementary system—grades K–6—devoted to kindergarten).

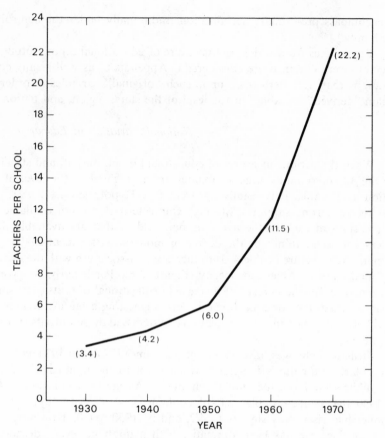

FIGURE 4–7. *Number of public teachers per public school by census year: 1930–70.*

system, differences that we argued would be a function of the varying modernity of lower environmental layers.

Regional Variation in Education

Input.   Table 4–4 presents regional educational input as measured by current per pupil expenditure, the salary of the average instructional staff member, and the proportion of teachers with a master's degree. Although in a few cases average input in the Far West is greater than that for the Northeast, in general the more modern the environment of a regional educational system the more modern its educational input.

Our formal test of Hypothesis 4.12 is based upon the number of inter-

TABLE 4–3   *United States Educational Input, Output, and Structure by Census Year, 1930–1970*

Variable	Year					Percent of Increase 1930–1970
	1930	1940	1950	1960	1970	
Educational Input						
1. Current expenditure per public pupil: 1970 Dollars (NSX)[b]	$197	$242	$339	$491	$780	296%
2. Salary per public instructional staff member: 1970 dollars (NSL)	$3274	$3959	$4806	$6734	$8775	168%
3. Percent of public school teachers with a master's degree (NMD)	3.6%	a	12.9%	22.0%	a	—
Educational Output						
1. Median year of schooling completed by persons 25 years or older (NME)	a	8.4	9.5	10.6	11.9	—
2. College graduates per 100 persons 25 years or older (NPC)	a	4.5	6.0	7.6	9.5	—
3. High school graduates per 100 estimated potential graduates (NGP)	27.8	49.1	55.6	70.4	75.6	172%
4. Secondary school enrollees per 100 estimated potential enrollees (NSP)	50.9	71.5	75.3	90.1	96.0	89%
Educational Structure						
1. Public teachers per public school (NTN)	3.4	4.2	6.0	11.5	22.2	553%
2. Multi-teacher public schools per 100 public schools (NMS)	40	48	61	83	98	146%
3. Public kindergarten FTE per 100 total public elementary FTE (NKP)	1.7	1.6	2.8	3.7	4.9	188%

[a] Appropriate data not available.

[b] See Appendix C for an explanation of all three-character codes.

region differences within Table 4–4 that are as predicted by the hypothesis. Given our identification of 5 ordered regions, there are 10 relevant inter-region differences.[k] If none of these differences is as predicted by the hypo-

---

[k] The 10 differences are as follows: 1) Northeast minus Far West, 2) Northeast minus Great Lakes, 3) Northeast minus Plains, 4) Northeast minus Southeast, 5) Far West minus Great Lakes, 6) Far West minus Plains, 7) Far West minus Southeast, 8) Great Lakes minus Plains, 9) Great Lakes minus Southeast, and 10) Plains minus Southeast.

TABLE 4–4   Regional Educational Input by Census Year, 1930–1970

Regional Educational Input	Year	Sociocultural Region					Number of Differences as Predicted (Maximum of 10)
		South-east	Plains	Great Lakes	Far West	North-east	
1. Current expenditure	1930	99	179	226	285	257	9
per public pupil:	1940	121	205	265	360	337	9
1970 dollars (RSX)	1950	218	346	361	446	408	9
	1960	340	453	518	558	613	10
	1970	600	628	775	891	986	10
2. Salary per public	1930	1919	2530	3375	4501	4496	9
instructional staff	1940	2340	2918	4002	5788	5590	9
member:1970 dollars	1950	3630	4574	5038	6366	5321	9
(RSL)	1960	5350	6087	6884	8302	7505	9
	1970	7530	7672	9330	9838	9338	9
3. Percent of public	1930	2.3	2.7	3.2	7.7	4.8	9
teachers with a	1940	a	a	a	a	a	—
master's degree	1950	6.7	11.6	15.4	11.3	17.9	8
(RMD)[b]	1960	14.4	25.9	22.1	18.8	27.7	7
	1970	a	a	a	a	a	—

[a]Appropriate data not available.
[b]Original data derived from rough estimates.

thesis we would suspect that the actual relationship is completely opposite to that predicted. If 5 of the 10 differences are as predicted we would be forced to conclude that there is no systematic evidence in support of the hypothesis. However, on the average, 8.9 of the 10 differences are as predicted, thus offering strong support for Hypothesis 4.12.

A particularly interesting pattern for per pupil expenditure is portrayed graphically in Figure 4–8, which clearly shows that in each region the average pupil received a greater dollar expenditure during each subsequent decade. However, also apparent is the fact that in recent years this increase was far greater in the Northeast, the Far West, and the Great Lakes regions than in the Plains or the Southeast; thus there was much greater variation in educational input among regions in 1970 than in 1930.

OUTPUT.   In general the relationship between the degree of modernity of regions and their educational outputs as measured by our four proxy variables is not as clearcut as in the case of inputs (Table 4–5). Although without exception the Southeast (the least modern region) has a lower output than the Northeast (the most modern region), the trend is not monotonic across the five regions, for in general the Far West has the highest output, whereas Hypothesis 4.22 predicted that the Northeast would be highest and the Far West second. In the case of median years of schooling

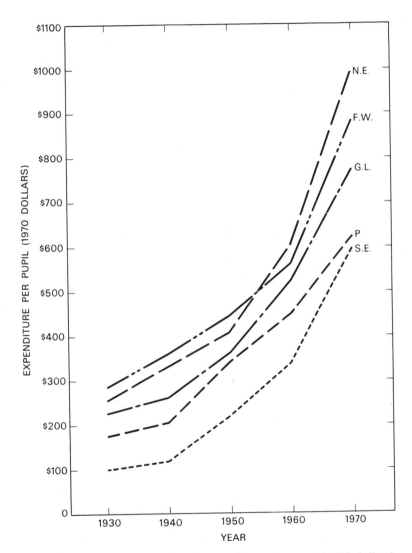

FIGURE 4–8. *Current regional expenditure per pupil (1970 dollars) by census year: 1930–70.*

completed and the percentage of college graduates, this might be due to the existence in the Far West of a younger population of persons 25 years or older, but the same pre-eminence of the Far West can be observed in the percentage of high school graduates and the percentage of secondary school enrollees, two measures far less affected by regional variation in age distributions or migration.

Since our measures of secondary school enrollees and high school graduates take into account private as well as public education, this discrepancy from the hypothesized relationship cannot be explained in terms of the relatively high proportion of students attending parochial schools in the Northeast. To some extent this discrepancy in the early part of the 1930–1970 time period can be explained in terms of differential immigration, but since the relationship does not vanish in the latter part (when immigration was minimal), that explanation seems inadequate. However, while immigration into the Northeast was diminishing, migration from the Southeast to the Northeast was increasing. But even this phenomenon seems inadequate to explain the magnitude of the discrepancy between what is predicted for the Far West by Hypothesis 4.22 and what is observable in Table 4–5.

In spite of these irregularities, a portion of which may be largely due to our inability to control for differential migration between where individuals received their education and where they were counted by the U.S. Bureau of the Census and the U.S. Office of Education, the data presented in Table 4–5 offer consistent support for Hypothesis 4.22, because on the average, 7.7 of the 10 relevant interregion differences are as predicted by the hy-

TABLE 4–5   *Regional Educational Output by Census Year, 1930–1970*

Regional Educational Output	Year	Sociocultural Region					Number of Differences as Predicted (Maximum of 10)
		South-east	Plains	Great Lakes	Far West	North-east	
1. Median year of schooling completed by persons 25 years or older (RME)	1930	a	a	a	a	a	—
	1940	7.4	8.6	8.5	9.7	8.4	6
	1950	8.2	9.7	9.5	11.5	9.6	7
	1960	9.3	10.9	10.6	12.1	10.7	7
	1970	11.0	12.0	12.1	12.4	12.1	9
2. College graduates per 100 persons 25 years or older (RPC)	1930	a	a	a	a	a	—
	1940	3.5	4.6	4.2	6.4	4.9	8
	1950	4.7	6.2	5.5	7.8	6.7	8
	1960	6.4	8.2	6.9	9.6	8.2	7
	1970	9.0	9.7	9.6	13.2	8.5	5
3. High school graduates per 100 estimated potential graduates (RGP)	1930	16.6	31.7	34.0	42.6	27.3	7
	1940	32.5	53.0	56.0	67.5	51.9	7
	1950	39.9	54.1	63.4	62.3	63.1	8
	1960	56.7	64.5	77.4	75.1	77.8	9
	1970	67.2	73.9	79.7	77.7	78.7	8
4. Secondary school enrollees per 100 estimated potential enrollees (RSP)	1930	34.4	56.7	59.1	73.8	50.7	7
	1940	51.0	74.2	78.1	88.3	79.2	9
	1950	59.6	70.5	81.5	87.2	84.4	9
	1960	80.2	88.5	94.4	93.0	94.9	9
	1970	88.0	95.9	97.1	101.9	98.9	9

aAppropriate data not available.

pothesis. Nevertheless, we should not overlook the possibility that differing regional values and ideology may be disturbing the predicted relationship between the outputs of regional educational systems and their environments. In other words, the classical American idea of the intrinsic worth of education as a practical necessity may be more prevalent in the Great Lakes and Plains regions than in the Northeast and thus produce forces there that cause children to continue their formal education regardless of its adequacy to meet the needs of a modern society. This is a point to which we will return in Chapter Seven.

STRUCTURE. The system-environment hypothesis also receives support as to school structure at the regional layer. In all five regions the size of schools has been increasing monotonically during the 1930–1970 period (Table 4–6). Nevertheless, the regions remain differentiated on this variable, with the Northeast and Far West generally having the largest schools. It is worth noting, however, that the average school in the Southeast is consistently larger than that in the Plains owing at least partly, we suspect, to climatic and topographical features in the Southeast that favor the transporting of pupils over relatively long distances.

The relationship between regional modernity and structural specialization (as measured by the percentage of multi-teacher schools) reflects a similar but changing pattern. From 1930 to 1950 there appears to be little

TABLE 4–6   *Regional Educational Structure by Census Year, 1930–1970*

Regional Educational Structure	Year	Sociocultural Region					Number of Differences as Predicted (Maximum of 10)
		South-east	Plains	Great Lakes	Far West	North-east	
1. Public teachers. per public school (RTN)	1930	2.9	2.5	3.2	4.2	5.6	9
	1940	3.8	3.1	3.6	6.6	6.9	7
	1950	5.1	4.2	5.5	11.1	9.4	8
	1960	10.4	7.6	10.7	17.6	17.2	8
	1970	22.5	15.6	21.6	24.9	27.6	8
2. Multi-teacher public schools per 100 public schools (RMS)	1930	46	37	28	70	47	6
	1940	57	38	36	69	67	6
	1950	66	50	50	85	79	6
	1960	88	66	80	95	96	8
	1970	99	92	99	99	100	9
3. Public kindergarten FTE per 100 total public elementary FTE (RKP)	1930	0.1	1.0	3.0	3.6	2.3	8
	1940	0.1	1.0	2.6	3.4	2.4	8
	1950	0.3	1.7	4.0	5.8	4.2	9
	1960	0.4	2.2	5.7	5.6	5.1	7
	1970	1.2	3.7	6.6	5.9	6.7	9

relationship, with multi-teacher schools least prevalent in the Great Lakes region and most prevalent in the Far West. However, by 1960 the hypothesized pattern emerges more clearly.

The most consistent relationship between the structural properties of regional educational systems and the degree of modernity of their regional environments occurs with respect to what we have termed "boundary expansion," as measured by the proportion of public elementary FTE devoted to kindergarten. Except for a reversal between the Far West and the Northeast, perhaps owing to the more recent development of the Far West, the more modern the environment the more extended (and thus modern) the educational structure.

In order to summarize these findings with respect to educational structure we have again computed the number of interregion differences that are as predicted by Hypothesis 4.32. This figure, when averaged across the various measures and years, is 7.7. Although somewhat below the comparable figure for the input of regional educational systems, this figure is nevertheless consistent with the hypothesis.

Interstate Variation in Education

In order to test the system-environment hypothesis at the level of the state educational system, a Pearsonian correlation coefficient was computed between state modernity and each measure of state educational input, output, and structure for each census year in which relevant data are available. This coefficient, when squared, reports the proportion of variance in educational input, output, or structure that is predictable from a knowledge of the state's degree of modernity.

TABLE 4–7   Correlation of State Educational Input with State Modernity by Census Year, 1930–1970

$(N = 48)$

State Educational Input	Year				
	1930	1940	1950	1960	1970
1. Current expenditure per pupil: 1970 dollars (SSX)	.70	.82	.74	.78	.71
2. Salary per public instructional staff member: 1970 dollars (SSL)	.88	.92	.84	.89	.83
3. Percent of public school teachers with a master's degree (SMD)	.59	a	.64	.62	a

[a]Appropriate data not available.
The median r across the 13 coefficients is .78.

INPUT. The system-environment hypothesis received strong support in the case of state educational input, for the 13 coefficients of correlation reported in Table 4–7 between state modernity and educational input range between .59 and .92, with a median value of .78. Some insight into the underlying processes being summarized by these correlation coefficients can be gained from an inspection of Table 4–8. There a detailed roster of the current per-pupil expenditure in 1970 dollars for the 48 coterminous states has been presented for each of the five census years. The states have been organized in terms of their rank order on the 1930–1970 average modernity index reported earlier (Table 4–2). Observable in Table 4–8 is the fact that all 48 states have consistently been increasing their per pupil expenditures for education during the 40-year period, a fact that attests to the generally increased modernity of American education noted earlier. However, of particular interest here is the fact that some states have been increasing their educational inputs more rapidly than others. Figure 4–9 presents graphically the data for New York, New Hampshire, New Mexico, and Mississippi, the four states whose degree of modernity was portrayed in Figure 4–2. Quite apparent is the association between degree of modernity and per-pupil expenditure, for the states high in modernity (Figure 4–2) are also high in per-pupil expenditure (Figure 4–9). Nevertheless, the rates of increase in expenditure vary somewhat from the rates of increase in modernity. For example, in 1930 the ranking of these four states in modernity is identical to their ranking in per-pupil expenditure. However, the rate of increase in expenditure for New Mexico from 1940 to 1950 increased far more rapidly than did that of the average state, so that by 1950 its expenditures per pupil had exceeded New Hampshire's. Nevertheless, in spite of such variations over time, the association of the inputs of a state educational system with its environmental modernity is remarkably uniform.

Similar consistencies exist with respect to each of the other two measures of educational input, thus offering strong support for Hypothesis 4.13.

OUTPUT. Table 4–9 reports by census year the correlation of state educational output with state modernity for the four available variables. Although data are not available in all cases for all years, Hypothesis 4.23 receives support from the analysis of output variation by state in each of the five census years, since the 18 coefficients of correlation range between .00 and .71, with a median coefficient of .53.[1] Of particular interest is the fact

---

[1]The correlation of .00 in 1970 between state modernity and high school graduates per estimated cohort is at first puzzling. Due to data limitations noted in Appendix C, our measure of the number of high school graduates in each state is no doubt weak, but it is unlikely to be weaker in 1970 than in the previous years. Although we cannot generalize with certainty, we suspect that the trend apparent in Table 4-9 whereby the correlation between state modernity and high school graduates per estimated cohort rose between

TABLE 4-8   Current State Expenditure Per Pupil (1970 Dollars) by School Year, 1930–1970

Stateª	School Year				
	1929–1930	1939–1940	1949–1950	1959–1960	1969–1970
1. New York	$319 (1)ᵇ	$435 (1)	$476 (1)	$736 (1)	$1237 (1)
2. Massachusetts	254 (9)	317 (6)	381 (15)	536 (17)	753 (20)
3. Connecticut	238 (12)	303 (7)	411 (9)	572 (7)	882 (9)
4. California	309 (3)	393 (2)	459 (2)	556ᶜ(10)	922 (4)
5. New Jersey	290 (5)	378 (3)	451 (3)	639 (2)	963 (2)
6. Rhode Island	222 (18)	291 (12)	388 (14)	542 (13)	904 (5)
7. Illinois	238 (13)	319 (5)	417 (8)	575 (6)	803 (16)
8. Maryland	186 (30)	232 (26)	344 (28)	515 (20)	882 (9)
9. Delaware	221 (21)	301 (9)	417 (7)	597 (3)	793 (17)
10. Pennsylvania	204 (27)	256 (17)	348 (26)	537 (16)	876 (11)
11. Ohio	222 (19)	267 (15)	326 (32)	479 (25)	680 (30)
12. Michigan	266 (6)	256 (18)	354 (23)	544 (12)	842 (13)
13. Colorado	257 (7)	255 (19)	354 (22)	519 (19)	695 (26)
14. Washington	233 (15)	292 (11)	399 (10)	551 (11)	743 (21)
15. Nevada	316 (2)	364 (4)	397 (11)	564 (8)	764 (19)
16. Oregon	240 (11)	270 (14)	439 (4)	588 (5)	891 (6)
17. New Hampshire	215 (25)	253 (20)	340 (29)	455 (28)	692 (27)
18. Missouri	163 (34)	223 (28)	280 (37)	451 (30)	714 (24)
19. Utah	174 (32)	217 (29)	288 (36)	423 (34)	600 (39)
20. Indiana	213 (26)	239 (23)	380 (16)	483 (22)	624 (34)
21. Minnesota	235 (14)	278 (13)	391 (12)	557 (9)	883 (8)
22. Florida	117 (38)	162 (38)	292 (35)	416 (35)	710 (25)
23. Arizona	253 (10)	267 (16)	388 (13)	529 (18)	766 (18)
24. Wisconsin	218 (22)	252 (21)	371 (19)	542 (14)	875 (12)
25. Kansas	215 (24)	229 (27)	353 (24)	456 (27)	721 (23)
26. Texas	127 (37)	183 (34)	337 (30)	436 (33)	581 (41)
27. Vermont	195 (29)	236 (25)	311 (33)	451 (31)	934 (3)
28. Maine	162 (35)	176 (36)	254 (38)	371 (38)	685 (29)
29. Wyoming	298 (4)	301 (10)	424 (6)	590 (4)	810 (15)
30. Nebraska	216 (23)	206 (32)	350 (25)	442 (32)	527 (46)
31. Iowa	223 (17)	240 (22)	372 (17)	482 (23)	890 (7)
32. Oklahoma	152 (36)	175 (37)	334 (31)	408 (36)	540 (44)
33. Virginia	103 (41)	133 (40)	235 (40)	359 (39)	691 (28)
34. Louisiana	112 (39)	157 (39)	345 (27)	488 (21)	620 (36)
35. Montana	254 (8)	302 (8)	432 (5)	539 (15)	822 (14)
36. West Virginia	167 (33)	177 (35)	242 (39)	339 (40)	626 (33)
37. New Mexico	179 (31)	212 (31)	359 (21)	475 (26)	724 (22)
38. Tennessee	99 (43)	123 (42)	213 (42)	312 (43)	560 (42)
39. Idaho	201 (28)	216 (30)	300 (34)	380 (37)	629 (32)
40. Georgia	74 (48)	117 (43)	199 (43)	332 (41)	600 (39)
41. Kentucky	107 (40)	130 (41)	195 (45)	306 (45)	612 (37)
42. Alabama	86 (45)	100 (46)	189 (46)	316 (42)	438 (48)
43. North Carolina	99 (42)	113 (44)	227 (41)	311 (44)	609 (38)
44. South Dakota	221 (20)	237 (24)	372 (18)	455 (29)	657 (31)
45. South Carolina	93 (44)	110 (45)	197 (44)	288 (47)	555 (43)
46. Arkansas	78 (47)	87 (47)	180 (47)	295 (46)	534 (45)
47. North Dakota	231 (16)	191 (33)	365 (20)	481 (24)	621 (35)
48. Mississippi	84 (46)	85 (48)	129 (48)	270 (48)	476 (47)

ªStates listed in descending order of *average* modernity during the period 1930–1970. (See Table 4–2 for details.)

ᵇFigures in parentheses represent the national ranking of each state as to current expenditure per pupil in each year.

ᶜEstimated by the authors.

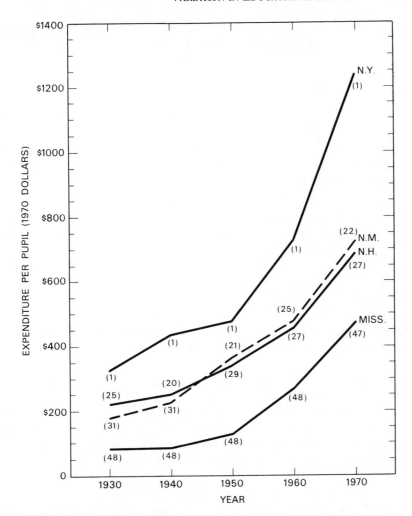

FIGURE 4–9.   *Current state expenditure per pupil (1970 dollars) for four selected American states by census year, 1930–70.*

that the state modernity-output correlations (median r = .53) typically are less than the state modernity-input correlations (median r = .78), suggesting the possibility that the input of state educational systems may be more de-

1930 and 1950 and then fell between 1950 and 1970 reflects the increasing and then decreasing relevance of high school graduation to the requirements of American society. In other words, although prior to 1950 high school graduation may have been important to the modernization of all sectors of American society, since then it may have lost its significance in the more modern sectors in favor of such alternative outputs as graduation from college and from graduate school.

TABLE 4–9 *Correlation of State Educational Output with State Modernity by Census Year, 1930–1970*
(N = 48)

State Educational Output	Year				
	1930	1940	1950	1960	1970
1. Median years of school completed by persons 25 years or older (SME)	a	.53	.53	.52	.54
2. College graduates per 100 persons 25 years or older (SPC)	a	.60	.71	.67	.67
3. High school graduates per 100 potential graduates (SGP)	.38	.43	.50	.39	.00
4. Secondary school enrollees per 100 potential enrollees (SSP)	.43	.58	.63	.45	.43

[a]Appropriate data not available.
[b]The median *r* across the 18 coefficients is .53.

pendent upon their sociocultural environments than is their output, a point to which we will return in Chapter Seven.

STRUCTURE. Hypothesis 4.33 receives strong support from the available data for school size, differentiation, and boundary extension, each of which is correlated with the degree of modernity of the state in each of the five census years. The relevant coefficients range from .24 to .74, with a median of .59 (Table 4–10). Particularly noteworthy is a shift over time in the degree of correlation between modernity and organizational specialization. In 1930 this correlation was rather low (.27), but during the ensuing 30 years it rose consistently to .44. Apparently, as American society became more modern between 1930 and 1960, the correlation between the modernity of its states and the degree of specialization of their educational structures increased. Viewed from another perspective, as American society became more modern, the more modern states moved more rapidly toward a more highly specialized educational structure than did the less modern states, a point to which we will also return in Chapter Seven.

SUMMARY

In this chapter we found consistent support for the system-environment hypothesis at the system levels of nation, region, and state, and with respect to the system properties of input, output, and structure. During the 40-year

TABLE 4-10   Correlation of State Educational Structure with State Modernity by Census Year, 1930–1970 (N = 48)

State Educational Structure	Year				
	1930	1940	1950	1960	1970
1. Public teachers per public school (STN)	.59	.68	.74	.70	.63
2. Multi-teacher schools per 100 schools (SMS)	:27	.40	.40	.44	.31
3. Kindergarten FTE per 100 total elementary FTE (SKP)	.62	.58	.68	.57	.70

The median *r* across the 15 coefficients is .59.

period between 1930 and 1970 American society became increasingly modern, and during this period *national* educational inputs, outputs, and structures changed in a similar fashion (Hypotheses 4.11, 4.21, 4.31). And at each of five time points, educational inputs, outputs, and structures were found to vary directly with the degree of modernity of their *state* environments, with inputs most highly related to environment, structure second, and output least (Hypotheses 4.13, 4.33, 4.23 respectively). The pattern at the level of the *region* was less consistent, but in general the more modern educational inputs, outputs, and structures were found in the more modern regions and the less modern in the less modern regions (Hypotheses 4.12, 4.22, 4.32). Inconsistencies in the output results obtained at the regional level may well be a function of the particular historical configuration of values and beliefs surrounding education in the various regions. After we have examined similar data for a national sample of *school districts* (Chapter Five) and *schools* (Chapter Six) we will return in our final chapter to consider the implications of all findings for both social theory and educational policy.

REFERENCES

[1]See, for example, Mary Wiley and Mayer Zald, "The Growth and Transformation of Educational Accrediting," *Sociology of Education*, 41 (1968), 36–56.

[2]For recent efforts in this direction, see Ray A. Bauer, ed., *Social Indicators* (Cambridge, Mass.: MIT Press, 1966); Eleanor B. Sheldon and Wilbert E. Moore, eds., *Indicators of Social Change: Concepts and Measurement* (New York: Russell Sage Foundation, 1969); and United States Department of Health, Education, and Welfare, *Toward A Social Report* (Washington, D.C.: Government Printing Office, 1969).

[3]For an overview of the national assessment project, see Frank B. Womer, *What Is National Assessment?* (Ann Arbor, Mich.: National Assessment of Educational Progress, 1970).

five

The School District as an Open Educational System

In the preceding chapter the degree of modernity of the input, output, and structure of the American educational system was shown to be systematically related at the *national* level to the increasing modernity of American society and in a manner consistent with our earlier conceptualization of American education as an open sociocultural system. In addition, within American society inputs, outputs, and structures of *state* and *regional* educational systems vary rather consistently with the degree of modernity of regional and state sociocultural environments. We now wish to extend our consideration of the system-environment hypothesis to the level of the *school district*. Again, it is our expectation that formal educational phenomena will vary directly as a function of the degree of modernity of their sociocultural environments.

THE ORGANIZATION OF AMERICAN PUBLIC SCHOOLING BY SCHOOL DISTRICTS

The earliest American public schools (those in New England) were generally governed by the town meeting or by the selectmen of the town. Later, as communities grew in size and as the administration of schooling became more complex, subcommittees of the selectmen were constituted as school committees to specialize in the problems of schooling. Today most communities have boards of education (a term we employ to encompass the variety of titles in use throughout the United States to characterize the governing boards of school districts). In most cases board members are elected, but in the largest cities they are often appointed, generally by the mayor. The community educational unit governed by a board of education is known variously as a "local educational agency," "school governance district," or most generally as a "school district." It is important to note that legally, school districts are subunits of state government rather than units of local government. They are created by states to execute state policy and generally can be abolished or altered at the pleasure of state legislatures. Although increasingly American school districts are constrained by state and federal law, most decisions regarding organization, curriculum, physical plant, qualification of staff, evaluation of pupil performance, and so on are still made at the local level. The United States is unique among modern nations in the degree to which major responsibility for the operation of elementary and secondary education resides with a multitude of local school districts.[a]

Although local school districts are generally autonomous, in many cases boundaries of school districts correspond with those of other geopolitical units. In general there are six types of local school districts: state, county, town, city, regional, and common. In Hawaii the school district boundary is that of the entire state. In 12 states (Nevada, Utah, Maryland, and nine states in the Southeast) the school district boundaries are coterminous with those of counties. In New England, New Jersey, Pennsylvania, Indiana, Wisconsin, Iowa, and Michigan, school districts are generally organized on a town or township basis. For most of the large cities the boundaries of school districts are generally those of the city itself. In parts of some states, most notably New Jersey, New York, Illinois, and California, regional districts have been formed by the consolidation of smaller districts at the secondary level, but not necessarily at the elementary level. Finally, in most of the states in the Plains region and in parts of New York, Ohio, Michigan, South Carolina, and Mississippi, schools are organized

---

[a]However, it should be recognized that in spite of this high degree of local autonomy with respect to decision making in American public education, there is considerable uniformity in the laws and policies under which local school districts operate. Although local school districts make the specific decisions regarding which teachers to employ, where to locate schools, and what curricula to offer, the standards applied in making these decisions are often determined at the state, regional, and national levels, not only by governmental agencies, but by accrediting agencies, colleges and universities, textbook publishers, and so on. American states now uniformly require at least a bachelor's degree for the certification of new teachers and uniformly require that youths attend a school until at least the age of 16. Even questions regarding taxing and bonding are subject to approval by state governments, and increasingly decisions regarding the criteria for pupil assignment are subject to approval by the federal government.

into "common school districts" that bear no direct correspondence to other geopolitical units. In rural areas these districts tend to be very small. "Sometimes they operate one-teacher schools; sometimes they operate no schools at all, sending their students to other districts on a tuition basis. Very often district boundaries were established through early surveys, sometimes along lines of latitude or longitude, rivers, Indian trails, highways, or other such landmarks."[1]

In the fall of 1967 there were 20,173 operating local public school districts in the United States. Over half (60 percent) offered instruction at both the elementary and secondary levels; more than one-third (36 percent) offered it only at the elementary level; and a small fraction (4 percent) offered only secondary instruction.[2] By state the largest number of school districts (approximately 1600) were in Nebraska, and the smallest (one) in Hawaii.

MEASURING THE MODERNITY OF COMMUNITIES
AS ENVIRONMENTS OF SCHOOL DISTRICTS

Ideally, in attempting to measure the degree of modernity of the immediate environment of school districts, one would obtain a series of objective measures of the community served by each school district in terms of the cultural, ecological, and structural phenomena identified in Chapter Two. Given multiple indicators of each dimension, one could conduct a principal components analysis of data from a large sample of communities similar to that performed in Chapter Four for the 48 coterminous American states. If the available data provided sufficient breadth of coverage, three components (rather than the single one noted in Chapter Four) would be expected to emerge, one tapping each of the three dimensions of the modernization process as we have described it in Figure 5–1. In this way one could assess directly the culture (e_{cc}), ecology (e_{ec}), and structure (e_{sc}) of the *community* environment of school districts. Unfortunately, nationwide data on the sociocultural characteristics of the over 20,000 American public school districts required for such a measurement process are currently unavailable.

Because of such limitations in the type of environmental data available for a national sample of American public school districts, we have had to approximate the ideal research design for testing the system-environment hypothesis at the level of the school district. We have selected a single indicator for the ecological and structural dimensions of modernity at the layer of the *community,* but to measure the cultural dimension we have had to rely (as we did in Chapter Four) upon simply the *region* in which the school district is located. Thus in considering school districts our measurement of their environments will tap the culture of the *region* (e_{cr}), the ecology of the *community* (e_{ec}) and the structure of the *community* (e_{sc}) (Figure 5–1).

Sociocultural Dimension	Instrumental-Functional Layer		
	Region	Community	Neighborhood
Cultural	e_{cr}	e_{cc}	e_{cn}
Ecological	e_{er}	e_{ec}	e_{en}
Structural	e_{sr}	e_{sc}	e_{sn}

Figure 5-1. *Characterization and coding of environment* (e) *of American public schools according to three instrumental-functional layers and three sociocultural dimensions. [See the final section of Chapter Three for the definition of all subscripts.]*

In order to conduct our test we obtained data from the 1967 Elementary-Secondary General Information Survey (ELSEGIS) of the U.S. Office of Education and performed a secondary analysis.[b] We omitted Alaska and Hawaii on the grounds that these states, rather than communities within them, are the primary basis of district organization. Similarly we omitted the District of Columbia on the grounds that it is controlled federally rather than locally. Then, in order to emphasize our focus on school districts rather than individual schools, we limited the sample further to districts containing more than one school.

The resulting subsample of 1,066 of the original random sample of 1,197 ELSEGIS school districts was then coded in terms of the degree of modernity of their sociocultural environments. Since data of the type required to characterize the ecological and structural dimensions of the environments were not available from the survey itself, we turned to data from the 1960 *Census of Population* of the U.S. Bureau of the Census, and matched data from census subdivisions with that from school districts. In 397 cases the boundaries of the school district were coterminous with those of a census "county" or "city" and the data could be taken directly from the *County and City Data Book*.[3] In 208 additional cases the school district boundaries were coterminous with those of a census "urban place," and the data could be taken directly from the *Census of Population*.[4] However, in the remaining 462 cases the school district boundaries were not coterminous with those of census subdivisions, and in such cases the county in which the superin-

---

[b]The basic data upon which the analyses reported in this chapter were performed were obtained from Kahn and Hughes, *Ibid.*, pp. 19–20. See Appendix C for further consideration of data sources and coding.

tendent of school's office was located was used as a proxy for the environment of the entire school district.[c]

In measuring the culture of the region (e_{cr}), because of limitations in our sample size and the fact that we desired to consider all three dimensions of the community environment simultaneously, we did not attempt to work with all five distinct regions discussed in Chapter Two and operationalized in Chapter Four. Rather we combined the Northeast, Far West, and Great Lakes into a single sociocultural region, which we called "high modern," and the Plains and South into a second region, which we called "low modern."[d] To measure the ecology of the community (e_{ec}) we chose to focus solely upon the degree of population concentration, which we defined as "high modern" for all school districts in communities having at least 550 persons per square mile (the 1960 median for all U.S. areal units in our study) and as "low modern" for all others. Finally, in order to measure the structure of the community (e_{sc}) we chose the percentage of males in the labor force in white-collar occupations. We defined all community environments with at least 40 percent white-collar males (the 1960 median for all U.S. areal units in our study) as "high modern" and those with fewer as "low modern."

In order to focus simultaneously upon both the independent and joint effects of the cultural, ecological, and structural dimensions of modernity upon educational inputs, outputs, and structure, we simultaneously cross-classified the 1066 school districts in terms of each dimension (Table 5–1). Although over half of the districts are either high or low on all three dimensions, reflecting the high degree of association among these three dimensions

---

[c]The process of match-merging data from the Census of Population of the U.S. Bureau of the Census with that collected by the U.S. Office of Education for school districts is greatly complicated by the fact that as of 1969 there existed no compilation of U.S. census data aggregated by school district. Since only a minority of school districts have boundaries coterminous with areal units whose socioeconomic characteristics are reported in detail by the census (primarily cities and counties), it was necessary for us to match manually the 1066 school districts with the best available *estimates* of their environmental characteristics. Although in cases where school districts were other than cities or counties this procedure contained error, we suspect that the error was far more likely to cause us to reject erroneously the system-environment hypothesis than to accept it erroneously. In other words, the existence of error in our measures of the modernity of the community environments of school districts has in general tended to attenuate the "true" relationship between community environment and measures of school district input, output, and structure.

[d]Although the combining of the Far West, the Great Lakes, and the Northeast into a single "region" violates an important component of traditional regional groupings (that of geographical compactness), our interest is in sociocultural regions rather than geographical ones. In a highly modern society, such as the contemporary United States, *sociocultural* regions need not necessarily have geographical compactness, for with the availability of such means of communication as airmail, the direct-dialing telephone, the interstate highway, and particularly the jet airplane, New York and California may be more closely linked socioculturally than, for example, Virginia and Arkansas.

TABLE 5-1   Conceptualization, Operationalization, and Distribution of Eight School District Environments of Varying Degrees of Modernity

Conceptualization of Modernity			Operationalization of Modernity			Distribution of School Districts
Cultural (e_{cr})	Ecological (e_{ec})	Structural (e_{sc})	Region	Population Concentration	Social Class	
High	High	High	Northeast, Far West, and Great Lakes	$\geqslant 550$ PSM	$\geqslant 40\%$ WC	297
		Low			$< 40\%$ WC	119
	Low	High		< 550 PSM	$\geqslant 40\%$ WC	75
		Low			$< 40\%$ WC	148
Low	High	High	Plains and South	$\geqslant 550$ PSM	$\geqslant 40\%$ WC	79
		Low			$< 40\%$ WC	34
	Low	High		< 550 PSM	$\geqslant 40\%$ WC	85
		Low			$< 40\%$ WC	229
All Environments			All Categories			1066

of the sociocultural environment of school districts, the districts are distributed among all eight cells of the $2 \times 2 \times 2$ classification, and thus permit a comparison of the independent and joint effects of each component.

RESEARCH DESIGN AND EMPIRICAL RESULTS

The specific hypotheses to be tested in this chapter are derived from the general hypothesis that was first presented in Chapter Three. At that time we stated:

$$S = F(EC),$$

which hypothesized that "the degree of modernity of an educational system (S) varies as a function (F) of the degree of modernity of its sociocultural environment (E), given certain constraints (C)."[e]

The constraints imposed in this chapter are that the educational system will be considered only at the level of the school district and the sociocultural environment only at the layers of the community and region. In using the available school district data to test the general hypothesis the system properties will take on only the values of input, output, and structure, and the dimensions of the sociocultural environment the values of cultural, ecologi-

---

[e]The reader unfamiliar with the symbolic notation presented in this chapter is referred to the final section of Chapter Three.

cal, and structural. However, the dimensions and layers of the environment will not be tested in terms of all six possible combinations, but (as noted earlier) only in terms of the culture of the region (e_{cr}), the ecology of the community (e_{ec}), and the structure of the community (e_{sc}).

Such a specification of the general hypothesis produces the following subsidiary hypotheses, which in general will be tested using educational data collected in 1967:

Hypothesis 5.1: $s_{id} = f_{ic}\ (e_{cr}) + f_{ie}\ (e_{ec}) + f_{is}\ (e_{sc})$.
The degree of modernity of the input (i) of a school district (d) varies as a direct function of the degree of modernity of the culture (c) of its regional (r) environment, the ecology (e) of its community (c) environment, and the structure (s) of its community (c) environment.

Hypothesis 5.2: $s_{od} = f_{oc}\ (e_{cr}) + f_{oe}\ (e_{ec}) + f_{os}\ (e_{sc})$.
The degree of modernity of the output (o) of a school district (d) varies as a direct function of the degree of modernity of the culture (c) of its regional (r) environment, the ecology (e) of its community (c) environment, and the structure (s) of its community (c) environment.

Hypothesis 5.3: $s_{sd} = f_{sc}\ (e_{cr}) + f_{se}\ (e_{ec}) + f_{ss}\ (e_{sc})$.
The degree of modernity of the structure (s) of a school district (d) varies as a direct function of the degree of modernity of the culture (c) of its regional (r) environment, the ecology (e) of its community (c) environment, and the structure (s) of its community (c) environment.

In order to assess the statistical significance of the results obtained in testing these hypotheses a statistical model was applied to our data to help assess whether trends that are consistent with that predicted by the hypothesis are real, or merely chance occurrences produced by the sampling process. In Chapter Four, when we tested the system environment hypothesis with state and regional educational systems, we presented data for all 48 coterminous states and all five regions; thus, sampling considerations did not apply. However, here we are basing our inferences about all 20,173 U.S. school districts in 1967 on a sample of only 1,066 and we need to be concerned with the issue of statistical significance. Therefore, to assist us in assessing the probability that the apparent results are not real ones, we have conducted a series of multivariate regression analyses using "dummy variables" (high modern = 1, low modern = 0), for each of the three components of modernity.[f] We have claimed support for the system-environment hypothesis at the

---

[f]For a technical discussion of our coding, see Daniel B. Suits, "Use of Dummy Variables in Regression Equations." *Journal of the American Statistical Association*, 52 (1957), 548–51; M. Davies, "Multiple Linear Regression Analysis with Adjustment for

level of the school district whenever any of the three components bears a statistically significant relationship with an indicator of educational input, output, or structure after controlling for the other two. Thus, we are testing for "net" (that is, partial) rather than "gross" (that is, zero-order) effects.

Although (as noted in the final section of Chapter Three) our formal model does not provide for the existence of "interactions" (that is, conditional predictability) among the dimensions and layers of modernity, such effects have been noted in past research using variables similar to ours.[5] Therefore, we augmented our statistical model to include the three possible first-order interaction terms (cultural by ecological, cultural by structural, and ecological by structural) as well as the one second-order interaction term (cultural by ecological by structural). All effects were tested for statistical significance at the .05 level, with the tests of the main effects being one-tailed and those of the interactions being two-tailed.

School District Inputs

Our measures of educational input for school districts are largely the same as those introduced in Chapter Four when we analyzed data for the American states and regions. From the data of the 1967 U.S. Office of Education ELSEGIS survey we computed for each of the 1066 school districts: 1) current per-pupil expenditure, 2) average instructional salary, and 3) percent of teachers who hold a master's degree. In addition we computed a fourth variable not previously discussed: expenditure per school for administration. As noted in Chapter Four the first variable is an excellent proxy for the overall level of energy input from the environment to the school system. The second and third variables tap characteristics of teacher input, and the fourth the level of administrative input.

Table 5–2 presents the mean educational input of each of these four variables in terms of the eight categories of the three dimensions of the environments of school districts described above. Consider the variable of per-pupil expenditure. The "average school district," regardless of modernity, spent $489 per pupil during the 1966–1967 school year. However, there was great variation in this expenditure according to the degree of modernity of the school's environment. In those environments characterized as highly

Class Differences," *Journal of the American Statistical Association*, 56 (1961), 729–35; or J. Johnston, *Econometric Methods* (New York: McGraw-Hill Book Company, 1963), pp. 221–30. For social science applications see, for example, Guy H. Orcutt *et al.*, *Microanalysis of Socioeconomic Systems* (New York: Harper & Row, Publishers, 1961), pp. 216–31; James N. Morgan *et al.*, *Income and Welfare in the United States* (New York: McGraw-Hill Book Company, 1962), *ad passim*; or Alan B. Wilson, "Social Stratification and Academic Achievement" in *Education in Depressed Areas*. ed. A. Harry Passow (New York: Bureau of Publications, Teachers College, Columbia University, 1963), pp. 217–35.

TABLE 5–2   Mean Educational Input in 1967 by Degree of Modernity of School District Environment

Modernity of Environment[a]			Measure of Educational Input			
Cultural (e_{cr})	Ecological (e_{ec})	Structural (e_{sc})	Current Per Pupil Expenditure (DCPE)	Average Instructional Salary (DAIS)	Percent of Teachers with Master's Degree (DZTP)	Per School Administrative Expenditure (DAES)
High	High	High	$596	$8086	31%	$15,500
	High	Low	514	7394	25	10,800
	Low	High	555	7449	23	13,500
	Low	Low	505	6513	15	9,200
Low	High	High	405	6799	24	8,100
	High	Low	381	6372	21	8,000
	Low	High	414	6553	24	7,700
	Low	Low	380	5808	17	5,300
All Environments			$489	$6991	23%	$10,400

[a]See Table 5–1 for operational definition of modernity of environment.

modern on the cultural, ecological, and structural components (operationally: high modern region, high population concentration, and high social class) the average per-pupil expenditure was $596, whereas as in their counterparts low on all three components the average was only $380 (Table 5–2). Of particular significance in testing Hypothesis 5.1 are comparisons in terms of each component of the modernization process when the two other components are controlled. To understand this analytic process, consider first the cultural comparison, controlling for ecology and structure. In each of the four cases, environments high on the cultural component spend more per pupil than do comparable ones low on the cultural component (compare $596 to $405, $514 to $381, $555 to $414, and $505 to $380). When similar comparisons are made in terms of structure controlling for culture and ecology ($596 to $514, $555 to $505, $405 to $381, $414 to $380) the same consistent pattern emerges. Finally, although showing the same general tendencies, the results in terms of ecology controlling for culture and structure ($596 to $555, $514 to $505, $405 to $414, and $381 to $380) produce one reversal.

Turning to other indicators of input that give additional insight into how much emphasis is placed upon varying aspects of the educational process in differing enviroments, it is readily apparent that average instructional salaries and per-school administrative expenditures in the school districts considered are influenced in a fashion consistent with our hypotheses by the regional culture of the district, as well as by its community's ecological and structural dimensions. Thus, environments high on the regional cultural dimension have a greater average instructional salary and per-school administrative expenditure, controlling for community ecological and social structural characteristics, than do comparable environments low on the regional cultural dimension. Similar comparisons of environments on their ecological and structural dimension reveal differences consistent with our expectations. Exceptions to this pattern occurred only when the percent of teachers with a master's degree is considered, and only on the regional culture dimension. In that instance, school districts in the less modern region and of low population density are found to have slightly higher percentages of teachers with a master's degree than similar school districts in the more modern region (23 percent vs. 24 percent, and 15 percent vs. 17 percent). Otherwise, the same pattern as on the other dimensions prevails.

In order to test statistically the results presented in Table 5–2, the dummy variable multiple regression analysis described earlier in this chapter was conducted and is presented in Table 5–3. Of particular importance to Hypothesis 5.1 are the regression coefficients for each of the three main effects, that is, the three dimensions of the sociocultural environment of these school districts. For all four measures of school district input the cultural

TABLE 5–3   *Unstandardized Partial Regression Coefficients for the Relationship of Modernity of School District Environment and Four Measures of Educational Input in 1967*

	Measure of Educational Input			
School District Environment Effects[a]	Current Per Pupil Expenditure (in hundreds) (DCPE)	Average Instructional Salary (in thousands) (DAIS)	% Teachers with a Master's Degree (DZPT)	Per School Administrative Expenditure (in thousands) (DAES)
Main				
Cultural (e_{cr})	1.48*	0.98*	1.9*	5.0*
Ecological (e_{ec})	0.11	0.58*	5.6*	1.6*
Structural (e_{sc})	0.48*	0.67*	5.7*	2.8*
Interaction				
$e_{cr} \times e_{ec}$	−0.14	−0.18	−3.7	−0.1
$e_{cr} \times e_{sc}$	−0.18	−0.11	−0.6	−1.6*
$e_{ec} \times e_{sc}$	−0.05	0.14	1.6	0.4
$e_{cr} \times e_{ec} \times e_{sc}$	0.11	0.02	0.5	0.7
Intercept	3.80	5.81	17.0	5.4
Multiple R	.47*	.30*	.43*	.34*

[a]See Table 5–1 for operational definition of school district environment effects.

* p. < .05.

effect (e_{cr}) makes a significant contribution to the overall relationship independent of the other two environmental effects. Similarly in all four instances the structural effect (e_{sc}) is significant, and the ecological effect (e_{ec}) is significant in three of the four instances (Table 5–3). In addition, the coefficients of multiple correlation for all four measures of school district input are statistically significant, and very few of the coefficients for the interaction effects are above chance levels. Thus the analysis presented in Table 5–3 offers extremely consistent support for Hypothesis 5.1, and we can feel confident in claiming support as well for the general system-environment hypothesis that is guiding our inquiry.

School District Outputs

Ideally one would like to examine at the level of the school district all of the relevant indicators of educational output suggested in Chapter Three. Unfortunately, the 1967 ELSEGIS study by the U.S. Office of Education did not touch on matters of output, and we know of no other recent national survey of a large sample of school districts from which such data would be available.[g]

However, in order to be able to give some attention to the question of community variation in educational outputs, we have taken the data from the 1960 Census of Population by the U.S. Bureau of the Census and examined variation in the median number of years of schooling completed by persons 25 years or older who reside in the communities sampled by the U.S. Office of Education in its 1967 ELSEGIS survey. Although this variable suffers from the limitations of intercommunity variation in population mobility and age structure noted in Chapter Four when we considered state and regional educational systems, it can certainly serve as a useful proxy variable until more valid measures of educational output become available for a large sample of American school districts.[h]

Table 5–4 presents a distribution of median years of schooling according to the eight sociocultural environments of school districts defined in Table 5–1. Clearly apparent is the fact that the highest median (11.7 years) is found in districts within those environments defined as most modern and the lowest

---

[g]Although the 1965 USOE Survey of Educational Opportunity contained several measures of educational output, the sample drawn for that study was designed to be representative of pupils by region and community size and thus can not be aggregated to provide estimates at the level of school districts. [See James S. Coleman *et al.*, *Equality of Educational Opportunity*, *Vol. I* (Washington, D.C.: Government Printing Office, 1966), 550–54].

[h]Unfortunately, in spite of the great need for such nationwide output data for both research and policy formulation, there appears to be little prospect of its being collected in the near future. At one time there was hope that the National Assessment of Educational Progress, currently being conducted by the Educational Compact of the States, would

TABLE 5–4   Mean Educational Output in 1960, by Degree of Modernity of School District Environment

Modernity of Environment[a]			Measure of Educational Output
Cultural (e_{cr})	Ecological (e_{ec})	Structural (e_{sc})	Median Years of Schooling (DMYS)
High	High	High	11.7
		Low	10.5
	Low	High	11.5
		Low	10.0
Low	High	High	11.2
		Low	9.5
	Low	High	11.2
		Low	8.9
All Environments			10.6

[a]See Table 5–1 for operational definition of modernity of environment.

median (8.9 years) in those defined as least modern. It can be further noted that all structural comparisons (11.7 vs. 10.5, 11.5 vs. 10.0, 11.2 vs. 9.5, and 11.2 vs. 8.9), and all cultural comparisons (11.7 vs. 11.2, 10.5 vs. 9.5, 11.5 vs. 11.2, and 10.0 vs. 8.9) favor the more modern environments. In addition, three of the four ecological comparisons (11.7 vs. 11.5, 10.5 vs. 10.0, and 9.5 vs. 8.0) favor the more modern environments, with the fourth comparison (11.2 vs. 11.2) being tied.

The formal test of statistical significance presented in Table 5–5 is equally conclusive. The multiple correlation of these three components of modernity (along with their interactions) with the median years of schooling found in the 1066 school districts is 0.72. In addition each of the three main effects (the cultural, the ecological, and the structural) is significant independent of the effects of the other two. Acknowledging the limitations of this variable

provide estimates of the output of individual schools and school districts. However, largely for what we suspect are political reasons, the decision was made to restrict the sampling design of that continuing national survey in such a way that estimates of output are not possible for areal units below the level of four broad regions or four broad categories of size of community. [See, for example, Frank B. Womer, *What is National Assessment?* (Ann Arbor, Mich.: National Assessment of Educational Progress, 1970).] Although plans are currently underway for several statewide assessments of educational output (most notably in Michigan and Florida) that will permit analyses at the level of the school district, such assessments are so scattered nationally as to obviate nationwide comparisons at the present time.

TABLE 5-5   *Unstandardized Partial Regression Coefficients for the Relationship of Modernity of School District Environment and One Measure of Educational Output in 1960*

School District Environment Effects[a]	Measure of Educational Output
	Median Years of Schooling (DMYS)
Main	
Cultural (e_{cr})	0.7*
Ecological (e_{ec})	0.3*
Structural (e_{sc})	1.7*
Interaction	
$e_{cr} \times e_{ec}$	0.0
$e_{cr} \times e_{sc}$	0.4*
$e_{ec} \times e_{sc}$	0.2*
$e_{cr} \times e_{ec} \times e_{sc}$	0.1
Intercept	8.9
Multiple R	0.72*

[a]See Table 5-1 for operational definition of school district environment effects.
*$p < .05$.

as a proxy for the more crucial measures of educational output identified in Chapter Three, the data presented in Tables 5-4 and 5-5, nevertheless, clearly suggest a substantial correlation between the degree of modernity of the environments of school districts and the degree to which they produce the types of output generally considered most functional in a highly modern society. Hypothesis 5.2 receives clear support from the analysis presented in Table 5-5.

School District Structure

The selection of potential measures of educational structure available from the 1967 ELSEGIS study is far more adequate for purposes of testing the system environment hypothesis than in the case of either input or output. From among many possible measures that could be constructed from the basic data of that study we have chosen six. To tap the important structural variable of organizational size we have computed the number of teachers per school in each of the 1066 school districts and averaged it within each of the eight environments. In order to give particular attention to the concept of organizational differentiation we have constructed four measures. First, we computed the percentage of schools in each district that contain all grades, one through twelve, on the assumption that such a form of age-grade organization represents the *lowest* degree of differentiation. As a second measure of differentiation we computed the grade span of each school in each district (a 1–12 school would have a span of 12 years, 1–8 school 8 years, and so on), and averaged within each of the 1066 districts to obtain district grade span. The districts were then averaged within each of the eight environments to obtain a summary for each type of environment. Again we have assumed that the larger the grade span the *less* the degree of differentiation. Two additional measures of differentiation were chosen that focus on the degree to which the staff of the schools in these 1066 school districts are specialized. One measure indicates the percentage of all professional staff who hold administrative or quasi-administrative positions (principals, assistant principals, and supervisors of instruction). The second reveals the percentage of all professional staff who are *not* assigned to either teaching or administrative positions (for example, librarians, guidance personnel, school psychologists, and audiovisual specialists). Both forms of specialization are expected to be found far more often in more modern environments than in less modern ones.

Our sixth measure of structure is identical to the one used in Chapter Four to tap the degree to which the boundary of an educational system has been extended to encompass a form of pre-primary socialization traditionally under the control of the family. We computed the percent of effort at the elementary school level that is devoted to the instruction of kindergarten pupils as indicated by the proportion of elementary pupil FTE enrolled in kindergarten, and it is our expectation that this percentage will be greater in the more modern environments than it is in the less modern ones.

Table 5–6 presents the results of our analysis when the mean value of these structural variables is tabulated within each of the eight environments. The pattern with respect to the frequency of undifferentiated schools (that is, those containing grades 1 through 12) is illustrative of what we have found. As predicted, all four structural comparisons (0.91 vs. 1.49, 1.51 vs. 3.77, 0.73 vs. 3.08, and 1.44 vs. 9.05), and all four ecological comparisons (0.91 vs. 1.51, 1.49 vs. 3.77, 0.73 vs. 1.44, and 3.08 vs. 9.05) favor the more modern environments (Table 5–6). In the case of the cultural comparisons, the results are less conclusive, with two comparisons as predicted (1.49 vs. 3.08 and 3.77 vs. 9.05) and two contrary to the prediction (0.91 vs. 0.73 and 1.51 vs. 1.44). However, this unexpected finding with respect to the cultural component of modernity is not apparent for all measures of school district structure. For example in the case of the percent of instructional staff in administrative or quasi-administrative positions, all four cultural comparisons (2.31 vs. 1.29, 2.18 vs. 1.40, 2.30 vs. 1.43, and 1.23 vs. 1.03) favor school districts in the more modern environments. In general, although for each of these six measures of school district structure there are slight deviations from what was predicted by the system-environment hypothesis, the exceptions are far outnumbered by the regularities and are quite likely attributable to measurement or sampling error.

TABLE 5-6   *Mean Educational Structure in 1967, by Degree of Modernity of School District Environment*

Modernity of Environment[a]			Measure of Educational Structure					
			% of Elementary FTE in Kindergarten (DZPK)	% of Schools Containing Grades 1–12 (DZUZ)	Grade Span of Average School (DZGS)	% of Instructional Quasi-Administration (DZIA)	% of Instructional Specialized Roles (DZIX)	No. of Teachers Per School (DTPS)
Cultural (e_{cr})	Ecological (e_{ec})	Structural (e_{sc})						
High	High	High	7.02%	0.91%	5.26	2.31%	4.42%	31.3
		Low	6.73	1.49	5.38	2.18	3.91	25.4
	Low	High	6.09	1.51	5.36	2.30	3.96	27.9
		Low	5.08	3.77	5.78	1.23	3.40	17.5
Low	High	High	2.92	0.73	5.43	1.29	3.68	26.7
		Low	1.01	3.08	5.32	1.40	3.40	22.6
	Low	High	1.61	1.44	5.53	1.43	4.00	26.1
		Low	0.85	9.05	6.53	1.03	3.44	16.6
All Environments			4.40	3.26	5.66	1.70	3.86	24.3

[a]See Table 5–1 for operational definition of modernity of environment.

In order to summarize these regularities statistically, we applied the dummy variable multiple regression model to the data underlying Table 5–6. Although the coefficients of multiple correlation vary from .20 (in the case of the percent of instructional staff in nonadministrative specialized roles) to .66 (in the case of percent of elementary FTE enrolled in kindergarten), each is statistically significant (Table 5–7). In addition, for all six measures of school district structure the sixth-order coefficients representing the cultural and the structural effects are significant, and in five cases the corresponding coefficients for the ecological effect are also significant. Clearly Hypothesis 5.3 is supported by these data. As in the case of school district input and output, these results with respect to school district structure offer consistent support for the system-environment hypothesis that has been guiding this inquiry.

SUMMARY

In the analysis of educational input, output, and structure presented in this chapter we have found consistent support at the level of the *school district* for the system-environment hypothesis presented in Chapter Three. Although the variables available to us for analysis are not ideal, for the most part they vary systematically in accordance with the degree of modernity of the cultural, ecological, and structural dimensions of the sociocultural environ-

TABLE 5-7   Unstandardized Partial Regression Coefficients for the Relationship of Modernity of School District Environment and Six Measures of Educational Structure in 1967

	Measure of Educational Structure					
School District Environment Effects[a]	% of Elementary FTE in Kindergarten (DZPK)	% of Schools Containing Grades 1–12 (DZUZ)	Grade Span of Average School (DZGS)	% of instructional Staff in Quasi-Administration (DZIA)	% of Inst. Staff in Specialized Roles (DZIX)	No. of Teachers Per School (DTPS)
Main						
Cultural (e_{cr})	4.7*	−1.69*	−.24*	.71*	.28*	2.48*
Ecological (e_{ec})	1.0*	−2.46*	−.45*	.29*	.13	4.38*
Structural (e_{sc})	0.9*	−3.26*	−.36*	.37*	.46*	7.42*
Interaction						
$e_{cr} \times e_{ec}$	−0.3	−0.98	−.20*	−.18	−.32*	−1.10
$e_{cr} \times e_{sc}$	0.3	−1.80	−.09	−.23*	−.05	−0.57
$e_{ec} \times e_{sc}$	−0.1	−1.80	−.33*	.34*	−.03	2.23*
$e_{cr} \times e_{ec} \times e_{sc}$	−0.4	−0.93	−.19*	.11	−.05	0.14
Intercept	0.8	9.25	6.50	1.06	3.51	16.9
Multiple R	.66*	.24*	.36*	.37*	.20*	.39*

[a]See Table 5-1 for operational definition of school district environment effects.

*p < .05.

ments of a national sample of school districts. Further, although the method of operationalizing modernity was not identical to that used in Chapter Four for the environments of state, regional, and the national educational systems, the same consistent results have been observed in this chapter with respect to school districts. After we have considered the system-environment hypotheses at the level of the *school* (Chapter Six) we will return in our final chapter to consider the implications of these findings for both social theory and educational policy.

REFERENCES

[1]D. Richard Wynn, *Organization of Public Schools* (Washington, D.C.: The Center for Applied Research in Education, Inc., 1964), p. 7.

[2]Gerald Kahn and Warren A. Hughes, *Statistics of Local Public School Systems, 1967* (Washington, D.C.: Government Printing Office, 1969), p. 3.

[3]Bureau of the Census, *County and City Data Book* (Washington, D.C.: Government Printing Office, 1967).

[4]Bureau of the Census, *Census of Population, Characteristics of the Population, 1960* (Washington, D.C.: Government Printing Office, 1963).

[5]See, for example, Charles B. Nam, A. Lewis Rhodes, and Robert E. Herriott, "School Retention by Race, Religion, and Socioeconomic Status," *The Journal of Human Resources*, 3 (1968), 171–90.

six

The School
as an Open Educational
System

In Chapter Four we began to consider empirically the association of the properties of educational systems with the degree of modernity of their sociocultural environments by examining American education at *state, regional,* and *national* levels at five points in time. Subsequently, we extended our test of the system-environment hypothesis by focusing on the environments of *school districts.* In this, our final empirical chapter, we consider how the degree of modernity of sociocultural environments affects the *school.* It is our expectation that the modernity of school inputs, throughputs, outputs, and structure also varies directly as a function of the degree of modernity of the school's most immediate environment.

THE ORGANIZATION
OF AMERICAN PUBLIC EDUCATION BY SCHOOLS

Formal public schooling did not begin immediately with the settlement of America. In the early colonial period, schooling was conducted exclusively in the home, in churches, or in private academies and dame schools. However, with the founding of the Boston Latin School in 1635, public or "town" schools came into existence. Initially a single school served an entire municipality, but with increasing population concentration within communities and with an increasing number of pupils attending school, the environments of schools became increasingly differentiated, with a school serving a specific neighborhood, rather than the entire community.[1]

The number of public schools has grown very rapidly during the past three centuries; in 1967 there were 93,581 public schools the United States.[2] Although in many cases a single school serves an entire municipality, most serve a more limited area (a "neighborhood"), the most extreme case being New York City, with a total of 894 public school neighborhoods under the jurisdiction of a single board of education.[3]

In spite of the fact that there are still many one-teacher schools in the United States (see Chapter Four) and that many schools contain all 12 grades (see Chapter Five), the typical school in contemporary America contains more than one teacher and fewer than all 12 grades. Thus, in general, there is a high degree of structural differentiation in contemporary American public education in grade levels, with grades 1 through 6 most frequently located in an "elementary" school, grades 7 through 9 in a "junior high" school, and grades 10 through 12 in a "senior high" school.[4]

MEASURING THE MODERNITY OF NEIGHBORHOODS AS ENVIRONMENTS OF SCHOOLS

Ideally, in attempting to measure the degree of modernity of the immediate environments of individual schools, we should obtain a series of objective measures of the neighborhood served by each school in terms of the cultural, ecological, and structural phenomena identified in Chapter Two. Given multiple indicators of each concept, a principal components analysis of data from a large sample of neighborhoods could be conducted, similar to that performed in Chapter Four for the 48 states and suggested in Chapter Five for a sample of communities. If the available data provided sufficient breadth of coverage, three components would be expected to emerge, one tapping each of the three dimensions of the modernization process as we have described it. In this way one could assess directly the culture (e_{cn}), ecology (e_{en}), and structure (e_{sn}) of neighborhoods.[a] Unfortunately, as was the case with respect to school districts, such nationwide data are unavailable.

Current limitations of data require us to approximate the ideal research design for testing the system-environment hypothesis with respect to schools. Therefore we have selected a single indicator for the structural dimension of environmental modernity at the layer of the *neighborhood,* but to measure the cultural and structural dimensions we have had to rely (as we did in Chapter Five) upon the *region* and *community,* respectively, in which the school is

---

[a]For a taxonomy of the dimensions and layers of the environments of educational systems and of our mneumonic codes, see Figure 5–1.

located. Thus, in considering schools as educational systems, we will measure the culture of the region (e_{cr}), the ecology of the community (e_{ec}), and the structure of the neighborhood (e_{sn}).

In order to conduct our test we have taken data from a minor part of the 1965 Equality of Educational Opportunity Survey of the U.S. Office of Education and performed a secondary analysis. The data we have used were not those from the main portion of the survey, commonly referred to as the Coleman Report, but those collected for the Office of Education by the U.S. Bureau of the Census through a supplement to the October 1965 Current Population Survey by means of a mailed questionnaire sent to the chief administrative officer of approximately 10,700 public and nonpublic schools.

Since the system-environment hypothesis, as it has been developed in Chapter Three, refers only to public schools, and since school level is itself an important structural variable in American public education, the analyses reported in this chapter are confined to a sample of 3,922 schools from the Census Bureau study that are *publicly* administered and that are either elementary (N = 1775), junior high (N = 963), or senior high schools (N = 1184).[b]

To represent the *cultural* component, as noted above, we chose simply the school's *region* (e_{cr}). Because of limitations in our sample size we did not attempt to work with all five regions. Again, as in Chapter Five, we combined the Northeast, Far West, and Great Lakes into a single sociocultural region that we call "high modern," and the Plains and South into a second region we call "low modern."[c]

To represent the *ecological* component of modernity we again chose to focus solely upon the degree of population concentration within the school's *community* (e_{ec}). However, instead of computing the population per square mile for each community, as we had done in Chapter Five, we were restricted by the coding of the available data to simply the school's location in terms of three major census categories. If a school was located in a "central city" of one of the Standard Metropolitan Statistical Areas (SMSA) it was coded as

---

[b]Considerable attention has been given to the problem of school nonresponse that plagued this study as well as the larger *Equality of Educational Opportunity* survey directed by James S. Coleman. For a more complete discussion of this and other methodological aspects of the study from which these data were obtained, see Herriott and Hodgkins, *Sociocultural Context and the American School,* especially chap. 9, Appendix A, and Appendix D.

[c]Owing to the manner in which the Bureau of the Census drew the sample of schools, it was not possible to combine the states into the exact sociocultural regions portrayed in Figure 4–4. However, the coding we were able to perform resulted in a very close approximation. For a comparison of the degree of modernity of the "ideal" and "actual" regions used in this portion of our analysis, see Herriott and Hodgkins, *Sociocultural Context and the American School,* Figures 9–1 and 9–2.

"high" on the ecological dimension of environmental modernity. If a school was located within the "ring" of a SMSA it was coded as "moderate." A school not located within an SMSA was coded as "low."[d]

To represent the *structural* component of modernity we chose to focus on the percent of males in white-collar occupations, as we did in Chapter Five. However, in this case our estimate was for the *neighborhood* served by the school (e_{sn}) and not for the entire community (e_{sc}). We defined all school neighborhoods with at least 35 percent white-collar male parents (the median for all schools in the study) as "high modern" and those with fewer as "low modern."

In order to focus upon the independent and joint effects of cultural, ecological, and structural dimensions of modernity upon the organizational properties of schools we simultaneously cross-classified the 3,922 schools as to school level (elementary, junior high, and senior high) and as to each of the three dimensions of modernity (Table 6–1). In Chapter Five, school

TABLE 6–1   Conceptualization, Operationalization, and Distribution of 12 School Environments of Varying Degrees of Modernity, by School Level

Conceptualization of Modernity			Operationalization of Modernity			Distribution of Schools		
Cultural (e_{cr})	Ecological (e_{ec})	Structural (e_{sn})	Region	Population Concentration	Social Class	Elementary	Junior High	Senior High
High	High	High	Northeast, Far West, and Great Lakes	Central City	$\geqslant 35\%$	149	109	112
		Low			$< 35\%$	208	98	105
	Moderate	High		Ring	$\geqslant 35\%$	302	217	248
		Low			$< 35\%$	208	101	153
	Low	High		Nonmetropolitan	$\geqslant 35\%$	76	58	62
		Low			$< 35\%$	117	39	67
Low	High	High	Plains and South	Central City	$\geqslant 35\%$	91	49	51
		Low			$< 35\%$	94	48	33
	Moderate	High		Ring	$\geqslant 35\%$	112	74	91
		Low			$< 35\%$	94	48	52
	Low	High		Nonmetropolitan	$\geqslant 35\%$	97	59	75
		Low			$< 35\%$	227	63	135
All Environments			All Categories			1775	963	1184

[d]Such an ordering of the three SMSA categories in terms of their population density is supported by data from the 1960 Census of Population. See Bureau of the Census, *County and City Data Book* (Washington, D.C.: Government Printing Office, 1967), for the basic data upon which this conclusion is based.

environments distributed themselves somewhat unevenly among the eight categories (see Table 5–1). Here e_{cr}, e_{ec} and e_{sn} are more evenly disbursed among all twelve cells of the $2 \times 3 \times 2$ classification and again permit a systematic comparison of the independent and joint effects of each dimension.

RESEARCH DESIGN AND EMPIRICAL RESULTS

The specific hypotheses to be tested in this chapter are derived from the general hypothesis first presented in Chapter Three. At that time we stated:

$$S = F(EC),$$

which hypothesized that "the degree of modernity of an educational system (S) varies as a function (F) of the degree of modernity of its sociocultural environment (E), given certain constraints (C)."[e]

The constraints imposed in this chapter are that the educational system will be considered only at the level of the school, and that the sociocultural environment will be considered only at the layers of the neighborhood, community, and region. In using the available school data to test the general hypothesis, the system properties will take on the values of input, throughput, output, and structure, and the dimensions of the sociocultural environment the values of cultural, ecological, and structural. However, the dimensions and layers of the environment will be tested only as to culture of the region (e_{cr}), the ecology of the community (e_{ec}), and the structure of the neighborhood (e_{sn}).

Such a specification of the general hypothesis produces the following subsidiary hypotheses, each of which will be tested using data for 1965:

Hypothesis 6.1: $s_{is} = f_{ic}(e_{cr}) + f_{ie}(e_{ec}) + f_{is}(e_{sn})$.
The degree of modernity of the input (i) of a school (s) varies as a direct function of the degree of modernity of the culture (c) of its regional (r) environment, the ecology (e) of its community (c) environment, and the structure (s) of its neighborhood (n) environment.

Hypothesis 6.2: $s_{ts} = f_{tc}(e_{cr}) + f_{te}(e_{ec}) + f_{ts}(e_{sn})$.
The degree of modernity of the throughput (t) of a school (s) varies as a direct function of the degree of modernity of the culture (c) of its regional (r) environment, the ecology (e) of its community (c) environment, and the structure (s) of its neighborhood (n) environment.

---

[e]The reader unfamiliar with the symbolic notation presented in this chapter is referred to the final section of Chapter Three.

Hypothesis 6.3: $s_{os} = f_{oc}(e_{cr}) + f_{oe}(e_{ec}) + f_{os}(e_{sn})$.

The degree of modernity of the output (o) of a school (s) varies as a direct function of the degree of modernity of the culture (c) of its regional (r) environment, the ecology (e) of its community (c) environment, and the structure (s) of its neighborhood (n) environment.

Hypothesis 6.4: $s_{ss} = f_{sc}(e_{cr}) + f_{se}(e_{ec}) + f_{ss}(e_{sn})$.

The degree of modernity of the structure (s) of a school (s) varies as a direct function of the degree of modernity of the culture (c) of its regional (r) environment, the ecology (e) of its community (c) environment, and the structure (s) of its neighborhood (n) environment.

To assess the statistical significance of the results we applied the same type of statistical model to these data that was used in Chapter Five. In developing our dummy variable form of multiple regression analysis we coded the cultural and structural dimensions of modernity just as we did in Chapter Five (high modern = 1, and low modern = 0). However, in the case of the trichotomous ecological dimension a slight modification from what was introduced in coding e_{ec} in Chapter Five was necessary, and so *two* dummy variables were created. The first (e_{ec_h}) considered high modern to be "1" and the other two categories to be "0." The second (e_{ec_m}) considered moderate modern to be "1" and the other two categories to be "0." Each of these two dummy variables must be introduced into the regression equation to fully tap e_{ec}.[f]

We have claimed further support for our hypothesis if any of the three dimensions bears a statistically significant relationship with an indicator of school input, throughput, output, or structure, after controlling for the other two.

We noted in Chapter Five that although our formal model does not provide for the existence of interaction effects among the dimensions and layers of modernity, such effects have been noted in past research. Because on occasion we found the first-order interactions to be statistically significant at the level of the school district (Chapter Five), we have created all five possible first-order interaction terms for our regression equations at the level of the school, but we have ignored all second-order interactions on the grounds that in our school district analyses they seldom proved to be statistically

---

[f]This represents the standard procedure for "dummying up" an ordered trichotomous variable. It involves a binary conversion of all the information available within the three categories in such a way as to preserve the ordinal properties and information of the original variable. If e_{ec} has the ordered effect predicted by the general hypothesis e_{ec_h} minus e_{ec_m} will be observed to be greater than zero. See Appendix C for further consideration of data sources and coding.

significant. Again, all effects were tested for statistical significance at the .05 level, with the tests of the main effects being one-tailed and those of the interactions being two-tailed.

School Input

In order to conduct a test of Hypothesis 6.1 we have relied upon four measures of the organizational input of schools. However, it is important to note that we do not necessarily expect the environment to affect the input of all types of schools uniformly. With respect to some indices of organizational input, different levels of school can be expected to be so highly specialized that the environment will have little effect. (For example, almost all senior high schools have a gymnasium, regardless of environment: on the other hand, far fewer elementary schools are likely to have a gymnasium, and so we would expect that the environment would be an important variable.)

Our first measure of school input is identical to one used and discussed in Chapters Four and Five—the percent of teachers holding a master's degree. This measure of the specialization of *personnel* input will be considered separately for elementary, junior high, and senior high schools. Three additional measures of the organizational input of schools tap the specialization of *material* input. They are: 1) the presence of a centralized library, 2) the availability of typing courses, and 3) the presence of a shop with power tools. Although from one perspective, these variables could be considered structural (that is organizational attributes associated with differentiation), they also indirectly indicate specialization. Thus, a library requires various facilities, equipment, and knowledge unique to itself; clerical courses require special curricula, technical equipment, and so on; and a shop requires specialized tools, materials, and so on.

Our measure of the degree to which a school is specialized in terms of its library emphasis (which is analyzed only at the elementary level) was taken from the elementary principal's report regarding the existence of a centralized library in the school. To measure the specialized material input associated with typing and a shop with power tools the analysis was restricted to junior high schools. We constructed a typing emphasis score based upon the junior high principal's answer to a question regarding the provision for typing instruction in the school. A school that offered no typing received a score of "0." If the school offered typing but had no room especially for that purpose, the school received a score of "1." Finally, a school that both offered typing and had at least one room especially for that purpose received a score of "2." Our third indicator of school material input taps the organization's emphasis on the teaching of mechanical skills, as reflected in a shop with power tools. Because 97 percent of the senior high schools have such a facil-

TABLE 6–2   Mean Educational Input in 1965, by Degree of Modernity of School Environment

Modernity of Environment[a]			Measure of Educational Input					
			Percent of Teachers with a Master's Degree (CTMD)			% Elementary Schools with Centralized Library (CCSL)	Junior High Typing Emphasis (CRTI)	% Junior Highs Having Shop with Power Tools (CSPT)
Cultural (e_{cr})	Ecological (e_{ec})	Structural (e_{sn})	Elementary	Junior High	Senior High			
High	High	High	18.6	35.9	52.6	87.0	1.40	99.1
		Low	19.6	31.5	43.3	73.5	1.50	96.9
	Moderate	High	19.4	31.8	47.9	76.4	1.02	98.6
		Low	12.5	26.3	38.1	66.2	0.86	99.0
	Low	High	13.7	24.2	37.4	72.0	1.02	93.0
		Low	10.9	25.5	32.4	59.1	0.79	86.8
Low	High	High	21.8	30.6	44.7	83.3	1.15	97.8
		Low	17.0	26.0	34.8	83.9	1.04	91.7
	Moderate	High	16.8	24.1	40.9	80.4	0.73	90.5
		Low	11.0	24.8	33.6	75.8	0.63	68.1
	Low	High	16.5	28.4	34.9	67.4	0.83	96.5
		Low	13.2	25.5	29.8	60.4	0.63	63.5
All Environments			16.1	29.0	40.6	72.8	1.01	92.7

[a]See Table 6–1 for operational definition of modernity of environment.

ity and 98 percent of the elementary schools do not, we confined our analysis to the 963 junior high schools, 93 percent of which have a shop with power tools.

Table 6–2 presents mean input scores for those schools within each of the 12 cells of the $e_{cr} \times e_{ec} \times e_{sn}$ classification. There it can be noted that in general the more modern the culture of the region (e_{cr}), the ecology of the community (e_{ec}), or the structure of the neighborhood (e_{sn}), the more modern the inputs of the school. Consider, for example, the percent of senior high school teachers with a master's degree (Table 6–2, sixth column). For all six e_{sn} comparisons, holding constant both e_{cr} and e_{ec}, the average senior high school in the more modern environment contains a higher percentage of teachers with a master's degree than does its counterpart in the less modern environment (compare 52.6 to 43.3, 47.9 to 38.1, 37.4 to 32.4, 44.7 to 34.8, 40.9 to 33.6, and 34.9 to 29.8). Similarly for all four e_{ec} comparisons, holding constant both e_{cr} and e_{sn}, the average senior high school in the high modern environment has a greater percentage of teachers with a master's degree than does its counterpart in the moderately modern environment, which in turn has more than does its counterpart in the low moderate environment (compare 52.6 to 47.9 to 37.4, 43.3 to 38.1 to 32.4, 44.7 to 40.9 to 34.9, and 34.8 to 33.6 to 29.8). In addition, for all six e_{cr} comparisons, holding constant both e_{ec} and e_{sn}, the average senior high school in the more modern environment contains a higher percentage of teachers with a master's degree than does its counterpart in the less modern environment (compare 52.6 to 44.7, 43.3 to 34.8, 47.9 to 40.9, 38.1 to 33.6, 37.4 to 34.9, and 32.4 to 29.8).

Although in general the same pattern holds at the junior high and elementary levels, it is not as consistent. At the junior high level in four of the six comparisons on the cultural dimension, the more modern environment had a higher percentage of teachers with master's degrees. On two of four ecological comparisons and four of six structural comparisons the expected results were obtained. At the elementary level, whereas three of four ecological comparisons and five of six structural comparisons were as expected, only three of the six cultural comparisons were in the anticipated direction. Overall, however, 37 out of 48 comparisons across the three levels of school were as expected.

In general the same consistent pattern can be observed with respect to each of the three additional measures of school input. In the case of the existence of a centralized library within elementary schools, five of the six structural comparisons and all four ecological comparisons are as predicted. In the case of the junior high school typing emphasis score, five of the six structural comparisons, all six cultural comparisons, and three of the four ecological comparisons are as predicted. Finally, in the case of the existence of a shop with power tools in junior high schools, five of the six structural comparisons, two of the four ecological comparisons, and five of the six cultural comparisons were as predicted by Hypothesis 6.1.

In order to summarize statistically this very consistent pattern across the four measures of school input, the dummy variable regression analysis introduced earlier was carried out. These results are also quite consistent and support Hypothesis 6.1 (Table 6–3). For all six tests of the hypothesis the coefficients of multiple correlation (R) are statistically significant. In addition both e_{cr} and e_{sn} are statistically significant for 5 of the 6 tests (Table 6–3). Because of its trichotomous nature e_{ec} produced 12 tests, 9 of which were statistically significant. Each of the interaction effects was statistically significant in at least one test, but only one interaction effect $(e_{cr} \times e_{ec_m})$ was significant in as many as three tests, suggesting that in general the main effects of these measures of school environments are much more important in predicting variation in school input than are the interaction effects.

TABLE 6–3   *Unstandardized Eighth-order Regression Coefficients for the Relationship of Modernity of School Environment and Measures of Educational Input in 1965, by School Level*

	Measure of Educational Input					
School Environment Effect[a]	Percent of Teachers with a Master's Degree (CTMD)			% Elementary Schools with Centralized Library (CCSL)	Junior High Typing Emphasis (CRTI)	% Junior Highs Having Shop with Power Tools (CSPT)
	Elementary	Junior High	Senior High			
Main						
Cultural (e_{cr})	1.1	5.3*	7.0*	−5.3*	.31*	11.0*
Ecological (e_{ecm})	1.3	1.0	6.5*	10.0*	−.01	4.5*
Ecological (e_{ech})	5.7*	5.3*	10.3*	17.2*	.45*	11.8*
Structural (e_{sn})	4.0*	3.9*	9.1*	7.1*	.06	8.3*
Interaction						
$e_{cr} \times e_{ecm}$	−2.5*	−3.8*	−1.6	4.5	−.05	−4.7*
$e_{cr} \times e_{ech}$	−1.3	−3.9*	−2.7	2.8	−.08	3.1
$e_{cr} \times e_{sn}$	0.8	−0.7	−0.4	−4.2	.02	8.9*
$e_{ecm} \times e_{sn}$	−2.0	−1.1	−1.8	1.7	.03	5.1*
$e_{ech} \times e_{sn}$	0.8	−1.5	−2.0	1.4	.12	6.8*
Intercept	3.1	26.6	29.9	60.7	.62	65.4
Multiple R	.20*	.20*	.33*	.19*	.30*	.39*

[a]See Table 6–1 for complete operational definition of school environment effects.
*p< .05.

School Throughput

In Chapter Three, organizational throughput was defined as the "raw materials" an organization receives from its environment for transformation into production output. In the case of the school, we noted that throughput may include pupil knowledge, skills, and orientations at the time of entry into the organization and until the pupil transfers, drops out, or graduates. Ideally, in order to tap school throughput, one would like to measure the knowledge, skills, and orientations of individual pupils at the time they enter the school. However, with the data available to us this was not possible, and we were forced to rely on the principal's estimate of these characteristics of all pupils enrolled in the schools under study. As one measure, we have chosen the percent of students who are one year or more behind grade level in reading, for in contemporary American society, students who do not know how to read well in English cannot easily achieve high-level technical knowledge. As a second measure we have chosen the average I.Q. score of the school, for such a score represents the competence of the student body in handling the types of complex intellectual tasks required by the larger society. As our third measure we have chosen the proportion of an age group that has been held back. Such a measure no doubt taps the acquisition of technical knowledge and skill, as well as "immature" social performance.

Table 6–4 presents means on the three measures of school throughput, for elementary, junior high, and senior high schools. Particularly noteworthy is the fact that although the effects of the culture of the region (e_{cr}) and the structure of the neighborhood (e_{sn}) are basically as predicted by Hypothesis 6.2, that of the ecology of the community (e_{ec}) is not. Whereas the general hypothesis predicts that the more modern the ecological dimension of the school environment, the more modern the school throughputs, Table 6–4 reveals that throughputs in schools in environments coded as "high modern" on the ecological dimension consistently are less modern than those in both "moderate modern" and "low modern" environments.

Our formal statistical summary of environmental effects on school throughput is presented in Table 6–5. For each of the 9 tests of Hypothesis 6.2 (three measures of throughput by three levels of school) the coefficient of multiple correlation (R) is statistically significant, with the average coefficient being higher for the junior high school than for either the elementary school or the senior high school (Table 6–5). For all 9 tests the effect of the structural dimension of the neighborhood environment (e_{sn}) is statistically significant, and in 5 tests the effect of the cultural dimension of the regional environment (e_{cr}) is also. However, only one of the 18 tests of the ecological dimension of the community environment (e_{ec}) of schools yields a statistically significant coefficient.

What is particularly noteworthy regarding this formal test of Hypothesis 6.2 is the rather general appearance (in five of the six tests) of a statistically significant interaction between the ecological dimension of community environment and the structural dimension of neighborhood environment where the measure of the ecological dimension focused on the central city ($e_{ec_h} \times e_{sn}$). What this significant interaction effect suggests is that the relationship between the community and neighborhood environments of schools and their throughputs is a conditional one. If the structural dimension of the neighborhood is high modern and the ecological dimension of the community is also high modern, the throughputs are most likely to be highly modern. But if, as in the urban ghetto, the structural dimension of the neighborhood is low modern while the ecological dimension of the community is high modern, the throughput is not likely to be highly modern. Such an interaction effect was not predicted by our general model.

To begin to understand this anomaly one must recognize that the operational measure of the modernity of the ecological dimension of school environments at the layer of the community that was used in this analysis (e_{ec}) dis-

TABLE 6-4 Mean Educational Throughput in 1965, by Degree of Modernity of School Environment and School Level

Modernity of Environment[a]			Measure of Educational Throughput								
			Mean IQ of Pupils (CPIQ)			% of Pupils 1+ Years Behind in Reading (CPBR)			% of Pupils 1+ Years Age Grade Retarded (CPBG)		
Cultural (e_{cr})	Ecological (e_{ec})	Structural (e_{sn})	Elementary	Junior High	Senior High	Elementary	Junior High	Senior High	Elementary	Junior High	Senior High
High	High	High	106.3	105.3	103.2	12.5	18.0	19.1	6.0	7.0	7.9
		Low	95.7	93.9	97.3	33.8	44.0	32.5	17.2	20.4	16.1
	Moderate	High	108.8	109.1	106.7	11.2	15.3	14.8	6.3	6.2	6.4
		Low	101.6	102.0	101.1	19.4	25.2	22.4	10.5	10.3	8.5
	Low	High	105.0	105.1	105.3	13.4	18.9	16.9	7.9	8.4	6.3
		Low	102.7	101.2	101.7	19.3	23.3	18.3	12.4	15.1	8.5
Low	High	High	104.3	105.9	103.4	16.3	18.8	19.4	9.5	9.3	8.5
		Low	93.1	94.9	94.3	33.2	41.7	38.7	20.1	20.5	25.3
	Moderate	High	107.2	107.2	103.7	11.7	16.5	16.9	7.0	7.8	7.2
		Low	96.5	100.1	102.2	23.6	26.1	24.4	14.6	11.5	10.4
	Low	High	105.9	106.1	103.7	14.1	16.9	19.9	7.8	7.0	7.0
		Low	99.9	99.3	99.9	21.6	22.4	27.4	13.2	12.0	10.2
All Environments			102.6	103.6	102.6	19.1	22.9	21.2	10.9	10.4	9.1

[a]See Table 6–1 for operational definition of modernity of environment.

tinguishes between central cities of SMSAs (high modern), rings of SMSAs (moderate modern), and non-SMSA areas (low modern) on the basis of their population density. Although there is no question that, on the average, the population is more concentrated in the central city than in the ring, our theoretical interest was in population concentration as a proxy variable for the pattern of social relationships that, as we noted in Chapter Two, traditionally have been associated with differences in population density.

Such a strict representation of the ecological dimension of the modernity of communities ignores several factors including the "ruralization" of the city[g] and the residential pattern of large numbers of white-collar workers in metropolitan areas. Thus, the recent and rapid migration to the central city of persons born and raised in areas of low population concentration has brought to the schools of the ghetto areas of many central cities a type of throughput more like that predicted for rural areas than for urban ones. This "migration effect" clearly points up one predictive limitation of a static model such as ours. Since it lacks a longitudinal component, our model could not take into account the fact that the modernity of the environment of the contemporary ghetto school is likely to be more influenced by where the residents of the ghetto previously lived than by where they live now.

In addition, our representation of the degree of modernity of schools and their environments does not take into account a "commuter effect." It draws heavily upon measures of the environment *by night* rather than *by day*. Although in many environments demographic measures by night and by day would lead to identical results, in the case of the central city they do not. Because many white-collar persons who work in the central city by day live elsewhere (generally in the ring), the throughput and output of schools in central cities is probably much less modern (and that of the ring much more modern) than would be observed if all white-collar persons who worked in the central city also lived there and sent their children to the public schools. Additional factors of a more cultural or sociopsychological nature are probably operative as well and together with the migration and commuter effects produce the "ghetto effect" noted in Table 6–5. However, aside from this important exception, which will be discussed further in Chapter Seven, the results presented above consistently support Hypothesis 6.2.

School Output

In open-systems terminology, production output is the product being exported by the system to its environment. Output is the final state of through-

---

[g]For a more extended discussion of this concept, see Norton Ginsburg, "The City and Modernization," in *Modernization: The Dynamics of Growth,* ed. Myron Weiner (New York: Basic Books, Inc. 1966), pp. 122–37.

TABLE 6-5 Unstandardized Eighth-order Regression Coefficients for the Relationship of Modernity of School Environment and Three Measures of Educational Throughput in 1965, by School Level

	Measure of Educational Throughput								
School Environment Effect[a]	Mean IQ of Pupils (CPIQ)			% of Pupils 1+ Years Behind in Reading (CPBR)			% of Pupils 1+ Years Age Grade Retarded (CPBG)		
	Elementary	Junior High	Senior High	Elementary	Junior High	Senior High	Elementary	Junior High	Senior High
Main									
Cultural (e_{cr})	2.8*	0.6	1.2	-1.8*	-0.1	-2.7*	-2.7*	-1.2	-3.0*
Ecological (e_{ecm})	0.2	1.8*	0.7	-0.7	0.3	-0.9	-0.7	-1.6	0.2
Ecological (e_{ech})	-3.5	-2.8	-2.9	6.9	10.2	6.6	2.9	3.7	6.3
Structural (e_{sn})	10.0*	9.3*	5.4*	-14.6*	-17.2*	-12.1*	-8.4*	-8.1*	-7.1*
Interaction									
$e_{cr} \times e_{ecm}$	-1.1	-0.8	0.2	0.3	1.3	-1.9	1.0	1.7	0.2
$e_{cr} \times e_{ech}$	-0.5	0.6	0.4	-0.1	0.4	-1.6	1.4	1.7	1.7
$e_{cr} \times e_{sn}$	1.3*	0.3	-0.5	-0.3	0.4	-1.7	-0.7	0.7	-1.4
$e_{ecm} \times e_{sn}$	-2.3*	-0.9	-0.2	1.3	2.3	1.8	0.3	-1.1	0.3
$e_{ech} \times e_{sn}$	-3.5*	-3.0*	-1.3	6.0*	9.9*	5.5*	3.2*	3.3*	4.3*
Intercept	100.0	99.8	100.0	21.5	21.9	27.0	13.3	12.1	10.4
Multiple R	.47*	.51*	.29*	.45*	.54*	.36*	.33*	.39*	.34*

[a]See Table 6-1 for complete operational definiton of school environment effect.

*p < .05.

put, the state at the time it is officially released by the system to its environment. As we have noted in Chapter Three, for the American public school, output occurs at the time the student's relationship with the secondary school is formally terminated. Such termination takes three basic forms: *negative* (dropping out before graduation from the twelfth grade), *neutral* (graduation from the twelfth grade and direct entry into the economic system), and *positive* (graduation from the twelfth grade and direct entry into college). In the analyses that follow we assume that the output of a senior high school meets modern American requirements best, and thus is modern, where negative termination is least and positive termination is greatest.

In this section, consistent with Hypothesis 6.3, we anticipate that the more modern the sociocultural context of American public schools, the more modern their system output. In so doing we will confine ourselves to only the senior high schools and only to negative and positive termination. As an indicator of negative termination we have chosen the proportion of former tenth graders who drop out before graduation. As one indicator of positive termination we have chosen the proportion of twelfth-grade *graduates* who go directly on to a four-year college or university. Finally, as a more comprehensive summary of the system output of American senior high schools, we have computed the proportion of previous tenth-grade pupils who graduate from the twelfth grade and then go directly on to some form of higher education. This last indicator of production output takes into account simultaneously both positive and negative termination.

The empirical results with respect to production output are rather similar to those just reported with respect to throughput. The e_{cr} and e_{sn} effects are as predicted by the hypothesis, but the e_{ec} effects are not. Consider, for example, the comprehensive summary in the form of the percent of former tenth graders in the average senior high school who go on to some form of college. For all six comparisons in terms of the structure of the neighborhood environment (e_{sn}), holding constant both the cultural dimension of the region (e_{cr}) and the ecological dimension of the community (e_{ec}), the schools in the more modern environments are more modern in their production output than are those in the less modern environments (Table 6–6). However, in only one of four comparisons in terms of the ecological dimension of the community (e_{ec}) does the predicted monotonic trend occur, and then only rather weakly (59.6 vs. 57.7 vs. 56.7).

A particularly interesting result observable in Table 6–6 is the consistent finding that the average senior high school in the *less* modern environment in terms of the culture of its region (that is, e_{cr}) consistently produces a larger percentage of graduates who go on to a four-year college than does its counterpart in the more modern environment (compare 42.4 to 41.7, 25.9 to 21.0, 42.9 to 39.7, 27.1 to 24.8, 40.9 to 33.0, and 29.4 to 27.2). Clearly this is contrary to that predicted by Hypothesis 6.3 and, given the consistency

TABLE 6–6   *Mean Educational Output in 1965, by Degree of Modernity of Senior High School Environment*

Modernity of Environment[a]			Measure of Educational Output		
Cultural (e_{cr})	Ecological (e_{ec})	Structural (e_{sn})	% Former Tenth Graders Who Didn't Complete the Twelfth Grade (CPDO)	% Twelfth-Grade Graduates Going to Four-Year College (CPFC)	% Former Tenth Graders Going to Some College (CPSC)
High	High	High	9.2	41.7	62.1
		Low	17.9	21.0	41.6
	Moderate	High	5.1	39.7	64.4
		Low	7.4	24.8	50.6
	Low	High	7.7	33.0	51.6
		Low	7.2	27.2	50.0
Low	High	High	11.2	42.4	59.6
		Low	19.9	25.9	38.5
	Moderate	High	7.0	42.9	57.7
		Low	10.7	27.1	43.2
	Low	High	6.6	40.9	56.7
		Low	10.6	29.4	47.1
All Environments			9.0	33.5	54.3

[a]See Table 6–1 for operational definition of modernity of environment.

of the e_{cr} effect in terms of the two other measures of school output, brings into question our assumption that the percent of twelfth-grade *graduates* going on to a *four-year* college is a reasonable measure of modern school output. In retrospect such a measure seems to ignore students who have dropped out before graduation and who thus do not appear in the denominator. But more importantly it also fails to consider that a measure of only the production of students who go to *four-year* colleges (thus ignoring two-year colleges and vocational schools) may not be sensitive to the full manpower requirements of a modern society.

As in the case of Hypothesis 6.1 and 6.2, the formal statistical test of Hypothesis 6.3 supports the more informal interpretation of the mean school output scores offered above. For all three measures of school output the coefficient of multiple correlation (R) is statistically significant with a value of approximately .40 (Table 6–7). Each of the three measures of the independent effects of the structural dimension of the school's neighborhood envi-

TABLE 6–7   *Unstandardized Eighth-order Regression Coefficients for the Relationship of Modernity of Senior High School Environment and Three Measures of Educational Output in 1965*

School Environment Effects[a]	Measure of Educational Output		
	% Former Tenth Graders Who Didn't Complete the Twelfth Grade (CPDO)	% Twelfth-Grade Graduates Going to Four-Year College (CPFC)	% Former Tenth Graders Going to Some College (CPSC)
Main			
Cultural (e_{cr})	−2.4*	−2.6*	5.2*
Ecological (e_{ec_m})	−0.5	1.1	2.6*
Ecological (e_{ec_h})	6.6	0.1	−0.9
Structural (e_{sn})	−6.2*	17.6*	18.1*
Interaction			
$e_{cr} \times e_{ec_m}$	0.7	−1.0	−4.1*
$e_{cr} \times e_{ec_h}$	0.4	−1.1	−1.9
$e_{cr} \times e_{sn}$	−1.0	0.6	1.6
$e_{ec_m} \times e_{sn}$	0.6	−3.1*	−4.4*
$e_{ec_h} \times e_{sn}$	3.4*	−5.3*	−7.8*
Intercept	10.2	30.0	47.9
Multiple R	0.43*	0.41*	0.43*

[a]See Table 6-1 for operational definition of school environment effects.

ronment (e_{sn}) is significant as predicted, as are two of the three coefficients for the independent effects of the cultural dimension of the school's regional environment (e_{cr}), the one exception being the measure of output, which focuses upon only the percent of graduates who go on to a *four-year* college. However, as in the case of throughput, the independent effects of the ecological dimension of the school's community (e_{ec}) typically is not significant, but the interaction effects of e_{ec_h} and e_{sn} are. Although we have received some support for Hypothesis 6.3 in terms of e_{cr} and e_{sn}, the results with respect to e_{ec} are not as predicted, an issue to which we will return in Chapter Seven.

School Structure

Many characteristics of the structure of schools, if our earlier discussions are correct, could be influenced by the degree of modernity of their sociocultural environments. Given our interests in the institutional role of education in modern society, as well as the limitations imposed by a secondary analysis of the available data, we have selected size and differentiation as the two structural characteristics to be considered at this time.

As noted in Chapter Two, modernity includes, among other things, an emphasis upon specialization and rationality directed toward the most efficient use of available technology. Thus, the emergence of a bureaucratic structure associated with education in modern societies can be at least partially explained as an attempt to meet the specialized manpower requirements of those societies. Though there is good reason to doubt that *unlimited* organizational size contributes to such ends, it is true that large organizational size permits a degree of bureaucratic efficiency not available to smaller organizations. Accordingly, other factors being equal, we would expect that schools in the more modern environments would be larger than schools in the less modern environments. However, although organizational bureaucracy is frequently associated with largeness, it does not necessarily follow that a large school organization is differentiated. Since we have chosen to examine the influence of modernization upon both school size and differentiation, it may be useful to consider briefly the nature of the relationship of these two distinct structural characteristics.

In our general discussion of the differentiation of open sociocultural systems in Chapter Three, we noted the ambiguous relationship of size to differentiation. Whether or not education reflects this relationship in its structural development is also unclear. Given the absence of empirical evidence to the contrary, it seems reasonable to assume that school size is a structural characteristic imperfectly related to differentiation as we have discussed it in Chapter Three. Thus, a small school may incorporate grades K-12, while a large school may include only grades 10–12. Or, a large school may have a curricular program that calls for teachers to be "generalists'" whereas a small school may encourage subject matter specialization. Therefore, although we expect school size to play some part in school differentiation, we would not expect the relationship to be perfect. Size, then, is viewed here as a structural characteristic of the organization distinct from its degree of differentiation.

In order to test our expectations regarding the structural property of size and modernity, we have related the number of full-time faculty members assigned to each school to the modernization environments of e_{cr}, e_{ec}, and e_{sn}. As in the case of school input, throughput, and output we have done this for these environments both singly and in combination. In addition, we have performed some analyses separately for elementary, junior high, and senior high schools.

As noted in Chapter Three the "enhancement of adaptive capacity" of the organization can be expected to result in organizational differentiation, and such differentiation, in turn, would be more likely to occur in the more modern sociocultural environments. Although up to this point in our analysis we have focused on elementary, junior high, and senior high schools, this modal grade structure (often referred to as the 6–3–3 plan) accounts for less than 33 percent of all public schools in the Census Bureau sample.[5] Clearly, there is considerable diversity in the organizational structure of public education in America. We contend that some of the various structural arrangements reflect a greater degree of organizational differentiation, and thus modernization, than do others. In particular, we shall assume (as we did in Chapter Five) that the fewer the grade levels located under a single school administration, the more modern the school.

To test Hypothesis 6.4 in terms of organizational differentiation, we have compared four types of public schools, each of which contains a twelfth grade but which vary in their degree of differentiation. The least differentiated of such schools in America is the school containing grades one through twelve (1–12). Somewhat more differentiated is the junior-senior high school, a school containing grades seven through twelve (7–12). Even more differentiated is the four-year senior high school containing grades nine through twelve (9–12). Most differentiated is the three-year senior high school containing grades ten through twelve (10–12). In presenting the data on degree of organizational differentiation, we have used two modes of analysis. For descriptive purposes we present the cumulative percentage of schools of differing degrees of differentiation, with 1–12 schools being considered "low" and the 10–12 schools "high." For the purpose of formally testing Hypothesis 6.4 in terms of organizational differentiation, the 1–12 schools will arbitrarily be assigned a score of "1." Then, since the 7–12 schools contain only half the grades that 1–12 schools do, they will be assumed to be twice as differentiated and assigned a score of "2." Similarly, the 9–12 schools will be assigned a score of "3" and the 10–12 schools a score of "4."

In Table 6–8 the size of the average elementary, junior high, and senior high school is presented in terms of each of the twelve categories of the sociocultural environments of these schools. Basically, the data are consistent with Hypothesis 6.4, with the predicted results most apparent in the cases of the senior high schools, where all four e_{ec} comparisons as well as all twelve e_{sn} and e_{cr} comparisons favor the more modern environments.

In Table 6–9 similar results are presented for the organizational differentiation variable in the form of cumulative percentages. When both the structure of the neighborhood environment (e_{sn}) and the ecology of the community (e_{ec}) are held constant through cross tabulation, in five of the six possible comparisons between the culture of the regions (e_{cr}) the more modern environment has fewer schools of low differentiation than does the less modern environment (compare 8.9 to 19.0, 9.5 to 32.7, 15.9 to 17.3, 25.4 to 38.1, 27.0 to 23.5, and 51.1 to 63.3). Similarly, when e_{cr} and e_{ec} are held constant, in all six of the possible comparisons in terms of e_{sn} the high modern environment contains fewer schools of low differentiation than does the low modern one. The picture with respect to e_{ec} holding constant e_{cr} and e_{sn} is also fairly consistent, for in three of the four possible comparisons

TABLE 6–8   Mean Educational Structure in 1965, by School Level and Degree of Modernity of School Environment

Modernity of Environment[a]			Measure of Educational Structure		
			Number of Full-Time Teachers (CFTT)		
Cultural (e_{cr})	Ecological (e_{ec})	Structural (e_{sn})	Elementary	Junior High	Senior High
High	High	High	23.6	57.6	105.1
		Low	28.8	64.6	93.7
	Moderate	High	21.6	46.0	77.4
		Low	19.6	38.2	64.2
	Low	High	18.7	40.3	59.1
		Low	16.3	27.2	46.4
Low	High	High	21.5	45.9	78.5
		Low	24.0	48.1	72.1
	Moderate	High	21.7	43.1	73.1
		Low	20.2	35.7	60.9
	Low	High	18.2	31.4	43.4
		Low	15.7	25.8	32.9
All Environments			21.0	44.4	68.6

[a]See Table 6–1 for operational definition of modernity of environment.

the high e_{ec} environment contains fewer schools of low differentiation than does the moderate e_{ec} environment, which in turn contains fewer than does the low e_{ec} environment (Table 6–9).

These rather informal results with respect to organizational size and differentiation have been summarized formally in Table 6–10, and offer consistent support for Hypothesis 6.4. In all four instances (organizational size in the case of elementary, junior high, and senior high schools, and organizational differentiation) the coefficient of multiple correlation (R) is statistically significant. In addition the effect of the culture of the regional environment (e_{cr}) and of the ecology of the community (e_{ec}) are significant in all cases, and in two of the four possible instances that of the structure of the neighborhood (e_{sn}) is significant as well (Table 6–10). Clearly, these measures of organizational structure offer strong support for Hypothesis 6.4.

SUMMARY

In this chapter we have examined the properties of schools as social

TABLE 6–9   Cumulative Percentage Distribution of One Measure of Educational Structure, by Degrees of Modernity of School Environment

Modernity of Environment[a]			Number of Schools	Measure of Educational Structure			
				Degree of Organizational Differentiation (CDOD)			
Cultural (e_{cr})	Ecological (e_{ec})	Structural (e_{sn})		1 (Grades 1–12)	2 (Grades 7–12)	3 (Grades 9–12)	4 (Grades 10–12)
High	High	High	123	1.6%	8.9%	53.7%	100.0%
		Low	116	1.7	9.5	50.9	100.0
	Mod-erate	High	295	2.7	15.9	53.2	100.0
		Low	205	12.2	25.4	64.4	100.0
	Low	High	85	8.2	27.0	55.3	100.0
		Low	137	31.4	51.1	80.3	100.0
Low	High	High	63	7.9	19.0	39.7	100.0
		Low	49	10.2	32.7	59.2	100.0
	Mod-erate	High	110	4.5	17.3	63.6	100.0
		Low	84	11.9	38.1	73.8	100.0
	Low	High	98	15.3	23.5	66.3	100.0
		Low	368	44.0	63.3	94.0	100.0
All Environments			1733	16.7%	30.7%	67.4%	100.0%

[a]See Table 6–1 for operational definition of modernity of environment.

systems in terms of the degree of modernity of the cultural dimension of their regional (e_{cr}), the ecological dimension of their community (e_{ec}), and the structural dimension of their neighborhood (e_{sn}). We have done this in terms of input, throughput, output, and structure. In general, the data available to us from a national sample of 3922 elementary, junior high, and senior high schools support our general hypothesis in the case of organizational input and structure. Our case with respect to throughput and output is less clear, with e_{cr} and e_{sn} generally being significantly related to these organizational properties but not e_{ec}. We have offered the tentative interpretation that the anomaly with respect to e_{ec} is due to the fact that our measurement of the relative degree of modernity of the central city may be invalidated by its failure to consider several aspects of the pattern of central city life including immigration from rural areas and commuting patterns. Certainly in the case of the urban ghetto (the $e_{ech} \times e_{sn}$ interaction terms in our regression analyses) there is considerable reason to suspect the

TABLE 6–10   *Unstandardized Eighth-order Regression Coefficients for the Relationship of Modernity of School Environment and Two Measures of Educational Structure in 1965*

School Environment Effects	Measure of Educational Structure			
	Organizational Size[b] (CFTT)			Degree of Differentiation[c] (CDOD)
	Elemen- tary	Junior High	Senior High	
Main				
Cultural (e_{cr})	1.6*	8.4*	13.9*	.20*
Ecological (e_{ec_m})	3.5*	9.4*	23.5*	.44*
Ecological (e_{ec_h})	7.3*	22.6*	41.8*	.67*
Structural (e_{sn})	−1.1	1.0	10.9*	.25*
Interaction				
$e_{cr} \times e_{ec_m}$	0.3	1.4	5.5*	.04
$e_{cr} \times e_{ec_h}$	−1.5*	−4.3*	−4.8*	.03
$e_{cr} \times e_{sn}$	0.3	−0.3	−1.2	.10*
$e_{ec_m} \times e_{sn}$	0.2	0.7	−0.4	.24*
$e_{ec_h} \times e_{sn}$	3.3*	7.3*	1.1	.36*
Intercept	15.7	24.3	32.9	1.99
Multiple R	.35*	.51*	.52*	.49*

[a]See Table 6–1 for operational definition of school environment effects.
[b]Size measured by the number of full-time teachers.
[c]Degree of organizational differentiation coded as follows: 1 = (1–12 schools), 2 = (7–12 schools), 3 = (9–12 schools), 4 = (10–12 schools).
*p < .05

validity of our model, and we will offer a more extended consideration of this in the next chapter.

REFERENCES

[1]D. Richard Wynn, *Organization of Public Schools* (Washington, D.C.: The Center for Applied Research in Education, Inc., 1964).

[2]Gerald Kahn and Warren A. Hughes, *Statistics of Local Public School Systems, 1967* (Washington, D.C.: Government Printing Office, 1969), Table A.

[3]*Ibid.*, Table 1.

[4]*Ibid.* See also Robert E. Herriott and Benjamin J. Hodgkins, *Sociocultural Context and the American School,* Final Report OEG-2–6–062972-2095; ED 028–502 (Washington, D.C.: U. S. Department of Health, Education and Welfare, January 1969), Table 9–10.

[5]See Herriott and Hodgkins, *Sociocultural Context and the American School,* Table 9–10.

seven

Summary

and

Conclusions

Throughout this book we have viewed American public education as an open sociocultural system in interaction with a sociocultural environment. In Chapter One, the institutional role of education in contemporary American society was identified as primarily that of socializing American youth in the skills and orientations necessary for the maintenance and development of a complex, technologically based social order. From this perspective, we traced the historical evolution of the formal structure of American education. To gain insight into the dynamics of this development, we considered the dominant values of American society during its period of development, particularly as they related to an emphasis upon the individual. We suggested that an intrinsic characteristic of the form taken by American education was a dialectical process wherein changes wrought in the educational system at different times varied as a function of the relative importance given to meeting either individual or societal needs. This varying emphasis, in turn, was related to the impact of industrialization upon American education, specifically as it has lead to the rationalization of the educational system and to the institutionalization of individual needs within it.

Although sociocultural environments can be viewed from many perspectives, we argued in Chapter Two that a particularly useful approach was to focus upon their degree of modernity, as indicated by the availability of advanced technology and the restructuring of social life in order to fully exploit that technology. Three *dimensions* of environments were distinguished: the cultural, or value orientations stressing man's mastery over nature, a futuristic time perspective, an emphasis upon action, and an emphasis upon the importance of the individual; the ecological, manifested as an increasing concentration and heterogeneity of population; and the structural, manifested as environmental complexity, interdependence, and functional specialization. In addition to these three dimensions, analytic *layers* of sociocultural environments were identified, consisting of the neighborhood, the community, the state, the region, the society, and the civilization. We then reviewed the available literature regarding how educational phenomena vary as a function of the degree of modernity of sociocultural environments with particular attention to the region, community, and neighborhood. In the latter part of Chapter Two we reported extensive informal evidence that such a relationship exists.

After making clear a series of assumptions regarding our view of "social reality," we presented in Chapter Three an open systems perspective and applied it to educational systems as a special type of sociocultural system. An open sociocultural system was defined as a set of lawfully related complex social relationships evidencing a high degree of stability in order to affect societally determined ends. Although we considered many *properties* of open sociocultural systems, four were singled out for particular attention: input, the material, personnel, and information imported by the system; throughput, the material, personnel, and information acted upon by the system; output, the material, personnel, and information exported by the system; and structural differentiation, the adaptive mechanism of systems manifested as increasing specialization. In addition, we identified a series of analytic *levels* for educational systems: the school, the school district, the state educational system, the regional educational system, the national educational system, and the civilization education system.

We then offered the general hypothesis that *the degree of modernity of an educational system varies as a function of the degree of modernity of its sociocultural environment.* From this general hypothesis, specific hypotheses were developed and tested empirically. In the sections that follow we summarize these empirical findings and consider their implications for both social theory and educational practice.

SUMMARY OF EMPIRICAL FINDINGS

At the level of *national educational systems,* the hypothesis was offered and tested in Chapter Four that the degree of modernity of the input, output, and structure of the American educational system varies over time as a direct function of the degree of general modernity of its societal environment. The time points chosen were 1930, 1940, 1950, 1960, and 1970. The degree of general modernity of American society was shown to rise consistently during this 40-year period. Associated with this consistent increase in societal modernity was a consistent increase in the degree of modernity of the inputs, outputs, and structure of the American educational system (Table 7–1, Section A).

At the level of *regional educational systems* the hypothesis was also offered and tested in Chapter Four that the degree of modernity of the input, output, and structure of a regional educational system varies as a direct

TABLE 7–1   Summary of Formal Tests Supportive of System-Environment Hypotheses, by System Levels and Properties and Environmental Layers and Dimensions

System Level and Property	Environmental Layer and Dimension							All Layers and Dimensions
	General Modernity[a]			Dimension of Modernity[b]				
				Cultural	Ecological	Structural		
	(e_{go})	(e_{gr})	(e_{ga})	(e_{cr})	(e_{ec})	(e_{sc})	(e_{sn})	
A. *Nation*								
1. Input	3/3[c]	—	—	—	—	—	—	3/3[c]
2. Output	4/4	—	—	—	—	—	—	4/4
3. Structure	3/3	—	—	—	—	—	—	3/3
B. *Region*								
1. Input	—	13/13	—	—	—	—	—	13/13
2. Output	—	18/18	—	—	—	—	—	18/18
3. Structure	—	15/15	—	—	—	—	—	15/15
C. *State*								
1. Input	—	—	13/13	—	—	—	—	13/13
2. Output	—	—	17/18	—	—	—	—	17/18
3. Structure	—	—	15/15	—	—	—	—	15/15
D. *School district*								
1. Input	—	—	—	4/4	3/4	4/4	—	11/12
2. Output	—	—	—	1/1	1/1	1/1	—	3/3
3. Structure	—	—	—	6/6	5/6	6/6	—	17/18
E. *School*								
1. Input	—	—	—	5/6	9/12	—	5/6	19/24
2. Throughput	—	—	—	5/9	1/12	—	9/9	14/30
3. Output	—	—	—	2/3	1/6	—	3/3	6/12
4. Structure	—	—	—	4/4	8/8	—	2/4	14/16
F. *All levels*								
1. Input	3/3	13/13	13/13	9/10	12/16	4/4	5/6	59/65
2. Throughput	—	—	—	5/9	1/12	—	9/9	15/30
3. Output	4/4	18/18	17/18	3/4	2/7	1/1	3/3	48/55
4. Structure	3/3	15/15	15/15	10/10	13/14	6/6	2/4	64/67
G. *All levels and properties*	10/10[c]	46/46	45/46	27/33	28/49	11/11	19/22	186/217[c]

[a]For the definition of all symbols see Chapter Four, section entitled "Research Design."

[b]For the definition of all symbols see Chapter Three, section entitled "A Formal Model."

[c]For all entries in this table the denominator represents the number of coefficients tested and the numerator the number of coefficients supportive of the hypothesis.

function of the degree of general modernity of its regional sociocultural environment. Five sociocultural regions of varying degrees of modernity were defined operationally (Northeast, Far West, Great Lakes, Plains, and Southeast) and the test of the hypothesis was repeated at five time points— 1930, 1940, 1950, 1960, and 1970. In general at all time points, the greater the regional modernity, the greater the modernity of the inputs, outputs, and structure of the regional educational system (Table 7–1, Section B).

At the level of *state educational systems* the hypothesis was also offered and tested in Chapter Four that the degree of modernity of the input, output, and structure of a state educational system varies as a direct function of the degree of general modernity of the state. Forty-eight states of varying degrees of modernity were identified, and the test of the hypothesis was repeated for each of five years—1930, 1940, 1950, 1960, and 1970. As in the case of the regional analysis, in general at all time points the greater the state modernity the greater the modernity of the inputs, outputs, and structure of the state educational system (Table 7–1, Section C).

At the level of *school districts* as educational systems an attempt was made to operationalize separately the three dimensions of modernity explained in Chapter Two. In Chapter Five we offered and tested the hypothesis that the modernity of the input, output, and structure of a school district varies as a direct function of the modernity of the culture of its regional environment, the ecology of its community environment, and the structure of its community environment. Using data from a 1967 national sample of 1066 school districts, in general we observed that the greater the modernity of the environment, the greater the modernity of the inputs, outputs, and structure of the school district as an educational system (Table 7–1, Section D).

At the level of *schools* we again represented separately the three dimensions of modernity. The hypothesis was offered and tested in Chapter Six that the modernity of the input, throughput, output, and structure of a school varies as a direct function of the modernity of the culture of its regional environment, the ecology of its community environment, and the structure of its neighborhood environment. Using data from a 1965 national sample of 3922 schools, in general we observed that the greater the modernity of the environment of schools, the greater the modernity of their inputs and structure (Table 7–1, Section E, Rows 1 and 4). However, in the case of throughputs and outputs, although the hypothesis was supported for the cultural (e_{cr}) and structural (e_{sn}) dimensions of modernity, it was generally not supported in the case of the ecological (e_{ec}) (Table 7–1, Section E, Rows 2 and 3). In interpreting this anomaly we paid particular attention to a "ghetto effect," which suppresses throughput and output in schools located within blue-collar neighborhoods of central cities. Although such an effect was not predicted by our general model, its implications are important, both for the further development of the model and for the analysis of educational systems—a point we will consider in greater detail in the next section.

In attempting to interpret and draw conclusions and implications from the findings just summarized, one should be aware of the many limitations of theory, data, and method that we have mentioned previously and which are discussed in greater detail in Appendix B. In spite of these limitations, our model and empirical analysis represent important advances in the sociological study of education and can provide considerable insight into the historical development and current state of the American educational system. Before we turn to these more general conclusions, several specific patterns in the input, throughput, output, and structure of the educational system at the national, regional, state, school district, and school levels merit further comment.

INTERPRETATIONS

Viewed from a macroscopic perspective, the relationship of the modernity of environment to the various properties of American schooling are clearly evident in the analyses in Chapters Four, Five, and Six. At the national level, it is apparent that American schooling has witnessed tremendous growth in inputs and outputs, particularly in the last two decades. Concomitant with that growth has been an increase in the size of the average school (22.2 teachers in 1970 vs. 3.4 teachers in 1930), and the structural complexity of the total system. These results are expected, of course, according to the pattern of development discussed in Chapter One. At the same time, however, they are strongly suggestive of the increasingly important role assumed by education in modern society, as well as of the interdependence of modern schooling and its environment. Logically, the tremendous increase in inputs over the 40-year period speaks both to the increasing value placed upon formal education by the society and to the growing affluence of the society as a whole. However, the relative importance of these two factors, as well as the degree to which such growth was stimulated by previous outputs of the system, cannot be verified systematically without data beyond those currently available to social scientists.

According to the framework set forth in Chapter Three, however, we would reason that the underlying explanation for the associations we have documented is to be found in the *gesellschaft*-like social characteristics of a modern society, wherein the technical services upon which the society rests led to a "rationalized" educational experience consistent with the required skills and orientations necessary to sustain it. In other words, the development of a rational educational system directed toward sustaining technical progress would logically be expected due to the dominant sociocultural thrust—an emphasis upon material mastery of the society's physical environment, expressed in higher standards of material well-being.

Of course, the growth of schooling over the last 40 years may be attributed primarily to the affluence of American society. Such an explanation undoubtedly contains a measure of truth. At the same time, however, an economic interpretation presupposes a causal nexus between national wealth and education more apparent than real. Thus, for example, although the United States is the most affluent nation on earth, its rate of literacy is roughly matched by those of nations far less wealthy, although these countries spend proportionately no more and sometimes less of their national income on education.[1] The absence of comparable data precludes similar comparisons on structural developments, although we suspect a similarity exists. The point is, that although wealth is important, it alone cannot explain the growth of American education. More important are the ecological, cultural, and structural dynamics associated with modernization that we described in Chapter Two.

Input

If we focus solely on the measures of input examined in the present study, it might seem legitimate to argue that affluence accounts for regional, state, or community disparities in educational input. However, although the affluence of the environment is important, one may argue that affluence is as much a product of modernity as is the growth of formal education. No doubt they are interrelated. However, some of the results reported in our analysis of community and school district relationships clearly reveal • that the wealthier communities in the less modern regions fall well below the poorer communities in the more modern regions on such economic variables as per-pupil expenditure ($405 vs. $505) and per school administrative expenditure ($8,100 vs. $9,200), while barely exceeding them in average instructional salary ($6,799 vs. $6,513) (Table 5–2). Although "cost of living" differences may explain a portion of these regional disparities, they would fail to account for all. Thus, economic reasoning provides only a limited insight into the variation in inputs reported in Chapter Five.

More significant, if one is willing to go beyond the dollar signs, is the pattern of input development over time within different environments, as well as the pattern of differences in input among environments. Thus, between 1930 and 1970, expenditure input per pupil has increased almost threefold nationally (Table 4–3), whereas in the least modern region during the same period such input has increased over fivefold. The same pattern of reduction in differences in input is apparent in average instructional salary and in the percent of teachers with a master's degree. Accordingly, whereas social inputs (both qualitatively and quantitatively) appear to have increased tremendously between 1930 and 1970, the magnitude of regional variation in such inputs has been reduced, suggesting that while regional variations in input are significant, the overall trend is toward greater national uniformity of input across regions.

In part, such convergence may be attributed to changing ecological and structural patterns in the less modern regions. Additionally, however, to the extent that original educational differences among regions were a function of variation in values among these regions, it would seem that the importance of regional traditions in dictating the nature and magnitude of educational inputs is gradually being weakened by those societal values previously identified as more consistent with modernization. Changing environmental conditions seem particularly important for the Southeastern region, whose educational development historically has been impeded by its traditionalism. On the other hand, the Plains region, with fewer historical traditions beyond that of the frontier, may be more strongly influenced by changing ecological and structural patterns, which have included a fairly rapid loss of rural population attended by a growth of "agri-business" and the beginning of industrial growth in some of its metropolitan areas.

Although regional variation in educational inputs seems to be decreasing, community variation in inputs exists—both within and among regions—and may be increasing. For example, the mean percent of teachers in a school district with a master's degree *within* more modern regions varies from 31 percent in districts in more modern communities to 15 percent in districts in less modern communities (Table 5–2). A similar pattern is evident in individual schools and neighborhoods, where, for example, senior high schools located in higher-class neighborhoods in more modern communities have a higher mean percent of teachers with a master's degree (52.6 percent) than do senior high schools in lower-class neighborhoods in the same modern communities (43.3 percent) (Table 6–2). With few exceptions, similar differences in the mean percent of teachers with a master's degree were found in all environments, with the disparity greatest between senior high schools in the more modern region, community, and neighborhood (52.6 percent) and those in the less modern region, community, and neighborhood (29.8 percent). Similar, but less dramatic, differences occurred at the junior high and elementary school levels.

Equally important is the *suggestion* provided by the input results reported in Chapter Five that differences between school districts predominantly of higher- or lower-class composition located in the same region and ecological community type are greater in every instance in the more modern region than in the less modern one. Thus, for example, the difference in average instructional salaries between school districts in communities of different degrees of structural modernity in the more modern regions was seen to be greater than in the less modern regions: $8086 vs. $7394 ($682) and $7449 vs. $6513 ($936), as opposed to $6799 vs. $6372 ($427) and $6553 vs. $5808 ($745) (Table 5–2). A similar pattern is evident for other input measures at the level of the school district (Table 5–2), but does not hold for the school (Table 6–2).

Part of the explanation for this phenomenon may undoubtedly be the traditional American pattern of local school financing, wherein monetary input is determined by a tax assessment on property in the school district. Since school district boundaries conventionally have been arbitrarily determined in metropolitan areas in accordance with either explicit or implicit residential patterns related to the cost of housing, it follows that the monetary input based upon property assessment in the wealthier middle- and upper-class areas would be greater. Since school districts in smaller communities and in less modern regions have tended either to include all types of residence, or to be less differentiated in terms of assessed value among school districts, the disparity in inputs derived from property taxes has been considerably less. Interpreted within the broader context of modernization, however, such variation in educational input is indicative of one of the major structural and ecological problems associated with urban life, wherein traditional social mechanisms used to provide inputs for education accentuate and reflect discrepancies in material well-being among sectors of the population.[a]

Throughput

Such a pattern is reflected in the educational system's throughputs as well. Whereas inputs reflect several important forms of variation, the most apparent and important variation in throughputs is the consistent discrepancy between schools in higher-class and lower-class neighborhoods. Regardless of grade level, the throughput of schools in predominantly lower-class neighborhoods is less modern than that of schools in predominantly higher-class neighborhoods. And, interestingly enough, in both the more and less modern regions the discrepancy by neighborhood in the percent of pupils behind in reading at the elementary, junior high, and senior high grade levels is greatest in the large cities (Table 6–4).

In Chapter Six this development, not predicted by our model, was referred to as the "ghetto effect" and attributed in part to our failure to consider theoretically the effects on the school of large-scale migration into the central city and the large numbers of white-collar commuters. Additionally, how-

---

[a]This development is clearly documented in a recent decision handed down by the California Supreme Court. See "Serrano vs. Priest: Implications for Educational Equality," The Supreme Court of the State of California, with a Commentary by William N. Greenbaum, *Harvard Educational Review,* Vol. 41, No. 4 (November 1971), 501–34.

ever, the cultural context of education in the central city must be considered, for a majority of the pupils attending the lower-class schools in the central cities are black, Puerto Rican, Mexican, or from other racial and ethnic minority groups that are not only poor but also discriminated against in employment. Thus, by virtue of both birth and cultural circumstance, members of these groups tend to be unprepared for education, unmotivated to succeed by the educational system, and unrewarded for school success. Given these considerations, the advantages of modern urban life *vis à vis* the educational system previously noted in Chapter Three are apparently more than offset by the disadvantages of the culture of the ghetto.[b]

Output

The output of the educational system at every level has increased over the 40-year period we have considered. Although longitudinal data are available only at the state, regional, and national levels, it is apparent that both nationally and within each of the five regions each of our four output measures has risen dramatically between 1930 and 1970 (Tables 4–3 and 4–5). The same is true for all the 48 states we considered, although we did not present the detailed data. Further, as in the case of our measures of input, the general trend for output at the regional and state levels reflects a reduction in the difference of output between more and less modern environments.

Some insight into the nature of these developments is provided by a consideration of output variation for school district and school. Thus, the median years of schooling in a school district was shown to be systematically related to the degree of modernity of both the ecological and structural dimensions of its community in both more and less modern regions (Table 5–4), suggesting the importance of these two dimensions in the determination of educational output. Further, for schools, the mean negative termination (dropout rate) is greater in schools in the less modern region than in the more modern region, holding constant both the ecology of the community and the structure of the neighborhood (Table 6–6). This is also true of the percent of former tenth graders going on to some type of higher education beyond high school (positive termination). But the opposite pattern of difference is evident when only the percent of twelfth-grade graduates going to a four-year college is considered. In this latter instance, the mean percentage is greater in schools in the less modern region than in the more modern

---

[b]Such a conclusion is, of course, consistent with that of Coleman and his associates, but from the standpoint of the system rather than that of the individual student. See James S. Coleman *et al., Equality of Educational Opportunity* (Washington, D.C.: Government Printing Office, 1966).

region, suggesting that increases in input in the less modern regions have until recently tended to facilitate primarily the more traditional academic aspects of the educational system.

Again, as with throughputs, a "ghetto effect" upon output was not anticipated by the model, but was evident in our analysis (Table 6–6). When contrasted to the predicted highly positive outputs found among middle-class schools in the central city, the suppressed output for schools in the urban ghetto is all the more evident. The high rate of dropouts and the relatively low proportion of graduates who go on to some form of higher education from these schools is certainly not surprising given our knowledge (noted earlier) of the throughput characteristic of these schools. Equally important, however, if our earlier consideration of the nature of the school in a more modern setting is correct, is the role the school plays in producing these results. Our data allow us to speculate that the ghetto itself is instrumental in the results obtained, for, as we suggested earlier, the school as an open system simply reflects the deprivation of its environment. Given our previous view of the school as a more efficient and effective social system in a more modern setting, there is also reason to argue that the system itself, as an expression of its "objectively rational" characteristics, is a major factor in explaining the negative results obtained by schools in the ghetto.

Finally, an interesting potential pattern in environmental-school relationships at the state level should be commented upon. In Chapter Four, we saw that the correlation between the modernity of the state and the inputs to state educational systems (Table 4–7) typically was higher than the correlation between the environment and the output of the system (Table 4–9), suggesting the possibility that inputs may be more dependent than outputs upon their environment. Unfortunately, our other data did not permit similar comparisons at other levels. However, the possible existence of such a pattern does raise the question of the extent to which state educational systems are influenced by national expectations as opposed to their immediate state environment. Generally, we suggest that at this level the institutional requirements of the educational system mitigate to some extent the influence of the immediate environment upon the productive processes in the system.

Structure

Structurally, there is little doubt that the modernity of the regional and state environments of educational systems is related to their size and complexity. Although the general pattern at the regional level is one of a reduction of structural differences over time, our longitudinal data on state educational systems suggest that as the society has become increasingly modern, the more modern states have moved more rapidly toward a highly specialized educational structure than have the less modern ones (Table 4–10). Viewed in the context of system development, such a finding indicates an important characteristic of the change associated with modernization, for beyond some unspecified point the system's movement toward a more complex and specialized structure increases rapidly as resistance to that type of change in the system's environment is overcome. Such a development is logically consistent with our earlier discussion of the dynamics of modernization, for the transition of the environment to a more modern form is expected to result in greater congruence between the objective rationality of the system and the subjective rationality of its immediate environment. Given such a state of affairs, feedback to the system tends to be more consistent with its institutional purpose and, therefore, makes structural change easier. Verification of such an explanation from our findings, of course, awaits further empirical study.

Structural differences in the school district are most evident in the size and specialization of individual schools (Table 5–6). Very evident in this instance is the tendency for the more modern community (ecologically and structurally) to have consistently larger and more specialized schools. The same pattern is found for junior and senior high schools but not for elementary schools. As to organizational differentiation, however, most of the more modern neighborhoods have more highly specialized schools.

Significant too in terms of the recent structural development of American education is the expansion of the boundaries of education's social role, as suggested by the association of community modernity with emphasis upon kindergarten education. Just how important the role of formal and rationalized early child rearing is to the requirements of a modern society is difficult to ascertain, although the recent emergence of pre-school day care centers and the Head Start program would suggest that such schooling meets the needs of many Americans. From the standpoint of the educational system, however, it seems reasonable to suggest that such a development enhances the control of the system over its throughputs, thereby increasing its probable effectiveness as an institution.[2]

Summary

In a broad sense, the foregoing comments document both the complexity and the developmental nature of education in American society. The very diversity of American environments precludes sweeping generalizations about "schooling." Thus, while we have chosen to look at only one aspect of that diversity, modernity, and in doing so have systematically demonstrated variation in the inputs, throughputs, outputs, and structure of the educational system, we suspect that concentrating on other environmental aspects would reveal additional educational variations although perhaps none of as much relevance to contemporary concerns. At the same time the systematic growth in education nationally in inputs, outputs, and structural characteristics between 1930 and 1970 attests both to the increasing importance of the educational system in American society and to the manner in which the system is responding to its societal role. With some exceptions, the overall pattern is one of increasing resources applied to increasing numbers of students in schools of increasing size and complexity.

Beyond this rather obvious generalization, however, we offer several further observations.

1) There is, generally speaking, clear evidence that the modernity of the environment of an educational system at the national, regional, state, community, and neighborhood layers is *systematically* related to the nature of educational input, throughput, output, and structure.

2) On the regional and state levels, educational systems are becoming increasingly uniform in their input, output, and structure, suggesting that *informally* (as opposed to the formal establishment of an administrative hierarchy) the general thrust of the institutional system of education is toward more centralized and standardized schooling.

3) Structurally, at all system levels, there is fairly consistent evidence that the educational system is becoming more differentiated and specialized, as well as expanding the boundary of its influence to earlier childhood.

4) At the same time as the region and state education is moving toward informal standardization and centralization, community and neighborhood variation in the educational system remains very high. Further, it is possible that with increasing modernity such variation may be accentuated.

5) With the increasing modernity of the environment, the social class context of the school becomes increasingly important in determining its inputs, throughputs, outputs, and structure.

6) In the central city of metropolitan areas, the lower-class school in the ghetto appears to be quite adversely affected by the modernization process, for in spite of relatively high inputs, its throughputs and outputs are more like those of schools located in less modern environments having significantly lower levels of input.

CONCLUSIONS

Viewed from an open systems perspective, and at the broad societal level, the American educational system has shown tremendous developmental growth in the 40-year period covered in this book. Both inputs and outputs have increased dramatically, and the structure of the system has become much more complex. A large part of this growth is unquestionably attributable to the training, allocation, and screening for occupations that schools do to fulfill their institutional role—a function of increasing importance in American society.[3] At the same time, however, the large variation in educational outputs in different sociocultural contexts *within* the society belies the commonly held belief that the phenomenal growth of the educational system is primarily, if not solely, attributable to this assumed requirement of modernizing societies. If this were indeed the case, we would find little systematic variation among schools. On the other hand we might reason that a modern society with increasing technical needs must "cull out" more and more potentially qualified individuals; and to do so would require the "processing" of more and more students, the majority of whom will not be selected.

Neither alternative seems consistent with our knowledge of the American educational system or the requirements of the larger society. More realistically, it seems that the recent growth of education is a logical consequence of the interaction of the cultural value system of American society, the requirements of modernization, and the systemic characteristics of formal education. Given the particular environmental emphasis upon individual and societal progress noted in Chapters One and Two, as well as the technical and social requirements of an industrial system, the rapid growth of the educational system (as an adaptive, rationally organized, and open system), although not inevitable, was to be expected. Since the underlying nature of modernity is relatively constant in technical requirements, and sociocultural and structural needs, the impetus for an educational system to meet these requirements was provided by the manifest benefits to be derived from industrialization and urbanization. The relative rate of such development and its peculiar nature in America was determined in large measure by the American sociocultural context. To the extent that the values and structure of the society were amenable to the changes required, the system's development and transition were rapid and subjectively rationalized in terms of the purposes held to be important to the society. The dominant American values noted earlier (emphases upon the individual, mastery over nature, and the future, and progress, achievement, equality, and materialism), insured the general implementation of educational needs and hence the rapid growth of the educational system.

Because of varying historical and sociocultural factors, some segments of the society were more resistant to such changes than other segments and less readily assimilated the institutional role of modern education. Given the open system characteristics of the educational system at all levels, development was less in these resistant areas of the society. Variations in the expected developmental pattern, then, reflect in part localized variations in societal values as they relate to the role of education. The systemic properties of the educational system, particularly those associated with its homeostatic characteristic, have insured an adaption of the system to such environmental variation.

Historical and sociocultural factors explain part of this variation in educational development, but also important is the role of schooling as a determinant of societal stratification. The importance of formal education for the productive process has been noted in Chapter Two. As an important "resource" for a modern technical system, its institutional significance for the individual is enhanced because educational achievement is an important determinant of one's position in the occupational hierarchy.[4] Viewed from the societal level, such a relationship can help explain why the social class composition of both the community and the neighborhood seems more important in determining the educational outputs in the more modern areas than in the less modern ones. To the extent that educational achievement becomes the *primary* basis for access to societal rewards, social class differences in educational achievement can be expected to become more pronounced. In more traditional contemporary settings, where family, religion, and ethnic origin continue to play an important role in determining such access, the relative importance of education to class and status is less. In the more modern settings, the public educational system performs a rather important secondary role for the society as a whole; as an integrative mechanism in both facilitating and legitimating the distribution of societal rewards.

On the face of it, such an interpretation would seem to contradict our argument in Chapter Two that the primary institutional role of education is the transmission of skills and orientations. However, such a role was deduced from assumptions about the nature of a modern industrial society and makes no claims regarding the manner in which those goals are met. It only presupposes that the social legitimation of the educational system rests upon the socially recognized and accepted needs of the sociotechnical order, not upon presumptions of an educational meritocracy wherein all individuals are developed to the best of their ability. Indeed, considerable evidence points to imperfect correlation between ability and educational success.[5] Further, from the viewpoint of the society, it is not an *economic* necessity that its technological requirements be met by the most able or talented individuals, however these terms might be defined.

Particularly important to an understanding of this phenomenon is the principle of the legitimacy of the role of education in selecting, sorting, and socializing youth *vis à vis* the acknowledged needs of the society. Once established, such a role becomes the principle upon which the system adjusts to the constraints of the environment by reacting to feedback based upon the subjective rationality of the system's membership. Thus, the apparent lack of success in meeting institutional goals of formal education in ghetto areas is often justified by the caliber of throughput available to the system. Such throughput requires tremendous energy to be spent for control, and may lead the system to expel students rather than attempt to socialize them. Or, to take a different example, the acceptance (or rejection) of educational innovations by schools seems invariably legitimated in the long run in terms of the institutional role of the school. Thus, computer-assisted instruction is only acceptable to educators if it facilitates the "learning process" as defined by the institutional role of the educational system. This is not to say that other reasons may not enter into the lack of success of education in ghetto areas, or with respect to the acceptance of innovations, but simply that the socially acceptable, and therefore organizationally rational, explanation will eventually be advanced to justify such decisions.

When American schooling is viewed as a system the apparent paradox of this whole process is revealed, for in spite of its many "failures" during the past century, noted in Chapter One, the educational system has thrived and grown as a social institution. The dimensions of this growth may be subsumed under the heading "bureaucratization." In very real terms, the history of education in America since the middle of the nineteenth century has been one of the growth of its bureaucratic characteristics. Yet, traditionally, in educational circles, to speak of bureaucracy is tantamount to raising images of the devil. No one is in favor of it, not even the most experienced bureaucrats. Yet bureaucracy is tolerated and seems to flourish in American education. Why? One obvious answer is that, in spite of our distaste as individuals for this form of social organization, it has served the interests of society well. Associated with increased bureaucratization have been dramatic increases in the output of the educational system. Although one may argue that the same results might have been possible without bureaucratic development, such an assertion has yet to be proved in education or in other areas of modern life. Indeed, the whole tenor of the social development we have referred to as modernization has been toward increasing bureaucracy in large areas of American society. Furthermore, as we have endeavored to point out in Chapter Two, bureaucratization is a logical social phenomenon, *given the emergence of a society with a complex division of labor resting upon an advanced technological base and whose social solidarity is contingent upon social differences rather than upon social similarities*

It should be remembered that a bureaucracy, like any social phenomena, is a particular pattern of relationships created by a society consistent with its dominant value orientations in order to come to terms with the objective reality of its environment. And, as such, if particular meanings are assigned to bureaucracy, the action of the bureaucracy is interpreted according to those meanings. Thus, consistent with the emphasis in modern society upon the future and upon mastery over nature, educational bureaucracy has meant that the most effective institutional pattern of relationships could be employed to meet the social and physical requirements of a modernizing society. Other meanings attributable to this form of organizational arrangement and particularly significant to individuals or various minority interest groups did not offset the dominant meaning of bureaucracy *for the society as a whole*. Just as the meaning of a bureaucratically organized economic system has emphasized a greater general measure of material prosperity, and the meaning of a bureaucratic centralized government has emphasized a political stability, growth, and individual autonomy (if not "freedom"), bureaucracy in education has emphasized the provision of the trained manpower necessary for a technologically advanced society, an increase in literacy, and a furtherance of a new type of normative integration accepted as functional for a complex modern society. Such meaning, from the societal viewpoin, is consistent with the dominant value orientations of the society and can be documented historically.

At the same time, as bureaucracy in American education is both theoretically understandable and objectively laudable from the standpoint of the society, critics justifiably point to a variety of inadequacies in current education. Thus, in a recent sociohistorical analysis of public urban education, Katz advances the thesis that "the structure of American urban education has not changed since late in the nineteenth century."[6] That structure, according to Katz is ". . . universal, tax-supported, free, compulsory, bureaucratically arranged, class-biased, and racist."[7] To him, "Bureaucracy provides a segmented educational structure that legitimizes and perpetuates the separation of children along class lines and insures easier access to higher status jobs for children of the affluent."[8] Essentially, Katz argues that most past educational innovations and reforms were not conducive to social change in the schools, but rather reinforced existing inequities, and he attributes this to the fact that the men who directed such change were basically conservative and fundamentally concerned with maintaining social order. Accordingly, the reforms and changes accepted into the educational system were primarily those that would make the system simply more of a "streamlined bureaucracy."[9]

Directly related to such concern regarding bureaucracy in education are those who advocate the decentralization of administrative authority. Such criticism has usually sprung from what Katz has referred to as a faith in the efficacy of "democratic localism" in overcoming the inequities and injustices of the present system. Analytically, we may suggest that the basis for such criticism rests more upon the type of authority exercised in a bureaucracy than upon its form. Following Weber, three types of authority may be identified: *traditional* authority rests upon an underlying acceptance of traditions; *charismatic* authority rests upon an underlying acceptance of the perceived extraordinary talents of an individual; and *rational* (that is, bureaucratic) authority rests upon an underlying acceptance of written ordinances and the authority of positions spelled out by those ordinances.[10] Critics of educational bureaucracy who are adherents of "democratic localism" are in effect subscribing to authority based upon tradition in contrast to the rational authority of the bureaucracy.

Additional concern regarding bureaucracy in schools can be identified. Such criticism, stemming from strongly humanistic commitments, emphasizes that the school is "dehumanizing" and intellectually emasculating the youth of the society—particularly the poor and those from disadvantaged minority groups. Stressing the inherently destructive nature of a variety of current educational practices, these critics basically argue for the restructuring of the total system so as to meet the developmental needs (both social and psychological) of the individual. Goodman, for example, envisions an educational system with little if any formal curriculum, very small informal schools at the elementary level, a diversity of educational paths at the secondary and college levels (including apprenticeships, on-the-job training, and academic preparation), and a university program geared to professional apprenticeship.[11]

IMPLICATIONS

Each of the types of criticism of bureaucracy in education noted above is to some extent well founded and suggestive of both the inadequacies of the present organizational form of education and the need for change. Unfortunately, when interpreted according to the concepts and empirical findings presented in this book, these changes often seem unrealistic. For example, although the results of our analysis support Katz's argument that American education is increasingly bureaucratic (at all levels) and class biased (certainly at the level of the school and school district), bureaucracy is not simply the instrument of oppression suggested by Katz—although there is little doubt it has been used in an oppressive fashion. It is also the logical outgrowth of organizational requirements of a modernizing industrial society. The class bias that our study and other research has shown to exist within the educational system (and possibly to be accentuated over time in the more modern areas of American society) is not provided or legitimated solely by the bureaucratic structure of American education, although it may well be perpetuated by it. Rather, as an open social system, the educational bureaucracy directly reflects the constraints placed upon it by its sociocultural environment. The educational system can no more ignore the negative feedback and input sources associated with its survival and its institutional role than can any other open social system. As Weber pointed out some time ago, ". . . one has to remember that bureaucracy as such is a precision instrument which can put itself at the disposal of varied . . . interests . . . ."[12] In Weber's terms the bureaucratic nature of the school system in contemporary American society is quite "normal" for a modern industrial state. The responsibility for the inequities would seem to lie in the sociocultural environment rather than in the educational system *per se*.

Those critics who champion a return to "democratic localism" as a solution to the problems of bureaucracy in education often fail to recognize that the effectiveness of such traditional authority rests upon a form of social organization where social solidarity is based upon "likeness of kind." Such *gemienschaft* bonds seem incompatible with the structural diversity and interdependence of a modern society, whose solidarity rests not upon likeness but upon differences. Further, given the historical development of American education, there is little to suggest that local control over the schools can provide a better or more meaningful education for students today than it did one hundred years ago. If the logic of our earlier argument about the effects of modernization on schooling in America is correct, a form of localized decentralization is likely to produce inequities in the system far beyond those apparent today, and probably very much like those of the elitist educational system of nineteenth-century Europe.

The data reported in Chapters Five and Six suggest that local control at the level of the school district and school, particularly in the less modern areas of American society, is presently much stronger than many critics seem to acknowledge. At these levels the acceptance of rational authority in terms of accreditation, university or state requirements, and the like has always been contingent upon its perceived legitimacy. As suggested previously, the open system characteristics of American education assure that feedback from local sources will be taken into account in greater or lesser measure, depending upon the sociocultural importance of those sources to the system's survival and purpose. That such importance does not necessarily increase or diminish with greater bureaucracy is evident in the fact that many of the least modern American states have a highly bureaucratic state educational system, yet individual schools are still strongly influenced by the traditional norms and customs of their communities and neighborhoods.

The reforms recommended by those critics who are justly concerned with the impact of a bureaucratized educational system upon the individual also seem problematic, for they presuppose an ability of society (in the interests of the well-being of the individual) to completely divorce education from both societal requirements and sociocultural constraints. As appealing as this type of reform may seem from a humanistic perspective, from the sociological perspective advanced in our preceding discussion, it seems highly unlikely. Given the interdependent nature of modern society, resting as it does upon an advanced technological base with great variance in existing social conditions, any attempt to fully implement such reforms (regardless of its good intentions and sound psychological base) is likely to be quickly challenged as usurping the social responsibilities of the school. There is no reason to question the validity of the criticisms. On the other hand, it does not necessarily follow that the amelioration of undesirable conditions associated with bureaucracy necessarily rests upon dispensing with bureaucracy, even if it were possible to do so.

What we are suggesting is that the development of a bureaucratic form of educational organization is logically consistent with the development of modern society. And to the extent that the United States continues to modernize, we can reasonably expect more bureaucracy in education. However, such a conclusion does not lessen the importance of these criticisms, nor is it meant to suggest that any hope for ameliorating contemporary educational problems is futile. Rather, we would like to suggest that the basic problem of education in contemporary America is not its bureaucratic form *per se,* but as noted by Israel, the need ". . . to control this bureaucracy in such a way that it does not become dictatorial or despotic . . . [so] . . . that, in exerting its power, it does not become independent of those in whose service it was originally created."[13]

Ideally, in spite of the coercive element involved in the school attendance of most children, there is a subjective rationality associated with their participation in the experience. Early in his life, the child perceives the rationality of learning the conventional elementary skills—reading, writing, spelling, arithmetic. Later, however, the subjective meaning of education becomes less immediate and concrete in its expression. Subsequent development is more closely controlled by the system to reflect what is deemed important, not to child, but to adult society. Thus, the subjective meaning of the experience, from the child's standpoint, is changed by the school into such relatively distant and abstract concepts as future occupational success, an appreciation of the cultural, historical, or political subtleties of his American heritage, or the desirability of educational achievement for parental approval. To the extent that the individual accepts these socially imposed reasons as legitimate and internalizes them, his experience remains subjectively rational and he seeks to comply with the school's behavioral and attitudinal norms and ultimately assumes his place as a responsible and productive citizen.

Of course, this description of the "meaning" of education to the individual is merely an idealized characterization of the transitional process by which children are socialized by the educational system into adult roles. If effective, the system produces individuals who have generally accepted the dominant values, attitudes, and beliefs of society, and have learned the skills and techniques necessary to interact in fairly autonomous fashion in a highly segmented, impersonal, and specialized social order.[c] However, the system is far from totally effective, and for many the subjective meaning

---

[c]In contrast to Reich, we do not believe that the educational system does little more than produce "training for the industrial order," although its importance for the productive system cannot be denied. Even when the system is not optimally effective it has an impact on the student far beyond simple "training." See Charles A. Reich, *The Greening of America* (New York: Random House, Inc., Bantam Books edition, 1971), p. 392.

of the experience is less than ideal. Such students often experience a sense of alienation and repressive control.

For many children the socialization process is confounded when, for a variety of reasons, they either fail to internalize the meaning associated with the educational system (and thus view their educational experience as something arbitrarily imposed upon them); or they internalize the abstractions but become disillusioned by the system itself before they complete compulsory schooling. Particularly, most lower-class and minority youths are unlikely to fully internalize the more abstract reasons for extending one's education beyond the compulsory period, owing primarily to the distinctive "middle-class" nature of education (which places them at an initial disadvantage) and to an apparent lack of relevance of educational curriculum to their own experience. On the other hand, for many middle-class youth, disillusionment can stem in some measure from the subjectively perceived restrictive, impersonal, and irrational nature of their educational experience.

Several social forces, in some sense extraneous to the educational system, contribute in an unknown measure to this apparent disjuncture in the formal socialization of many contemporary youth. Technology and the economy itself, for example, provide other activities and material gratifications, which young people either obtain easily or which the mass media promote as desirable. So, also, traditional attitudes and values may work at cross purposes to the assumed role of the formal educational system, thereby undermining the efforts of the educator. Particularly important, however, is the growing value placed by society upon the individual and his development. Compatible with both the rational emphasis upon the individual as a concomitant of modernization, previously noted, and with a major American value configuration centering upon the individual and humanism,[d] such a development tends to result in pressures for a more democratic and egalitarian social structure.[e] Whatever their sources, however, these elements can be viewed as contributing to disenchantment and alienation among

———

[d]What Parsons has referred to as "individualistic utopianism" is in some respects related to this emphasis, wherein "*both* individual and collective rights are alleged to be promoted only by *minimizing* the positive organization of social groups." See Talcott Parsons, "Distribution of Power in American Society," in Talcott Parsons, *Politics and Social Structure* (New York: The Free Press, 1969), p. 201.

[e]That this is not unique to American society, nor necessarily results in a more egalitarian system, has been noted by several authors. See, for example, C. B. MacPherson, "Democratic Theory: Ontology and Technology," in David Spitz, ed., *Political Theory and Social Change* (New York: Atherton Press, 1967), pp. 203–20; Mulford Q. Sibley, "Social Order and Human Ends: Some Central Issues in the Modern Problem," in Spitz, *Political Theory and Social Change,* pp. 221–55; and Joseph LaPalombara, "Distribution and Development," in Myron Weiner, ed., *Modernization: the Dynamics of Growth* (New York: Basic Books, Inc., 1966), pp. 218–29.

students about the "meaning" of their educational experience, somewhat independent of the content and structure of the educational system itself.

At the same time as social forces contribute to a sense of alienation on the part of many students, their reciprocal effect upon the rationalization process of education noted in Chapter One has undoubtedly accentuated the alienation. For example, pressures for a more democratic social structure tend to conflict with increased educational bureaucracy. Such a development was, in general, foreseen by Weber, who noted that "democracy as such is opposed to the 'rule' of bureaucracy in spite of and perhaps because of its unavoidable yet unintended promotion of bureaucratization."[14] Thus, even though bureaucracy in education in the more democratic societies has tended to promote universal enrollment, a "rationalized" procedure for learning,[15] and evaluation on the basis of merit, it has at the same time tended to reduce the individual's freedom of choice[16] and to promulgate a meritocracy based upon expertise. In effect, by reducing socialization to a calculated procedure whereby the individual is "slotted" into a system of learning, the institution ignores or actively discourages possible variations in the subjective meaning of his experiences in education, in favor of institutional requirements.

In pre-modern society, where formal schooling was restricted to the few and thus of more limited importance, individual dissatisfaction was of relatively little significance and the response of the educational system to it was fairly predictable. However, as suggested in Chapter One, collective dissatisfaction with the American educational system historically can be characterized as a dialectical process whereby different groups of critics of the system have stressed either a greater emphasis upon individual concerns or a more rigorous program of education to meet the needs of the society. The system assimilated both types of criticism, changing in some fashion consistent with the rationality of its institutional role, although not necessarily with individual desires. This gradualism was possible only as long as formal education did not hold great importance for most members of the society. However, with formal education so critical to socialization, current dissatisfaction and alienation suggest the need for more significant institutional changes.

This development is not unique to education in American society, but is a manifestation of a larger social problem associated with modernization, the relationship of the individual to society. The problem is expressed in education as that of maintaining a rationality *vis à vis* an institutional role that encourages increased bureaucracy while attempting to lessen the depersonalizing effects of bureaucracy on the individual. If we are correct in our characterization of modern society, the solution to this problem does not lie in abolishing the present bureaucratically organized educational system, for in spite of all its flaws it performs many essential services that cannot be provided by a nonbureaucratic arrangement. Nor is it realistic for the system to increasingly institutionalize individual needs (as we have outlined this process in Chapter One), thereby increasing the discrepancy between what many individuals expect from the educational system and what it actually gives them. The solution to the current educational "crisis" is most likely to be found in a social redefinition of the institutional role of education as one that more nearly approximates a balance between the subjective meaning of individual needs and the objective requirements of the larger society. A primary institutional directive which sensitizes the educational system to both kinds of requirements must be built into the bureaucratic purpose underlying the rationality of the educational system.

It is important to note that the success of such a transformation will lie not within the educational system, but within the larger society. As an open system *within a sociocultural environment,* the school depends upon continuous information feedback from that environment to determine the nature and direction of its efforts. The results of our study have clearly demonstrated the systematic nature of that interdependency. If we are correct in our assessment of these results, then change must originate outside the school, within the various environmental layers we have identified. Accordingly, values will have to shift not only nationally, but in the region, state, community, and neighborhood as well. Like racial integration in the schools, the national policies and directives of the federal government will have very limited success in school district and school if they are not accepted by local people.

What decisions are necessary to effect needed change in education rests in part upon a conscious effort to incorporate into the institutional role of education the growing individual and humanistic values characteristic of so many of America's youth. The basis for such an effort has to some extent already been laid by the educational system itself. For, in effect, by raising the educational level of the American population, recent educational development has created an important "condition for social change."[17] Such a condition has not been created deliberately but rather is the result of reciprocal effects between education and the social context. Educational development is both a logical product of modernization and a catalyst for further social change.

Beyond efforts to incorporate individual and humanistic concerns into the institutional role of education, the most difficult aspect of the transition that we perceive to be currently taking place is likely to be associated with the need for a redefinition of the relationship of education to existing status interests and to the productive processes of American society. Since in a modern society collective status interests are becoming increasingly subordinate to the productive process, this relationship is particularly critical. To the extent that educational attainment is directly related to subsequent status and class consideration, as a function of occupational opportunity,[18] the incorporation of individual and humanistic concerns will serve as little more than a subtle mechanism for the maintenance of class, race, and possibly ethnic and religious differences. A major problem, then, is to find ways either to reduce the importance of formal education as a requisite for occupational success or to restructure education so that social background is totally irrelevant to both educational success and subsequent job opportunities.

Each alternative has both attractive and undesirable aspects. By reducing the importance of formal education for occupational success, one makes possible a broader service orientation to both the local community and the individual, thereby increasing the likelihood of broader individual and community participation in and identification with the school. At the same time, some attention must be paid to the basis for occupational qualification and subsequent stratification in a modern society. If the society is not to revert to the traditional stratification criteria of formal and social ascription, other "achievement-oriented" criteria must be found. Thus, if it is possible to significantly divorce educational status from social background, more equal educational and occupational opportunity will surely evolve. In doing so, however, American society will run the very great risk of developing a "meritocracy" as irrational in its own way as are current systems of stratification.[19] Thus, any attempt to modify the nature of the relationship of modern education to the productive system entails a measure of risk between the "Scylla" of a retreat to a system of stratification based upon ascription and the "Charybdis" of a meritocracy.

No obvious safeguards against these risks seem to exist. Our understanding of the nature of modern society and of the educational system, however, leads us to suggest that the most likely development will be toward a meritocracy wherein educational success becomes the key to one's position in the stratification system. To soften the effects of such a development, a host of egalitarian reforms in the larger society, aimed primarily at a more equitable distribution of material rewards as well as a greater sense of participation in community decisions, will be necessary. Whether or not such reforms will de-emphasize the role of education as a producer of status or even reduce its significance in the broader social milieu is difficult to predict.

Incorporating individual and humanistic concerns into the institutional role of education and reducing the importance of status to educational achievement will, of course, make the task of education and of educators much more complex than it is today. Indeed, in the long run it is likely to contribute significantly to making the teaching force more professional, for it will call for an expertise in working with students in educational planning and reform not required of most teachers today.[1] Further, a redefinition of the institutional role of education will force the educational system both to restructure its current forms of specialization and to seek different types of innovation. The current structure, with its age-grade, organizational, and role specialization has evolved in a fashion rationally consistent with previous societal requirements. Incorporating individual needs will require new forms of specialization that can more adequately cope with those needs. Thus, age-grade specialization is likely to make little sense in such a context, whereas a large variety of specialized individual programs may. Also, whereas acceptable current innovations tend to be judged as to their success in transmitting a standardized body of knowledge to homogeneous groups of students, future innovations will need to be evaluated as to their usefulness in providing a variety of information to diverse individuals.

At the same time that this transition develops, the basic societal requirements cannot be ignored and must undoubtedly act as a constraint upon structural changes and individualized innovations. In contrast to the contemporary system, however, these requirements must not be the sole criteria for organizational and institutional rationality in decision making, as we have described them in Chapter Two. Thus, although the educational system's conventional age-grade specialization must be restructured according to the throughput being processed, it probably cannot be entirely abandoned. And innovations acceptable to meet the requirements of individualized instruction cannot completely ignore the realities of the social context, for they will have to have socially perceived utility.

Needless to say, concrete suggestions as to how to implement these changes are very complex and largely beyond the scope of this book. We predict, however, that the result will be an American educational system more centralized and bureaucratic than the present one. And yet at the same time the local environment will continue to play an important role in the nature of the educational experience. This will occur, we suspect, through a redefinition of those aspects of the individual's educational experience that are a matter of societal concern, that are a matter of concern to his local sociocultural setting, and that are unique to his own identity as a human being. Matters of societal concern will be determined in large measure

---

[1]A particularly insightful analysis of the implications for the educational system of increased professional expertise among teachers is provided by Corwin, who concludes, among other things, that "in organizations with a substantial segment of professionally oriented employees, conflict is produced by the organization itself and involves one aspect of the organization against another: professional opposed to bureaucratic principles of organization . . . [for] . . . professional employees differ from other militant employees in that the cause they champion concerns more than the 'rights of an individual'; their cause is a defense of the role of experts within complex organizations." Ronald G. Corwin, *Militant Professionalism: A Study of Organizational Conflict in High Schools* (New York: Appleton-Century-Crofts, 1970), p. 358.

by a centralized national bureaucracy, and the rest will be more amenable to local decision. Thus, whereas the qualifications of teachers and administrators are likely to be systematically controlled nationally, local variation in individual needs will be taken into account in determining the ideal outputs for individual schools and school systems. Further, such changes will occur at a differential rate in the society until the point is reached where more people realize that the institutional role of education is a dual one, and must serve much more equitably than it does today *both* the individual and the society.

The extent to which this predicted development of American schooling will occur is, of course, open to debate. By addressing ourselves in the final pages of this chapter to a generally acknowledged concern of both contemporary educators and their critics, we have extrapolated our theoretical model and empirical findings to consider their possible implications for the future state of American education. Additional implications could have been considered as well. It is our hope, however, that others—armed with more comprehensive data and methodological tools, and perhaps with a greater insight garnered from the conceptual framework and results reported in this study—will pursue further our line of theoretical development and empirical inquiry. For it is our firm conviction that a basic fact of modern life is that as individuals we are part of a scientific and technically rational social system with which we must continually come to terms. Such a social system is neither inherently good nor inherently bad, but as we have attempted to demonstrate above, it greatly constrains our present social institutions.[g] Unfortunately, to cope successfully with these constraints, we must understand far better than we do today the dynamics of the developmental process of modern social life. We hope that this book has provided a small step in that direction.

REFERENCES

[1]Bureau of the Census, *Statistical Abstracts of the United States: 1969*, 90th ed. (Washington, D.C.: Government Printing Office, 1969), Table 1268, pp. 859–60.

[2]See, for example, Urie Bronfenbrenner and J. C. Condry, Jr., *Two Worlds of Childhood: U.S. and U.S.S.R.* (New York: Russell Sage Foundation, 1970).

[3]Wilbert E. Moore, "Developmental Change in Urban Industrial Societies," in *Per-*

---

[g]As Mesthene has observed in discussing the effects of technological change on society, "New technology creates new opportunities for men and societies, and it also generates new problems for them. It has both positive and negative effects, and it usually has the two *at the same time and in virtue of each other*." Emmanuel G. Mesthene, *Technological Change: Its Impact on Men and Society* (New York: The New American Library, Mentor Books, 1970), p. 27 (italics are those of the author).

spectives in Developmental Change, ed. Art Gallaher, Jr. (Lexington, Ky.: University of Kentucky Press, 1968), pp. 201–30.

[4]For a more extended discussion of this relationship, see Gerhard Lenski, *Power and Privilege: A Theory of Stratification* (New York: McGraw-Hill Book Company, 1966), p. 392.

[5]*Ibid.,* p. 391.

[6]Michael B. Katz, *Class, Bureaucracy and Schools* (New York: Frederick A. Praeger, Inc., 1971), p. 105.

[7]*Ibid.,* p. 106.

[8]*Ibid.,* p. 122.

[9]*Ibid.,* p. 125.

[10]For a critical discussion of this distinction, see Raymond Aron, *Main Currents in Sociological Thought,* Vol. II (New York: Basic Books, Inc., 1967), 231–42.

[11]Paul Goodman, "No Processing Whatever," in *Radical School Reform,* ed. Beatrice and Ronald Gross (New York: Simon and Schuster, Inc., 1969), pp. 98–106.

[12]*From Max Weber: Essays in Sociology,* trans. and ed. H. H. Gerth and C. Wright Mills (New York: Oxford University Press, paperback edition, 1958), pp. 231–32.

[13]Joachim Israel, *Alienation from Marx to Modern Sociology* (Boston: Allyn and Bacon, Inc., 1971), p. 282.

[14]Gerth and Mills, *From Max Weber,* p. 231.

[15]*Ibid.,* pp. 240–44.

[16]For a further discussion of this point, see N. P. Mouzelis, *Organization and Bureaucracy* (London: Routledge & Kegan Paul, Ltd., 1969), p. 41.

[17]Reece McGee, "Education and Social Change," in *On Education—Sociological Perspectives,* ed. Donald A. Hansen and Joel E. Gerstl (New York: John Wiley & Sons, Inc., 1967), pp. 86–93.

[18]Lenski, *Power and Privilege,* p. 392.

[19]For an interesting, as well as provocative, essay on the dangers inherent in such a development, see Michael Young, *The Rise of the Meritocracy, 1870–2033: The New Elite of Our Social Revolution* (New York: Random House, Inc., 1959).

appendix A

The Measurement of
State, Regional, and
National Modernity

In order to begin to tap empirically some of the variation in modernity within contemporary America suggested by the discussion in Chapter Two, we desired a "modernity index" using available data for recent years. Because, as noted in Chapter Four, few data are currently available to tap the cultural and structural dimensions of modernity, we chose to focus our measurement of modernity on a "general modernity" score rather than on separate scores for each of the three dimensions. Since the state is the smallest areal unit for which reasonably relevant and comparable longitudinal data currently exist, we chose it as the primary unit of analysis. To describe regions and the nation as a whole we chose to aggregate state data. Further, we confined our measurement to the years 1930, 1940, 1950, 1960, and 1970 to maximize data comparability.

In distinguishing the process of modernization among American states we began by considering carefully the three dimensions (the cultural, the ecological, and the structural), thereby reducing the likelihood of "fractional coverage."[a] The next step in the construction of this modernity index consisted of a review of the numerous indicators (well over 100) used in cross-

---

[a]Amitai Etzioni and Edward W. Lehman, "Some Dangers in 'Valid' Social Measurements," *The Annals of the American Academy of Political and Social Science*, 373 (1967), 1–15.

cultural research.[b] We kept in mind: a) the relevance of each possible indicator to the three dimensions, b) its possible sensitivity to differences in a relatively modern society, and c) the availability of recent data for all American states. Many indicators that did not meet these criteria were eliminated. Ultimately, five indicators for the 48 coterminous states were chosen as particularly appropriate and reasonably representative: 1) percent of males in the labor force engaged in nonagricultural work, 2) percent of the population located in urban areas, 3) per capita annual income, 4) number of physicians per 100,000 people, and 5) number of telephones per 100 people. Justification for each indicator was offered in Chapter Four (see Figure 4–1). It is doubtful that five other *carefully justified* indicators would lead to a very different ranking of the states.[c]

We first identified or computed the relevant data for each of the 48 coterminous states at each of the five relevant time points. These data are presented in roster form in Tables A–1 through A–5. Because of minor errors in data comparability, noted in Appendix C, and because of differences among the three dimensions of modernity, the covariation across the five indicators could not be expected to be perfect, and an inspection of Tables A–1 through A–5 shows that it is not. However, the comparative ranking of the states generally reflects a strong association among the five indicators at each time point during the 1930–1970 period.

To permit comparison across the five time points it was desirable to develop a common operational definition of modernity. To facilitate this we selected the year 1950 as the reference year in computing weights for data for all five years. Principal components factor analysis was selected as the best method for deriving these weights.[d]

The matrix of zero-order Pearsonian correlation coefficients computed from the 1950 data (Table A–3) is presented in Table A–6. There it can be noted that the degree of correlation varies from a low of .65 between the percent of males in nonagricultural work and per capita income, to a high

---

[b]Most of the indicators originally selected were drawn from Norton Ginsburg, *Atlas of Economic Development*, Department of Geography Research, Paper No. 68 (Chicago: University of Chicago Press, 1961), pp. 1–5.

[c]There is, however, one particularly appropriate indicator of modernity that we could not include in our index for states—the *consumption* of electrical energy. Although this indicator is central to the concept of modernity as we have discussed it, and has been widely used in cross-cultural studies, reliable data are not available for geopolitical units within the United States. Data on the *production* of electrical energy are available, but we chose not to use this as a proxy variable because of lack of correspondence between where electrical energy is produced and where it is consumed.

[d]For one discussion of factor analysis, see Harry H. Harman, *Modern Factor Analysis* (Chicago: University of Chicago Press, 1960); for computer program performing principal components factor analysis, see William W. Cooley and Paul R. Lohnes, *Multivariate Data Analysis* (New York: John Wiley & Sons, Inc., 1971), chap. 4.

Rank[a]	State	Modernity Score (SMO)	Percent Nonagricultural (SNA)	Percent Urban (SPU)	Per Capita Income[b] (SSI)	Physicians Per 100,000 Population (SPY)	Telephones Per 100 Population (STR)
				Indicator of Modernity			
1.	New York	4.70	93.7	83.6	$ 2688	160	21
2.	Massachusetts	3.80	95.8	90.2	2117	148	20
3.	California	3.36	83.5	73.3	2307	172	23
4.	Illinois	2.37	86.1	73.9	2219	149	20
5.	Rhode Island	2.26	95.9	92.4	2020	114	16
6.	Connecticut	2.09	92.9	70.4	2386	125	19
7.	New Jersey	1.85	95.2	82.6	2159	113	16
8.	Pennsylvania	0.29	91.6	67.8	1797	127	14
9.	Ohio	-0.02	85.4	67.8	1811	126	15
10.	Maryland	-0.03	84.2	59.8	1802	153	13
11.	Michigan	-0.64	84.6	68.2	1839	113	13
12.	Washington	-0.66	81.5	56.6	1739	127	18
13.	Delaware	-0.83	78.4	51.7	2358	120	14
14.	Nevada	-0.91	76.5	37.8	2036	159	16
15.	New Hampshire	-0.95	84.9	58.7	1600	117	17
16.	Oregon	-1.25	76.0	51.3	1584	139	18
17.	Colorado	-1.42	68.3	50.2	1477	164	17
18.	Missouri	-1.82	69.1	51.2	1456	152	16
19.	Indiana	-2.20	76.0	55.5	1419	125	14
20.	Maine	-2.86	79.2	40.3	1394	118	16
21.	Wisconsin	-2.95	69.3	52.9	1582	103	16
22.	Minnesota	-3.18	62.8	49.0	1387	125	17
23.	Florida	-3.46	74.2	51.7	1208	123	10
24.	Vermont	-3.65	67.0	33.0	1454	131	16
25.	Iowa	-3.83	56.7	39.6	1338	126	20
26.	Utah	-3.90	71.4	52.4	1296	100	12
27.	Kansas	-4.27	61.1	38.8	1241	116	18
28.	Nebraska	-4.40	53.7	35.3	1368	129	18
29.	Arizona	-4.91	73.0	34.4	1371	110	8
30.	Wyoming	-5.35	62.6	31.1	1570	98	12
31.	West Virginia	-5.73	76.9	28.4	1071	102	8
32.	Texas	-5.94	57.3	41.0	1108	110	9
33.	Montana	-6.23	58.0	33.7	1380	93	10
34.	Oklahoma	-6.36	58.0	34.3	1053	106	10
35.	Virginia	-6.57	63.8	32.4	1009	100	8
36.	Louisiana	-6.81	60.2	39.7	962	97	6
37.	Tennessee	-6.98	54.6	34.3	874	116	7
38.	Idaho	-7.21	54.2	29.1	1166	86	11
39.	Kentucky	-7.33	54.9	30.6	907	109	7
40.	Georgia	-8.29	51.5	30.8	812	98	5
41.	New Mexico	-8.53	52.9	25.2	944	90	5
42.	South Dakota	-8.91	39.4	18.9	967	86	13
43.	Alabama	-9.27	49.7	28.1	751	82	4
44.	North Carolina	-9.46	50.5	25.5	775	73	5
45.	Arkansas	-9.59	38.7	20.6	707	110	5
46.	North Dakota	-10.16	35.9	16.6	870	75	10
47.	South Carolina	-10.47	46.8	21.3	626	73	3
48.	Mississippi	-11.58	32.3	16.9	661	76	3

[a]In terms of modernity score.
[b]1970 dollars.

TABLE A–2   Roster of 48 Coterminous American States on Five Indicators of Modernity: 1940

Rank[a]	State	Modernity Score (SMO)	Indicator of Modernity				
			Percent Nonagri-cultural (SNA)	Percent Urban (SPU)	Per Capita Income[b] (SSI)	Physicians Per 100,000 Population (SPY)	Telephones Per 100 Population (STR)
1. New York		5.46	94.8	82.8	$2411	196	22
2. Massachusetts		4.91	97.1	89.4	2172	164	24
3. Connecticut		3.95	95.2	67.8	2541	145	27
4. California		3.62	87.0	71.0	2328	159	27
5. New Jersey		3.56	96.4	81.6	2278	142	21
6. Rhode Island		3.51	97.7	91.6	2059	130	21
7. Illinois		2.42	87.8	73.6	2089	146	22
8. Delaware		1.65	83.2	52.3	2782	125	24
9. Maryland		1.60	87.6	59.3	1973	162	20
10. Pennsylvania		0.81	93.1	66.5	1796	131	17
11. Ohio		0.58	87.0	66.8	1843	130	18
12. Michigan		0.52	86.2	65.7	1882	117	21
13. Washington		–0.18	84.4	53.1	1834	121	22
14. New Hampshire		–0.58	88.8	57.6	1604	114	19
15. Nevada		–0.64	83.3	39.3	2427	131	15
16. Colorado		–0.81	74.6	52.6	1513	146	21
17. Oregon		–1.16	78.9	48.8	1726	128	19
18. Indiana		–2.06	78.9	55.1	1532	113	15
19. Missouri		–2.22	71.4	51.8	1452	132	16
20. Utah		–2.44	77.7	55.5	1349	100	18
21. Maine		–2.84	83.6	40.5	1449	105	16
22. Florida		–2.90	80.6	55.1	1422	108	10
23. Wisconsin		–3.02	70.3	53.5	1535	108	14
24. Minnesota		–3.10	64.6	49.8	1458	122	16
25. Vermont		–3.61	70.3	34.3	1405	129	15
26. Arizona		–3.96	74.5	34.8	1377	112	14
27. Wyoming		–4.42	67.4	37.3	1685	91	14
28. Kansas		–4.45	63.3	41.9	1180	115	15
29. Montana		–4.77	64.6	37.8	1579	95	13
30. Iowa		–4.78	58.2	42.7	1388	115	12
31. Nebraska		–4.92	55.8	39.1	1216	120	15
32. Texas		–4.93	65.6	45.4	1197	98	12
33. Virginia		–4.97	71.3	35.3	1291	98	12
34. West Virginia		–5.45	82.7	28.1	1128	91	9
35. Louisiana		–5.82	63.9	41.5	1006	99	10
36. Oklahoma		–6.12	61.7	37.6	1034	96	11
37. Idaho		–6.30	59.9	33.7	1286	79	13
38. Tennessee		–6.69	60.4	35.2	939	94	10
39. New Mexico		–7.16	62.4	33.2	1039	80	8
40. Georgia		–7.39	59.6	34.4	942	82	8
41. Kentucky		–7.73	58.3	29.8	887	90	7
42. North Carolina		–8.53	59.6	27.3	909	72	5
43. South Carolina		–8.63	56.1	34.5	851	66	5
44. Alabama		–8.87	56.2	30.2	781	66	6
45. South Dakota		–8.91	44.6	24.6	995	78	9
46. North Dakota		–9.76	39.1	20.6	970	80	7
47. Arkansas		–9.84	44.0	22.2	709	86	5
48. Mississippi		–11.31	38.0	19.8	604	61	5

[a]In terms of modernity score.
[b]1970 dollars.

Rank[a]	State	Modernity Score (SMO)	Percent Nonagri-cultural (SNA)	Percent Urban (SPU)	Per Capita Income[b] (SSI)	Physicians Per 100,000 Population (SPY)	Telephones Per 100 Population (STR)
					Indicator of Modernity		
1.	New York	8.56	96.5	80.3	$3036	207	36
2.	Massachusetts	7.33	97.9	86.7	2682	178	34
3.	Connecticut	7.02	96.7	69.3	3065	162	39
4.	New Jersey	6.35	97.3	81.0	2887	146	34
5.	California	5.34	91.5	68.1	2966	159	31
6.	Rhode Island	5.28	98.4	87.0	2665	125	30
7.	Delaware	4.94	89.2	46.5	3461	140	37
8.	Illinois	4.92	91.1	74.5	2945	143	29
9.	Maryland	4.14	92.9	60.8	2549	166	28
10.	Pennsylvania	3.36	95.1	66.5	2526	133	26
11.	Michigan	3.32	92.2	65.4	2713	113	30
12.	Ohio	3.13	91.8	67.3	2600	123	27
13.	Colorado	2.76	82.1	57.4	2329	147	32
14.	Washington	2.42	90.1	53.6	2695	116	29
15.	Nevada	1.80	88.7	52.5	3126	127	17
16.	New Hampshire	1.78	92.0	58.6	2123	121	27
17.	Oregon	1.44	86.6	48.1	2581	121	26
18.	Utah	1.44	85.2	62.9	2068	116	28
19.	Missouri	1.01	78.4	57.9	2332	129	24
20.	Indiana	0.75	86.0	56.4	2452	103	23
21.	Minnesota	0.32	73.0	53.9	2253	135	23
22.	Wisconsin	−0.05	78.9	56.8	2366	105	21
23.	Texas	−0.10	81.4	59.8	2160	99	22
24.	Wyoming	−0.36	77.8	49.8	2618	84	24
25.	Kansas	−0.40	73.4	47.4	2226	120	24
26.	Florida	−0.52	87.6	56.5	2076	107	16
27.	Maine	−0.75	88.7	41.5	1924	105	23
28.	Arizona	−1.07	82.8	36.5	2089	117	21
29.	Vermont	−1.14	77.5	36.4	1916	133	22
30.	Montana	−1.19	71.5	42.8	2581	95	22
31.	Nebraska	−1.23	64.9	45.8	2374	111	23
32.	Louisiana	−1.34	80.3	51.4	1753	112	19
33.	Oklahoma	−1.66	75.9	49.6	1848	97	22
34.	Iowa	−1.77	66.0	46.9	2337	107	19
35.	Virginia	−1.80	83.6	41.4	1990	99	18
36.	New Mexico	−2.60	81.4	46.2	1874	83	16
37.	Idaho	−2.77	69.3	39.8	2063	82	22
38.	West Virginia	−3.04	88.6	31.9	1771	85	16
39.	Tennessee	−3.50	73.1	38.4	1605	94	18
40.	Georgia	−3.85	74.8	41.4	1640	83	15
41.	South Dakota	−5.06	53.5	33.1	1961	82	17
42.	Kentucky	−5.20	69.7	33.5	1545	83	12
43.	Alabama	−5.33	71.3	40.1	1402	70	12
44.	North Carolina	−5.62	70.7	30.5	1632	76	10
45.	North Dakota	−6.02	49.3	26.6	2045	76	15
46.	South Carolina	−6.33	70.0	30.8	1423	69	9
47.	Arkansas	−6.56	60.1	32.3	1302	80	11
48.	Mississippi	−8.16	52.9	27.6	1182	63	10

[a]In terms of modernity score.
[b]1970 dollars.

TABLE A–4 Roster of 48 Coterminous American States on Five Indicators of Modernity: 1960

Rank[a]	State	Modernity Score (SMO)	Percent Nonagri-cultural (SNA)	Percent Urban (SPU)	Per Capita Income[b] (SSI)	Physicians Per 100,000 Population (SPY)	Telephones Per 100 Population (STR)
1.	New York	10.47	97.8	72.8	$3645	194	49
2.	Massachusetts	9.75	98.8	86.8	3283	173	46
3.	Connecticut	9.64	98.2	69.0	3730	159	51
4.	New Jersey	9.20	98.5	82.6	3475	144	48
5.	California	7.81	94.7	71.7	3567	156	40
6.	Rhode Island	7.37	98.9	89.9	2866	131	41
7.	Maryland	6.88	96.1	56.2	3132	168	42
8.	Delaware	6.54	94.0	32.6	3928	133	49
9.	Illinois	6.48	94.2	75.9	3440	128	36
10.	Colorado	6.24	90.2	62.1	3010	147	44
11.	Pennsylvania	5.76	96.9	65.6	2948	137	38
12.	Michigan	5.73	95.9	65.0	3032	122	41
13.	Ohio	5.32	95.6	67.4	3056	124	36
14.	Washington	4.96	92.8	58.4	3022	121	40
15.	Nevada	4.55	94.6	66.3	3705	129	21
16.	Oregon	4.30	91.6	53.4	2930	125	38
17.	Utah	4.22	92.5	66.5	2518	118	38
18.	Arizona	3.88	90.4	69.9	2653	114	34
19.	New Hampshire	3.76	96.4	59.8	2726	103	36
20.	Missouri	3.75	87.7	61.3	2879	120	34
21.	Minnesota	3.42	81.5	61.0	2709	138	33
22.	Texas	3.25	89.5	72.7	2517	101	33
23.	Florida	2.83	93.9	62.2	2577	115	28
24.	Kansas	2.83	82.2	56.4	2697	126	33
25.	Oklahoma	2.76	87.8	61.0	2414	109	35
26.	Wyoming	2.57	82.9	56.8	3009	76	38
27.	Indiana	2.49	91.7	56.8	2859	95	30
28.	Vermont	1.82	84.5	37.0	2454	151	30
29.	Louisiana	1.58	91.7	56.2	2100	104	31
30.	New Mexico	1.55	91.0	61.8	2369	87	29
31.	Virginia	1.47	90.1	48.7	2429	113	28
32.	Wisconsin	1.21	94.6	35.8	2827	92	29
33.	West Virginia	1.14	86.5	62.1	2185	102	27
34.	Maine	0.85	93.7	39.9	2450	91	30
35.	Iowa	0.70	73.4	52.2	2644	107	28
36.	Nebraska	0.62	72.0	52.0	2802	116	24
37.	Montana	0.54	78.0	46.3	2634	86	32
38.	Tennessee	0.39	85.6	45.7	2014	108	30
39.	Georgia	0.32	88.8	49.8	2111	93	28
40.	Idaho	−0.57	77.1	41.4	2310	83	31
41.	Alabama	−1.28	87.7	51.7	1915	70	23
42.	North Carolina	−1.97	83.8	36.2	2049	87	21
43.	Kentucky	−2.11	81.1	37.7	2008	88	21
44.	South Dakota	−2.39	61.2	39.0	2429	78	26
45.	Arkansas	−2.52	81.8	41.4	1753	84	20
46.	South Carolina	−2.87	85.6	34.3	1807	74	20
47.	North Dakota	−3.62	58.3	35.1	2286	80	21
48.	Mississippi	−4.23	73.7	36.2	1533	68	20

[a]In terms of modernity score.
[b]1970 dollars.

TABLE A–5   *Roster of 48 Coterminous American States on Five Indicators of Modernity: 1970*

Rank[a]	State	Modernity Score (SMO)	Percent Nonagri-cultural (SNA)	Percent Urban (SPU)	Per Capita Income[b] (SSI)	Physicians Per 100,000 Population (SPY)	Telephones Per 100 Population (STR)
					Indicator of Modernity		
1.	New York	16.30	98.4	85.5	$4797	236	64
2.	Connecticut	14.42	98.9	77.3	4807	191	63
3.	California	14.35	96.5	90.8	4469	191	62
4.	Massachusetts	13.69	99.1	84.5	4294	206	57
5.	New Jersey	13.05	99.1	88.9	4539	145	61
6.	Maryland	12.19	97.7	76.6	4247	181	56
7.	Illinois	12.00	96.1	83.0	4516	138	59
8.	Delaware	11.03	96.6	72.1	4233	133	61
9.	Rhode Island	10.92	99.2	86.9	3920	154	51
10.	Colorado	10.89	93.7	78.6	3751	175	55
11.	Nevada	10.84	97.0	80.8	4544	112	56
12.	Pennsylvania	10.68	97.7	71.4	3893	152	58
13.	Ohio	9.94	97.3	75.3	3983	132	54
14.	Washington	9.91	94.7	72.6	3993	146	53
15.	Florida	9.79	94.7	80.5	3584	154	52
16.	Michigan	9.62	97.7	73.8	4043	124	53
17.	Minnesota	8.92	88.4	66.4	3793	151	53
18.	Oregon	8.71	93.6	67.0	3700	144	51
19.	Missouri	8.64	92.5	70.0	3659	128	54
20.	Utah	8.60	95.1	80.5	3210	138	51
21.	Arizona	8.51	95.3	79.5	3542	143	45
22.	Texas	8.19	93.7	79.7	3515	116	50
23.	New Hampshire	7.86	97.9	54.2	3608	140	50
24.	Kansas	7.78	87.0	66.0	3804	116	53
25.	Indiana	7.45	95.2	64.9	3773	102	50
26.	Virginia	7.20	95.5	63.0	3586	120	47
27.	Wisconsin	7.04	90.3	65.8	3722	105	49
28.	Nebraska	6.91	79.3	61.5	3700	115	54
29.	Vermont	6.82	91.4	32.1	3491	187	46
30.	Oklahoma	6.81	92.4	68.0	3269	101	52
31.	Wyoming	6.41	86.2	60.4	3420	100	54
32.	Iowa	6.28	80.4	57.2	3714	103	53
33.	Louisiana	6.20	95.0	66.1	3065	119	45
34.	New Mexico	5.98	94.0	69.9	3044	112	44
35.	Georgia	5.76	94.1	60.2	3277	106	45
36.	Tennessee	5.53	93.8	58.7	3051	119	44
37.	Maine	5.25	95.5	50.9	3243	110	44
38.	Montana	4.91	82.1	53.6	3381	104	47
39.	Idaho	4.14	82.5	54.3	3206	94	45
40.	West Virginia	4.09	97.5	38.9	2929	120	41
41.	North Carolina	4.05	92.2	44.9	3188	109	40
42.	Alabama	3.95	94.8	58.4	2828	89	41
43.	Kentucky	3.89	90.1	52.3	3060	101	40
44.	South Carolina	3.20	94.0	47.5	2908	91	39
45.	Arkansas	2.70	88.3	50.0	2742	92	39
46.	North Dakota	2.62	68.4	44.3	2937	94	49
47.	South Dakota	2.15	66.9	44.5	3182	80	46
48.	Mississippi	1.39	89.4	44.5	2561	83	35

[a]In terms of modernity score.
[b]1970 dollars.

TABLE A-6   Product-moment Correlations, Means, and Standard Deviations of Five Indicators of the Degree of Modernity of 48 Coterminous American States in 1950 (N = 48)

Indicator of Modernity	1	2	3	4	5	Mean	S.D.
1. Percent of males in non-agricultural work (SNA)	–	.79	.65	.71	.72	80.6	12.3
2. Percent urban (SPU)		–	.70	.78	.79	51.4	15.6
3. Per capita income (SSI)			–		.75	.84	2245	523
4. Number of physicians per 100,000 population (SPY)				–	.84	113	30.8
5. Number of telephones per 100 population (STR)					–	22.7	7.5

TABLE A-7   Factor Weights Resulting from a Principal Components Analysis of Five Indicators of the Degree of Modernity of 48 Coterminous American States: 1950 (N = 48).

Indicator of Modernity	Factor				
	I (Modernity index) (SMO)	II	III	IV	V
1. Percent of males in non-agricultural work (SNA)	.86	−.43	−.20	.19	.00
2. Percent of population in urbanized areas (SPU)	.91	−.22	.10	−.34	.04
3. Per capita income (SSI)	.87	.36	−.29	−.04	.14
4. Number of physicians per 100,000 population (SPY)	.91	.09	.33	.19	.13
5. Number of telephones per 100 population (STR)	.94	.19	.03	.01	−.29
Latent root	4.03	0.41	0.25	0.19	0.13
Cumulative percent of trace	80.6	88.7	93.7	97.5	100.0

of .84 between the number of telephones per 100 of population and both per capita income and the number of physicians per 100,000 of population, with a median coefficient of .75. Since in this work our primary interest is not in modernity *per se*, but rather in its relation to educational inputs, outputs, and structures, such variations as can be noted in Table A-6 are not as important as is their commonality. To summarize this commonality we conducted a principal components factor analysis of the correlation

TABLE A–8   Product-moment Correlations, Means, and Standard
Deviations of Modernity Indices for 48 Coterminous
American States: 1930, 1940, 1950, 1960, and 1970 and
a 1930–1970 Average (N = 48)

Year	Year					1930–1970 Average	Mean	Standard Deviation
	1930	1940	1950	1960	1970			
1930	–	.986	.968	.935	.932	.980	–3.71	4.17
1940		–	.987	.962	.950	.993	–3.10	4.32
1950			–	.980	.959	.994	0.00	4.03
1960				–	.973	.983	2.86	3.66
1970					–	.975	7.87	3.52
1930–1970 Average						–	0.78	3.88

matrix presented in Table A–6. The results presented in Table A–7 reveal a very high degree of internal consistency among the five indicators and suggest that the first factor, explaining over 80 percent of the variance in the correlation matrix, is an excellent summary of "general modernity." Therefore, we applied the weights from the first factor to the data of Tables A–1 through A–5 (standardized using 1950 means and standard deviations to compute z-scores) and summed within each year in order to arrive at a modernization score for each state at each of the five time points. Tables A–1 through A–5 present the result of this "component scoring" in the column labeled "modernity score."

To obtain a simple summary of the relative position of each state during the entire 40-year period (1930–1970), the modernity scores for each state were averaged across the five time points. Table A–8 presents the zero-order correlations, means, and standard deviations of the modernity indices for the five time points as well as for the 40-year average. There it can be noted that in no case is the association between time points less than .93, with the median being .97. Clearly there is a strong association in the degree of modernity for each pair of the time points.

To obtain a modernity score for each of the five sociocultural regions at each of the five time points, we computed the average of the state modernity scores for the states in each region (weighted by each state's population in the appropriate year) for each region for each of the five time points. The results of this weighting and averaging have been presented in Figure 4–5 (Chapter Four).

To obtain a modernity score for the United States as a whole at each of the five time points, we computed the average of the state modernity scores for all of the 48 states (weighted by each state's population in the appropriate year) for each of the five time points. The results of this weighting and averaging have been presented in Figure 4–6 (Chapter Four).

appendix B

Limitations of
Theory, Data, and Method

In this book we have viewed American education as an open sociocultural system highly dependent upon its environment. In addition, we have defined that environment in terms of its degree of modernity and have hypothesized a relationship between properties of the educational system and the degree to which its environment has been influenced by modernization. We then tested a portion of this model through a secondary analysis of data available at five levels of the American educational system. Given this experience it may be useful to expand upon our discussion of limitations presented at various points in the text to note some additional limitations apparent within our work, limitations that will need to be overcome before a more complete understanding of American education as an open sociocultural system can be achieved. These limitations occur particularly with respect to our view of the environments of educational systems; our view of the structure and function of educational systems; and sampling errors, measurement errors, and uncontrolled extraneous variation.

THE ENVIRONMENT OF EDUCATIONAL SYSTEMS

Our exploration of variation in the structure and functioning of American education has placed heavy emphasis on the effects of the sociocultural environment in which schooling takes place. We argued that these environments can be defined as a variety of geographical areas and political subdivisions of differing degrees of modernity. However, we were particularly limited in our documentation of the validity of such an assertion by the absence of appropriate data. Our comparison of 48 states as to modernity as measured by five indicators at five points in time is obviously only an example of the type of evidence required. Particularly disappointing to us has been the fact that data on variation in values and ideology currently are not available for all American states, communities, and neighborhoods.

Our research has also been restricted by a rather narrow definition of the concept of environment itself. We have focused on the environment of educational systems primarily in terms of the culture of their regional environment (e_{cr}), the ecology of their community environment (e_{ec}), and the structure of their neighborhood environment (e_{sn}). Although the explication of just these three contexts turned out to be a mammoth undertaking, a more complete treatment of the environment of American schools is desirable. Particularly important to further attempts to measure the effects of such environments will be the need to distinguish between the present condition of the environment, its previous condition, and the rate of change between the two. Our view of the effects of the environment on educational systems was static, for it took into account merely the present condition of the environment and did not allow for the possibility that rapid changes in the social composition of some environments (particularly certain central cities of the Northeast and Great Lakes regions and certain rural areas of the Southeast) could modify their degree of modernity rather dramatically.

Particularly troublesome in this respect in our research has been the measurement of the ecology of the community. In Chapter Six we argued that, on the average, the central cities of the United States are more modern than either the rings or the nonmetropolitan areas. However, the frequent correspondence of central city and low social class raises doubts about the validity of this assumption. A view of the ecology of the community that takes into account the impact upon the central city of migration, commuting patterns, ethnic composition, race, primary economic base, and the like seems essential. Such a concern can provide a clearer notion of the influence of modernity on both rural and urban life and can provide a more complete understanding of the system-environment relationship within American education.

AMERICAN EDUCATION AS AN OPEN SYSTEM

In speaking of American education as an open system, we have used primarily a holistic or organic framework. Our justification for such a framework, in contrast to the more commonly accepted behavioristic or mechanical conceptions of social behavior, is handicapped by a paucity of empirical documentation at the subsocietal level. This is particularly true of research on the school. Almost all past research on the school has focused on a role (for example, pupil, teacher, or principal) as the unit of analysis rather than on the school itself. Nevertheless, whenever appropriate systematic evidence on schools has been available, we have provided it, but we have also drawn upon our own personal observations regarding the organizational properties of schools. Clearly, a more complete documentation of those properties of open systems that we attribute to American public education is needed.

Another aspect of education as an open system that needs more systematic development is the extent to which educational systems are open, in both comparative and absolute terms. We have argued that all social systems are "open," but we have not attempted to posit any variation in openness across different types of educational systems. Yet it seems reasonable to expect, for example, that public and nonpublic schools would differ appreciably in their openness to environmental influences. Further efforts directed at the school as an open system should include a more systematic delineation of the "parameters" of the openness of schools as social systems in differing institutional contexts. Such specificity will undoubtedly contribute to a clearer understanding of the effects of various environmental forces upon different types of educational system.

A problem of some magnitude, which we now see as a possible limitation of our approach, is the manner in which we have excluded pupils from membership in the school as a social organization, defining them instead as the "raw materials" acted upon by the school. We readily acknowledge that this exclusion can be construed as unrealistic from some perspectives, for obviously a great deal of intraschool activity and interaction includes pupils. On the other hand, by excluding pupils from organizational membership, we could focus more sharply on those organizational properties of schools shared with other social organizations. Further, in addition to this analytic advantage, removing pupils from organizational membership has the heuristic value of permitting the observer to view the school more clearly in terms of its institutional role than is possible when pupils are defined within organizational boundaries. Certainly the decision as to whether or not pupils should be considered organizational members is a very complex one, dependent upon the purposes of the analysis.

Related to this issue is the inherent limitation associated with defining pupils as production throughput or "raw materials." Such a definition speaks of students as inanimate, which of course they are not. Although for preliminary analyses, such as that performed in this monograph, it seems useful to view the student body in such a fashion, ultimately it will be necessary to weigh carefully other ideas of pupil-organization relationships that are consistent with the wholistic model of the school in society we have set forth. It is possible that a greater use of analogies may offer creative insights into this issue. For example, pupil-organization relationships may be likened to those of plants in a nursery, for pupils, like plants, are subject to the artificial environment of the school wherein certain genetic characteristics are developed to a degree not normally achieved in their "natural environments." Such an analogy can be carried a step further for, like some nurseries, the school returns the pupils to their natural environments periodically. A different analogy, suggestive of a more active pupil-organization relationship, might see the relationship as similar to that between animals and a circus. The behavior of school pupils, like that of circus animals, can be in opposition to that intended by their "trainers."

Analogies are useful for they suggest possible properties of the pupil-organization relationship that might otherwise be overlooked. Perhaps we need to think of the pupil-organization relationship in such a way that we can specify the conditions under which particular properties of this relationship are most operative. However, the fact that we have not yet been able to do this should not negate the heuristic value of our model as one of many needed approaches to the organizational analysis of schools as open sociocultural systems.

SAMPLING ERROR

Past research on the school as a formal organization has been characterized by two major limitations: the tendency to overgeneralize from case studies of only a few schools, and the use of pupils or teachers as the unit of analysis when the primary focus is on the school itself. In our efforts to avoid these limitations in testing our view of the system-environment relationship, we obtained data from national samples of schools and school districts. However, although our samples were very large by contemporary standards, our approach has not been without its own limitations.

Ideally, in studying the system-environment relationship at the level of the school, one would draw a large probability sample of schools that had been stratified on the three dimensions of the sociocultural environment at all relevant layers of the environment. Complete cooperation from all sampled schools would be essential, for in this way accurate estimates of sampling errors could be made and reported. Unfortunately, our empirical analysis of schools is based upon neither a stratified probability sample nor a 100 percent response rate. The sample of schools we used arose through the probability sampling of households, not schools, and the response rate was only 73 percent.

It should be noted, however, that there are currently many rather formidable obstacles to obtaining a more scientifically defensible sample of American schools. Although a roster of all public and private schools in the United States is currently available from the U.S. Office of Education, the schools on this roster have not been identified in terms of variables that would permit stratification on important sociocultural dimensions of the environment of the school district, or school attendance district. Such data are available for communities and census tracts from the U.S. Bureau of the Census, but the lack of correspondence between the areal units in which schools are located and governed and those for which census data are available currently makes the complete identification of schools in terms of census data impossible. Until such important background variables are available at the time a sample is being selected, the development of scientifically precise probability samples for investigating the system-environment relationships of schools will not be possible.[a]

It should also be noted that even if appropriate sampling data were currently available, research of the type proposed would still be greatly inhibited by the reluctance of many public school officials to supply "sensitive" data. School officials, particularly those in less modern areas, are reluctant to answer questions about the environment of their schools, and particularly about their inputs, throughputs, and outputs. Thus, even if a scientifically sound sample could be drawn, the researcher is still greatly limited by selective nonresponse. Although efforts can be made to learn enough about the recalcitrant schools so that the responding portion of the sample can be adjusted to provide more accurate population estimates, the data required to do this are generally also under the control of school officials. Barring sudden willingness of public school officials to supply the necessary data, the existence of unknown sampling errors due to selective nonresponse are likely to continue to limit the type of generalizations that can be made regarding the system-environment relationships of American public schools.

MEASUREMENT ERROR

Our efforts to explore empirically the system-environment relationships were also limited by measurement errors with respect to variables describing both the system and its environment. One consequence of such error is that

---

[a]Efforts are currently underway by the National Center for Educational Statistics of the U.S. Office of Education to aggregate small area data from the 1970 censuses of population and housing by school district. Should the results of these efforts be made available to researchers on computer tapes, many of the problems we faced in matching school districts to census data can be overcome. We know of no comparable effort for individual schools.

coefficients summarizing the relationship between measures of the environment and of the system have very likely been underestimated. This has not
been a serious problem in this study, for the objective here was merely to explore the general hypothesis that environment and system are related in a
particular way. However, many scholars concerned with both the sociological
study of schools and strategies for their reform will want to ask more
strenuous questions of data comparable to ours. Under such circumstances
it will become extremely important that measurement errors that distort the
fit between concepts and data be reduced below the level apparent in our
study.

The measures of the educational system itself that we used in this report
dealt with its structure, inputs, throughputs, and outputs. It was particularly
encouraging to us that the relationships most consistent with the general
hypothesis occurred with respect to measures of organizational size and
specialization—measures that are likely to be subject to very little error.
However, a more complete description of the structure of schools will require additional measures of such important dimensions as complexity and
degree of bureaucracy.

All of our measures of input were at best merely indirect proxies for
what we view as the degree of modernity of the organizational input of
educational systems. Far more valid and reliable measures of personnel input
could be obtained by submitting questionnaires to the teachers themselves
and then aggregating their replies in order to characterize the school. Similarly, more systematic procedures than single questions addressed to the
principal are needed to characterize the curriculum and plant of the school.
No doubt it will often be necessary to make direct observations in each school
to obtain appropriate data on these aspects of organizational input.

Probably the weakest measures used in the empirical portion of our studies were those for production throughput. Ideally, one would want to obtain
direct measures of pupil knowledge, skill, and orientations at several points
in time. Particularly important would be measures of the knowledge, skill,
and orientations possessed by the pupils at the time they entered the initial
year of each level of school, and again when they completed the terminal
years of the same schools. It is particularly important to note that such
measures should not be of the normative type so typical of individual
psychological assessment in American education. In characterizing the
throughput of schools one needs to know the percentage of pupils at different
stages within the organization who know a certain fact, possess a particular
skill, and hold a particular orientation. The typical normative data does not
provide this, and in relying (as we did in Chapter Six) on the principal's
estimates of the percentage of pupils who were above a particular grade level
in reading (a normative measure) we no doubt permitted a good deal of error
to creep into our estimates. In addition, the particular variables we selected

as proxies for knowledge, skill, and orientation were indirect at best. Currently there is great need for an extensive effort to develop criterion measures of various dimensions of pupil socialization by the organization, measures comparable in quality and scope to those that now exist for the normative description of the cognitive behavior of pupils.

Our measures of organizational output were more direct and no doubt more reliable. At the level of the school, most high school principals reported that they could provide accurate estimates of the number of pupils going to various forms of further education. However, our measure of negative termination (dropping out) was distorted by the fact that it included only those pupils who had dropped out after entering the tenth grade. This was necessary in our study because of the fact that close to 50 percent of the American schools having a twelfth grade do not contain a grade lower than the tenth and thus principals would not be aware of the degree of dropping out before the tenth grade. However, further research may want to concentrate more on 9–12, 7–12, and 1–12 schools in which a more comprehensive estimate of school dropout rates could be computed. In this way more complete data can be obtained for some of the less modern areas in which early dropping out is most frequent, thus providing a more accurate estimate of the strength of the system-environment relationship.

It is particularly important to note that throughout our examination of the effects of the environment upon educational systems we have relied upon single items to measure the properties of educational systems. Given the exploratory nature of this research, and the fact that we were constrained by the lack of more comprehensive data, it did not seem appropriate to attempt to build summary measures. However, a more precise assessment of the strength of the relationship between the sociocultural contexts of educational systems and their organizational characteristics is desirable and will require the development of reliable summary measures of structure, input, throughput, and output.

UNCONTROLLED EXTRANEOUS VARIATION

In any survey of organizations there is always the possibility that variables other than those that have been conceptualized, measured, and introduced into the analysis are affecting the relationships under examination and thus are confusing the interpretation of results. To guard against this possibility we have gone to great lengths in Chapters Five and Six to make simultaneous distinctions among the three dimensions of the sociocultural environments of educational systems. By so doing we could identify their independent effects on the structure and functioning of school districts and schools, and thus not confuse, for example, cultural effects with ecological effects. In general we have found that each of the three dimensions bears an association with measures of organizational structure and functioning above and beyond that attributable to either of the other two dimensions with which it is generally correlated. However, the possibility still remains that the "independent" effects we have observed may be attributable to environmental variables (particularly measures of wealth) that were not included in our conceptualization. In addition, there exists the possibility that owing to the limitations of the size of our samples of educational systems, our control on the three dimensions was not tight enough to reveal their "true" independent effects.

Before computing the effects of context on school inputs we attempted to control for the possible "extraneous" effects of structure.[b] To do this we entered a measure of organizational size into all regression equations for context on input. This procedure is obviously limited by the extent to which our measure of size actually captures the essence of what we described as the organizational structure of schools. A far more rigorous test of the effects of context on input, which are independent of structure, would require the prior introduction of a summary or composite measure of the several dimensions of structure.

A similar criticism can be leveled at our failure to control for input in looking at the environment-throughput and environment-output relationships. However, our case may not be as weak as it may at first seem, for the results of our analysis are rather similar to those of others who have also found that the environment-output relationship is affected very little by the introduction of variables similar to those we have conceptualized and measured as organizational structure and input.[c]

One major limitation in our attempts to study the system-environment relationship is the result of our inability to control for changes taking place in the environment of educational systems. In extending our work, a more precise characterization of the sociocultural environment at prior points in time will be required. Because of the unexpected observance of interaction effects among the several environmental dimensions, it has become quite apparent that the effects of changes in the environment of schools are likely to act in different ways upon organizational structure, input, throughput, and output. Structure seems only slightly affected by change in the environment. (For example, once a school with a particular number of classrooms is

[b]This methodological study was reported in Robert E. Herriott and Benjamin J. Hodgkins, *Sociocultural Context and the American School*, Final Report CEG–2–6–062972–2095; ED 028–502 (Washington, D.C.: U.S. Department of Health, Education and Welfare, January 1969), chap. 12.

[c]See, for example, James S. Coleman *et al.*, *Equality of Educational Opportunity*, Vol. I (Washington, D.C.: Government Printing Office, 1966), chap. 3.

built it is not easily changed.) Thus organizational size is likely to be more highly related to a condition of the local environment at the time a school was built than to that of the present.

Inputs also seem to be institutionalized and thus lag behind changes in the environment. However, what is particularly apparent is that throughputs and outputs are very sensitive to environmental changes, particularly changes in the structure of the neighborhood environment of the school. Because we lacked measures of the context at different points in time we were unable to control for such changes and to examine systematically their differential effects upon organizational structure and functioning. To understand more fully the environment-organization relationship, future studies will need to take into account very systematically this developmental nature of environments as well as of educational systems themselves.

appendix C

Sources and Coding of Data

A detailed description of data sources, a roster of all original variables, and the computing formulas applied to these variables to obtain derived variables could not be included in this book due to space limitations. What follows is a brief overview of the more complete Appendix C which can be obtained by writing directly to the authors.[a]

STATE, REGIONAL, AND NATIONAL DATA

The data analyzed and reported in Chapter Four were obtained from a variety of published sources that report data for American states. In some cases the measures could be obtained directly from these original sources. In other cases computations were performed using two or more "original" variables to compute "derived" variables.

Most of the original variables were obtained from eleven major sources.[b] A roster of all variables and a listing of specific sources and computing

---

[a]For a photocopy of the 80-page detailed version of Appendix C, please send $5.00 to Dr. Robert E. Herriott, Senior Social Scientist, Abt Associates, Inc., 55 Wheeler Street, Cambridge, Massachusetts 02138.

[b]Office of Education, *Biennial Survey of Education, 1928–1930*, Vol. II. Washington, D. C.: U. S. Government Printing Office, 1932; Office of Education, *Biennial Survey of Education, 1938–1942*, Vol. II. Washington, D. C.: U. S. Government Printing Office,

formulas are presented in the more detailed version of Appendix C. To simplify the presentation of computational formulas, all variables have been identified in the tables in Chapter Four and in the expanded Appendix C through the use of three-character mnemonic codes. The first character of each code is either N (for nation), R (for region), or S (for state), depending upon the level of aggregation of the variable. All regional and national variables were obtained by aggregating the corresponding state variable, adjusted by appropriate weighting factors.

SCHOOL DISTRICT DATA

The empirical findings presented in Chapter Five were obtained through the analysis of data from two major sources.[c] The school district questionnaire, the computing formulas used to convert responses to questionnaire items into derived variables, the sources used to identify the district's environment, and a table describing how the regional and community environments of school districts were made operational are presented in the more detailed version of Appendix C. All relevant variables have been given a four-character mnemonic code to facilitate their identification and to simplify the presentation of computing formulas. The first character of this code is always D (for district).

1943; Office of Education, *Biennial Survey of Education, 1948–1950*. Washington, D. C.: U. S. Government Printing Office, 1954; Office of Education, *Statistics of State School Systems, 1959–1960*. Washington, D. C.: U. S. Government Printing Office, 1963; U. S. Bureau of the Census, *United States Census of the Population: 1930*. Vol. II, *General Report Statistics by Subjects*. Washington, D. C.: U. S. Government Printing Office, 1933; U. S. Bureau of the Census, *United States Census of the Population: 1940*. Vol. II, *Characteristics of the Population*, Part I, *United States Summary*. Washington, D. C.: U. S. Government Printing Office, 1943; U. S. Bureau of the Census, *United States Census of the Population: 1950*. Vol. II, *Characteristics of the Population*, Part I, *United States Summary*. Washington, D. C.: U. S. Government Printing Office, 1953; U. S. Bureau of the Census, *United States Census of the Population: 1960*. Vol. II, *Characteristics of the Population*, Part I, *United States Summary*. Washington, D. C.: U. S. Government Printing Office, 1964; Simon, Kenneth A. and W. Vance Grant, *Digest of Educational Statistics: 1970*. Washington, D. C.: U. S. Government Printing Office, September 1970; National Center for Educational Statistics, *Statistics of Public Schools: Fall 1970*. Washington, D. C.: U. S. Government Printing Office, March 1971, U. S. Bureau of the Census, *Census of Population: 1970. General Social and Economic Characteristics*. Final Report PC(1)–CXX. "State Name." Washington, D. C.: U. S. Government Printing Office, 1972.

[c]Gerald Kahn and Warren A. Hughes, *Statistics of Local Public School Systems, 1967* (Washington, D. C.: U. S. Government Printing Office, 1969), Table A; Bureau of the Census, *Census of the Population, 1960* (Washington, D. C.: U. S. Government Printing Office, 1963).

SCHOOL DATA

The empirical findings presented in Chapter Six were obtained through the analysis of data from a single source.[d] The school questionnaire, the computing formulas used when necessary to convert questionnaire responses to derived variables, the sources used to identify the school's environments, and a table describing how the regional, community, and neighborhood environments of schools were made operational are presented in the more detailed version of Appendix C. All relevant questionnaire items and other sources have been given a four-character mnemonic code to facilitate the identification of variables and to simplify the presentation of computing formulas. The first character of this code is always C (for *school*).

---

[d]For the methodological details of this project, see Robert E. Herriott and Benjamin J. Hodgkins, *Sociocultural Context and the American School,* Final Report OEG-2-6-062972; ED 028-502 (Washington, D. C.: U. S. Department of Health, Education and Welfare, January 1969), Chap. 9.

Name Index

Name Index

Subject Index

Subject Index